Reading the Nineteenth-Century Novel

READING THE NOVEL

General Editor: Daniel R. Schwarz

The aim of this series is to provide practical introductions to reading the novel in both the British and Irish, and the American traditions.

Published

Reading the Nineteenth-Century Novel	**Alison Case and Harry E. Shaw**
Reading the Modern British and Irish Novel 1890–1930	**Daniel R. Schwarz**
Reading the Novel in English 1950–2000	**Brian W. Shaffer**

Forthcoming

Reading the Eighteenth-Century Novel	**Paula R. Backsheider**
Reading the American Novel 1780–1865	**Shirley Samuels**
Reading the American Novel 1865–1914	**G. R. Thompson**
Reading the Twentieth-Century American Novel	**James Phelan**

Reading the Nineteenth-Century Novel

Austen to Eliot

Alison Case and
Harry E. Shaw

Blackwell
Publishing

BLACKWELL PUBLISHING

350 Main Street, Malden, MA 02148–5020, USA
9600 Garsington Road, Oxford OX4 2DQ, UK
550 Swanston Street, Carlton, Victoria 3053, Australia

First published 2008 by Blackwell Publishing Ltd

1   2008

Library of Congress Cataloging-in-Publication Data

Case, Alison A., 1961–
Reading the nineteenth-century novel: Austen to Eliot / Alison Case and Harry E. Shaw.
p. cm.—(Reading the novel)
Includes bibliographical references (p.) and index.
ISBN 978-0-631-23149-3 (hardcover : alk. paper)—ISBN 978-0-631-23143-1 (pbk. : alk. paper)
1. English fiction—19th century—History and criticism.   2. Literature and society—Great
Britain—History—19th century.   3. Fiction—Technique.   I. Shaw, Harry E., 1946   II. Title.
PR861.S525 2008
823'.809—dc22
2007013164

A catalogue record for this title is available from the British Library.

Set in 10/12.5pt Minion
by Graphicraft Limited, Hong Kong
Printed and bound in Singapore
by Utopia Press Pte Ltd

The publisher's policy is to use permanent paper from mills that operate a sustainable
forestry policy, and which has been manufactured from pulp processed using acid-free
and elementary chlorine-free practices. Furthermore, the publisher ensures that the text
paper and cover board used have met acceptable environmental accreditation standards.

For further information on
Blackwell Publishing, visit our website at
www.blackwellpublishing.com

To my past and present students at Williams College, who keep me focused on how and why novels matter.
A. C.

To Robert W. Shaw, who in a single, brief conversation led his younger brother to hear voices in Victorian novels.
H. S.

Contents

Introduction

On one level, nothing could seem more familiar to readers on both sides of the Atlantic (and beyond) than the tract of British novels extending from Austen and Scott to George Eliot. It is natural enough to see them as a set of vivid scenes and characters, and there's much to be said for such an approach, which was certainly the majority approach of their first readers. But the fissures that may lie beneath seeming continuities have lately become a staple topic in and beyond literary criticism, and for good reasons. Over a century has passed since the novels we will discuss in this book first appeared, and changes in literary conventions and taste, and perhaps more important in society itself, have intervened that may make a full experience of nineteenth-century British fiction less available than it might appear to be. Our purpose is to help allow readers to enjoy as rich an encounter as possible with the novels and novelists we discuss. One of our principal means of doing this will be to focus on differences – differences between novelists, and differences between the assumptions and background experience modern readers may bring to these works and the assumptions and experiences from which they were written.

Despite some obvious continuities, nineteenth-century fiction tends to have what we might call a different center of gravity from that of more recent and distinctively "modern" fiction. (In saying this, of course, we are setting aside the large number of more recent novels that simply continue in the tradition of fiction-writing established by the great nineteenth-century novels – which includes a good deal of popular fiction.) The great and distinctive achievements of nineteenth-century fiction were, on the one hand, to bring into the novel a rich and detailed depiction of the workings of society and history, and on the other to extend the novel's grasp of individual psychology. These elements persist in more recent fiction, but with a difference. Modern fiction has pushed its depiction of the individual consciousness deeper, using such techniques as the "stream of consciousness." At the same time, its relationship to society and history has become more indirect and vexed. When Stephen Daedalus in *Ulysses* tosses off the line "history is a nightmare from which I am trying to awake," he points not just to the attempt by many novelists to evade the depiction of history and society in favor of what they take to be more fundamental realms and issues (individual psychology, myth), but also an equally important tendency for historical forces to be registered, not by a realist depiction, but in the modes of expressionism or symbolism we might well associate with dreams and nightmares (as in Pynchon). In a vast oversimplification, we might say that "serious" modern novels have tended to abandon nineteenth-century realism for other fictional modes, centered on the individual psyche or the collective unconscious or on the play of language itself.

This change coincided with a crucial shift in thought and writing about the novel. The critical discourse on novels was, until the early twentieth century, largely a matter of book reviewing for the general literate public, the sort of reviewing that persists to our own day in newspapers and periodicals. In the early twentieth century, however, another, more "professional" and more self-consciously theorized discourse about novels arose, as part of the movement whereby authors of "modern" fiction (above all Henry James) attempted to break free from the line of fiction it is the purpose of the present book to illuminate. This more "professional" kind of criticism became, with the passage of time, the basis for criticism of the novel as it was presented to students in schools and universities. It was useful for many purposes, among them encouraging a focus on the craft of the novel, on how novels create their effects. But a criticism based on a set of aesthetic priorities that were developed as part of a rebellion against the nineteenth-century social novel would seem likely to have certain limitations for those who want to understand nineteenth-century novels, not leave them behind. The combination of more modern novelistic practice (at least in "serious" novels) and of the institutions of novel criticism as it has developed since the modernists, has created a situation in which, for all their familiarity, certain crucial aspects of the novels of Austen and Thackeray and Eliot may be obscured for modern readers. This is a pity, because whatever changes of taste and artistic practice may have occurred, the world the nineteenth-century novelists faced and the problems they grappled with remain ours.

The Nineteenth-Century World

In the nineteenth century, a series of developments that began in the previous century grew and solidified to a point where society began to assume a configuration and character that is the basis of the world we ourselves inhabit. Technological changes provided a prime impetus, and Britain was for much of this period at the forefront. Travel and communication became rapid and efficient to an extent earlier periods could hardly have imagined possible. A series of industrial revolutions, centered in its first wave on the manufacture of cloth and in its second on creation and expansion of railways, were accompanied by profound demographic shifts involving both a strong growth of population and the growth of cities. The latter development was perhaps the most striking in the eyes of contemporaries, as two small villages became within a generation the large cities of Manchester and Birmingham. The problems of infrastructure caused by the headlong, uncontrolled growth were considerable. The lack of all but the most primitive sanitation meant that disease struck these cities, and London, repeatedly. Political agencies had to be invented to cope with problems on such a scale, and they were on the whole and in the long run reasonably successful with many of them. But the rise of administration also meant the by-now familiar rise of bureaucracy and red tape.

During the same period, and at least partly as a result of the economic, technological, and demographic changes we have mentioned, conflict between social classes intensified and sometimes erupted. The most spectacular example of this, of course, occurred across the Channel, just before the turn of the nineteenth century. The specter of the French Revolution haunted England (and for that matter all of Europe) throughout the period this book covers. This was not only because the guillotine provides such an evocative symbol and (to the genteel classes) threat. The conditions of the huge working class in England, through at least the middle of the nineteenth century, were dreadful, especially in cities, as novels like *Mary Barton* and *Bleak House* make painfully apparent. But the issue of how to deal with the potential for class warfare was only the extreme case of a more general problem. Social and economic changes on the scale we have been describing can hardly occur without making traditional political forms obsolete. The system of parliamentary government that had served England for centuries had no means of representing the most vital components of the new order, whether they were manufacturers or working men. The latter had, typically, no vote at all; the former had much less influence on national policies than their economic importance would seem to justify. During the middle ages, Old Sarum had been a thriving community; by the nineteenth century, its only year-round inhabitants were sheep. Yet until the Reform Bill of 1832, Old Sarum (or more precisely, the man who owned the land on which it had stood) sent two members to Parliament, while Manchester sent none. "Reform" was a prime concern in the period. It meant many things: the invention of appropriate governing bodies for the hugely expanded cities, the adjustment of parliamentary representation to better reflect the social and economic realities of the age, the implementation of laws to curb child labor and to create sanitary conditions in cities. Such reforms were among the great achievements of nineteenth-century Britain; they also were never adequate to the complex problems that a growing rate of social and economic change continued to produce.

The implications of this rapid pace of change were, of course, hardly lost on the people to whom it was happening, and had a profound impact on their perceptions of the social world. Victorians were well aware that they lived in a very different world from their grandparents', and that their children would probably grow up to take their place in a world different from their own. They wanted to pass on the values and traditions most dear to them, but they also recognized the need to equip themselves and their descendants to face new circumstances. This is a perception familiar to us, but relatively new to them. To call a period "an age of transition" is one of the most tired of historical clichés – all ages by definition constitute transitions from what came before to what came after. But the Victorians were distinctive in perceiving their *own* age as predominantly transitional in character: "the first of the leading peculiarities of the present age is, that it is an Age of Transition," wrote John Stuart Mill in "The Spirit of the Age" (1831). "Mankind have outgrown old institutions and old doctrines, and have not yet acquired new ones."[1] They found this condition by turns threatening, debilitating, and exhilarating. Matthew Arnold would describe himself, more elegiacally, as "Wand'ring between two worlds, one dead/The other powerless to be born."

For women, the shakeup of structures and values often felt more like an opportunity than a threat. The question of women's proper capacities, duties, and rights was openly and hotly contested enough that the debate had a name: the Woman Question. Mill published his *On the Subjection of Women*, the most lucid and sophisticated analysis and indictment of women's inferior status yet, in 1869, and as a Member of Parliament routinely introduced bills for women's suffrage and equal property rights. Women themselves were agitating for the reform of women's legal status and challenging the male monopoly on higher education and the professions, while steadily infiltrating the less heavily defended fields of literature, journalism, and the arts.

Along with their vision of nineteenth-century novels as insufficiently subtle in their narrative forms, the modernists have bequeathed us a vision of the Victorians themselves as stuffy, hidebound, and obsessed with propriety. This was understandable since, for most modernists, the Victorians were actually their parents. There is also an element of truth in it. The nineteenth century was an age of codification – of the rules of games and sports, for example, and only slightly less formally, of codes of behavior, especially for women. But rules only need to be codified and written when we can no longer count on people to absorb them by more traditional means. Focusing only on the more widely celebrated assertions of women's "proper" place, such as Dickens's relentlessly self-sacrificial heroines, Ruskin's famous "Of Queens' Gardens" lecture in *Sesame and Lilies*, or Coventry Patmore's poem "The Angel in the House," though, can lead us to see this code as more uniform than it was, punctuated only by a few voices of lonely outrage like Charlotte Brontë's. But values are most vehemently insisted on when they are under threat. Most of the novels we discuss, by men or women, engage directly or indirectly with the Woman Question, and they do so from a wide variety of perspectives.

Novels provided a crucial social forum in which such issues were explored. Part of their power to perform this function stemmed from significant changes in the publications of books and the constitution of audiences. Literacy was expanding steadily, increasing both the social range and the sheer volume of the reading public. The rise of circulating libraries in the early and middle part of the century also vastly increased the accessibility of novels: for a moderate annual fee, subscribers could read as many new works as they pleased. To keep patrons satisfied, circulating libraries bought large quantities of newly released novels likely to be much in demand (rather like video rental stores today). Their status as the largest single purchasers of new novels in turn gave the library buyers considerable influence over what got published, as publishers saw little chance of profits with a new novel if, say, Mudie's (the largest network of libraries) decided not to buy it. The many libraries had strict rules about sexual content, for example, which produced a *de facto* censorship against which authors often chafed. Since subscribers paid an annual fee based on how many volumes they wanted to have out at a time, the libraries also preferred the three-volume format for novels. The expansive Victorian "triple-decker" novel, then, derives partly from market pressures of the day. Serial publication and, later in the century, cheap paperback editions, also made novels available to less wealthy patrons, and as costs steadily declined, eventually crowded out the libraries.

The expansion of audience and sales brought with it an expansion of authorial profits. Jane Austen was never paid more than fifty pounds for a manuscript, but bestselling authors, male or female, could become quite wealthy, particularly once they had established a name and an audience for themselves. Writing was in fact one of the few ways genteel women could get rich by their own unaided efforts – one reason that so many, talented or not, tried their hands at it. Nearly all the authors we cover here wrote novels at least partly to make money, a motivation which they did not see as necessarily at odds with the aim of producing good art. (The highbrow/lowbrow distinction, with its implication that truly sophisticated art must resign itself to an audience drawn only from the small circle of the truly sophisticated, is another legacy of modernism it would be well to eschew for our purposes.)

The novelists we discuss in this book, then, faced the coming of modernity, in which traditional values were weakening, mass culture was growing, technology was transforming lives and even the landscape, and social realities were altering with ever increasing speed. So do we. Their attempts to come to grips with the beginnings of a modernity we now inhabit are worthy of our attention. At the very least, a serious encounter with nineteenth-century fiction can remind us of how our present condition arose. The attempt to incorporate into the novel the representation of the complexities of societies as they move through history may be the most distinctive achievement of nineteenth-century fiction, and an ability to imagine and evaluate our own place in history is something we continue to be sorely in need of, for reasons that include not only political decision-making but the hope of understanding what it means to be human in our own times. It was certainly an attempt that has far-reaching consequences for all elements of the form of the novels in which it is most deeply felt. For example, all the novels we here consider are based upon the most traditional of novel storylines, the love plot. Yet even here differences arise; as subsequent chapters will suggest, the function and status of this ubiquitous element vary greatly when we turn from *Wuthering Heights* to *Waverley*, and the difference is largely a result of Scott's focus, not so much on the passions of individuals, as on the historical context in which those passions exist. The same could be said for other seemingly conventional aspects of these novels: identifying common elements among them often helps us to bring into focus important differences in their social vision.

Narrators and Narrative Focus

In our view, the key to a full experience of nineteenth-century novels is sensitivity to their narrators. All novels have narrators of one kind or another, and it is always important to keep in mind that the voice we hear arising from the pages we read is something that an author has created, not simply the voice of the author speaking to us. But the narrators of the works we will be discussing have a particular prominence and interest. We experience the characters and the setting, and we come to understand the larger significance of the novels, through our developing relationship with the voice or voices that tell us these stories. In the discussions of individual novels that follow, we take considerable pains to characterize the distinctive perspectives and discursive practices of the narrators. Before doing so, though, it will be helpful to settle on some general terms and classifications.

The most common general kind of narrator in nineteenth-century fiction is one positioned outside the story – that is, a narrator who does not appear as a character in the story – who reports a range of information unavailable to any one character within the story (and in fact unavailable in principle to any individual in real life), such as the secret thoughts and actions of multiple characters, or scenes said to be taking place simultaneously in widely different locations. For decades, most students of literature have been taught to call such narrators "omniscient" (sometimes with the oxymoronic qualifier "limited omniscient" if the narrator restricts his or her privileged knowledge to the thoughts or private actions of only one or two characters). "Omniscient," though, can be a misleading term in at least a couple of significant ways. One is that very few realist narrators actually exhibit a universal knowledge of their characters – in fact, they not infrequently explicitly *disclaim* specific kinds of knowledge, as when the narrator of *Vanity Fair* tells us what he "hoped" Mr. Osborne was thinking on his deathbed (see chapter 5). Thinking of all such narrators as "omniscient," then, can obscure for us the variety of kinds and extents of knowledge individual narrators lay claim to or actually display, which can be highly consequential for our understanding of what a particular novel is up to (see, for example, the significant geographical limitations in Austen's fiction on the narrator's access to consciousnesses other than the heroine's which we discuss in chapter 2). The belief that an author is adopting an omniscient perspective on the narrated world – a perspective that in real life is presumed to be available only to God – can also subtly predispose a reader to see "omniscient" narrators as presumptuous, grandiose, or authoritarian, as interested in "playing God" in relationship to the reader or the narrated world. We would suggest that there is little evidence in the texts of these novels of such ambitions – that instead narrators are far more likely to remark on their own limitations. Even passages of narratorial discourse in which the narrator refers to him- or herself as author of the story are rarely celebrations of absolute power. More often they reflect on the limits of the author's ability to evoke desired responses in their readers, or to forestall negative ones. Typical nineteenth-century realist narrators, in other words, neither seek the pedestal of omniscience nor require to be pushed off it. Instead of referring to such narrators as "omniscient," then, we will follow the lead of some recent narrative theorists in using the term "authorial" to refer to narrators who stand apart from the fictional world, have privileged knowledge of its inner workings, and address the reader rhetorically in ways that invite us to identify them with the voice of the author.[2]

In the discourse about novels that arose in the early twentieth century, there was much talk of "objectivity" and the "disappearing narrator," and a certain amount of condescension was shown to the "intrusive" and "garrulous" narrators created by the likes of Thackeray and Trollope. As with "omniscience," we would caution our readers to be attentive to such loaded terms and aesthetic assumptions. It is certainly true that nineteenth-century narrators do anything but disappear, but this need not be a failing. They are, indeed, fundamentally social creatures, and we will get most out of reading them if we engage with them on those terms.

For narrators who tell a story in which they themselves feature as a character, narratologists usefully distinguish between those who are themselves the main character, termed "autodiegetic" (e.g., Jane Eyre) and those who are only, as it were, witnesses on the sidelines, or "homodiegetic" (e.g., Nelly Dean). We will use these terms when precision requires them, but more often will rely on the more familiar "first person narrator" to refer to a narrator who figures as a character.

First person narrators such as Nelly Dean and Jane Eyre are clearly entities we should refer to using feminine pronouns; they have a gender, as do male first person narrators. What of authorial narrators? Although the question of whether there are male and female styles of narration is much debated, we have opted for the simple solution of referring to narrators created by males by using male pronouns and narrators created by females by using female pronouns. Thus Austen's narrator is referred to in these pages as a "she," Thackeray's narrator as a "he." We do this partly to keep the issue of the gender of narration alive (though in the background), partly to emphasize the "humanness" of nineteenth-century narrators, and partly to avoid the unappealing choice between using "he" to refer to both sexes or resorting to the unwieldy "he or she."

An important issue involving narrators is narrative focus. The great narratologist Gérard Genette made a decisive step in conceptualizing the issues involved when he introduced a vital distinction between (in his roughest formalization) "who sees" and "who speaks" as the narration proceeds. (Before Genette's intervention, these two issues had been lumped together under the rubric of "point of view.") As Jane Eyre narrates her story, we hear her voice speaking and see things through her eyes. But in what is often thought of as Hemingway's typical narrative practice (the standard example is his story "The Killers"), the voice that tells us the story appears to belong to no one in it, but we nonetheless see more or less only what one of the characters would be seeing at any given moment. The set of possible variations here is quite large. Genette himself refined his definition of "who sees" to become "who perceives" and to focus on the flow of what he calls information (a concept not without its difficulties). In the scene from *Vanity Fair* to which we briefly referred above, the narrator restricts what he sees and knows to what somebody in the

Osborne household could have seen and known during the days leading to old Osborne's death, even though that same narrator elsewhere in the novel commands a much wider view of scenes and information (including the thoughts of all the characters). Austen is celebrated for her use of narrative focus to shape our experience of her novels and help create their meaning. As might be expected with regard to such a central aspect of the novelist's craft, a good deal of challenge and attempted revision has arisen around Genette's distinction and terminology. We have chosen not to enter the fray; instead, we employ common-language explanations of moments in the novels where narrative focus is important.[3]

The Implied Author, Free Indirect Discourse, and "Sentiment"

Another useful bit of terminological clarification involves a concept we will not always employ when, if we felt the need to be quite precise, we probably should – the "implied author."[4] This concept was invented by the eminent theorist of narrative Wayne Booth. Its purpose is to give us the best possible way of talking about the structure of values that lies behind a given novel. The most basic problem it solves is a tendency to confuse the values assumed and projected by a novel with the values of its author. Booth's invention of the implied author has the virtue of shifting our attention away from what we think we know about the views of the author as a real person. Instead of asking, "What did Austen believe about marriage?" one asks, "What would you have to have believed about marriage to have made the series of artistic choices that resulted in *Persuasion*?" Real-life authors change their minds; often the reason they write novels is precisely that doing so expresses what they really have in their minds (and souls) in a way clearer than any other form of their expression (say, a letter to a friend). Speaking in terms of the implied author forces one to concentrate on the evidence of the novel's text, and not, say, on facts we know or think we know about the author. It immerses one in the task of reading the novel, not speculating on biography.

We will reserve a full explanation of a final bit of terminology, "free indirect discourse," for the appendix to this book. Free indirect discourse is a method of reporting the thought or speech of a character that is important in nearly all of the novels we will be treating. In our experience, once readers grasp how it works, it can add a great deal to their understanding of a novel and the pleasure they take in it. This entire book might indeed have been taken up with discussions of how the various authors employ this device. We have reluctantly decided instead to define it in the appendix, mention its presence in a key passage from *Persuasion*, and add a few brief mentions in subsequent chapters.

Moving from matters of form to those of ideology, a reader of nineteenth-century novels can greatly profit from paying close attention to what the texts actually say and do with regard to feelings, and especially "sentiment." The use of pathetic scenes in fiction to evoke tearful responses from readers is generally termed "sentimentalism." With their philosophical roots in Adam Smith's "Theory of the Moral Sentiments," sentimental scenes in novels are supposed to work roughly like this: sympathetic identification with the suffering object produces a gush of feeling – ideally signaled by a gush of tears – that affirms and strengthens the reader's innate capacity for good – his or her "moral sentiments." Fictional sentimentality, the theory goes, promotes real benevolence by heightening and reinforcing our sensitivity to claims, via our feelings, on our benevolence: they help, in other words, to cultivate the right kind of feeling.

In its present usage, though, the term "sentimental" tends to conflate the descriptive with the pejorative, suggesting, by most definitions, the evocation of emotions that are excessive or disproportionate to their occasion, or cloyingly false in tone, and when called up in service of social or political judgments, a dishonest desire to swamp hard reasoning with easy tears. We would suggest, however, that it is important to acknowledge the same potential for complexity, aesthetic ambition, and intellectual weight in novelists' treatments of emotional connections both within novels and between novel and reader as we do to their other representational strategies. These novels' engagements with feelings and "sentiment" are inextricably bound up with – indeed, part of – their aspirations to engage adequately with "the real" in its cultural and historical specificity: that is, with their realism.

How this Book Proceeds

Some introductions to literary genres proceed as "casebooks." As the institution of literary criticism has grown over the years, certain approaches have proved to be useful and interesting; a "casebook" is organized on the principle of giving examples of a variety of such approaches. In its purest form, a casebook feeds the same literary work through a variety of critical machines whose nature and workings it wishes to reveal, thus showing what each one would make of the text in question. We share the view that one of our responsibilities is to provide our readers with some sense of what different kinds of reading practices active on the current critical scene can accomplish. But our focus is on individual works and authors, not on methods. Still, in several of the chapters that follow we do give some indication of the nature of several important approaches to the novel: Foucauldian criticism, for instance, makes an appearance in the chapter on Trollope, Bakhtinian criticism does likewise in the chapter on Thackeray, and issues arising from postcolonial criticism enter into the discussions of Scott and the Brontës. In our view, one of the most important critical approachs to prose fiction (and much else) to have appeared in the past forty years is feminist criticism. The reader will find that issues involving gender and the place of women appear repeatedly in the pages that follow.

The scope and purpose of this book have precluded any attempt to tackle the daunting task of bringing readers up to speed on the large critical literature about the various novels we discuss. We mention a few studies and try to acknowledge major debts. We provide at the end of each chapter suggestions for the most significant critical work on that novelist. In the last few decades, the majority of the best work on nineteenth-century fiction has occurred in books that discuss a range of authors in the period. A brief bibliography of this work is also provided.

In this sort of study it is hard to imagine doing anything approaching full justice to those who have influenced us in person or in print, the more so because of the sheer volume of work on nearly all of the novels we discuss. But we do not wish to deprive ourselves of the pleasure of thanking those who have provided direct and indirect assistance with this volume. Alison Case would like to thank Heather Morton, Bojana Mladenovic, Christian Thorne, Brian Martin, Theo Davis, Karen Swann, and Samreen Kazmi for commenting on versions of this work. Harry Shaw is grateful for the expert advice of Wendy Jones and James Eli Adams, and for the assistance of Sarah Cote and Daniel Wilson in canvassing critical studies. It is a particular pleasure for him to extend thanks to Richard Fischer for his observations and suggestions.

Our approach to the very different novels and novelists we discuss varies. Our aim is to focus on the aspects of the novels which, when fully grasped, promise to make them live for modern readers; we also hope to forestall misunderstandings likely to flow from "modern" assumptions about what novels should be and do. In some cases, problems can arise because it may not be immediately apparent that the task the novelist has set himself or herself means that some of the pleasures we normally associate with novel-reading may be truncated. Scott, for instance, can be disappointing for readers who are looking for depth-psychology or a passionate and moving love story, but subtle and fascinating for those who recognize that his real interest is in exploring social identity and our place in history. By the same token, Gaskell's fiction needs to be understood in the context of her wish to convey the plight of working men and women in times of explosive social unrest, and certain aspects of Trollope's *The Warden* come into focus for us when we grasp his horror at the coming of mass society and all it implies. When we move to the Brontës, quite different issues arise. With *Wuthering Heights*, a fundamental question is whether the novel can in the end be understood at all in any conventional sense; with *Jane Eyre*, it seems important to come to terms with the power but also the limitations of fiction so firmly planted in the consciousness of an individual character.

In some of our chapters, we spend a good deal of time on relatively brief passages from the novels, because only such careful attention to the moments that constitute the minute-by-minute experience of novels can adequately define what it means to be fully alive to them. To read a novel richly means to perform it, as one would perform a musical score. We hope that our readings of passages will provide a model for this kind of performance that will carry over into our readers' own approach to works of fiction. Since this is a book for readers, we focus on a number of occasions on moments when the novels we study seem to be commenting on what it means to read.

We conclude this introduction by returning to the centrality of the narrator. For all of these authors, despite their manifest differences, attention to the role of the narrator pays rich aesthetic dividends and can also guide us to the issues that matter most, different though they may be from novel to novel. It is our hope that this book will help its readers recognize the remarkable intelligence the novelists we treat bring to issues and problems that matter to modern men and women, and will also come to share our gratitude for the novelists' insights into what it means to be human. Last but not least, we hope that these pages will help enhance the wonder and delight with which readers will react to the sheer artistic skill of the authors we treat.

Chapter 1

Pride and Prejudice and *Persuasion*

Jane Austen is an author readers think they know. At least one reader of Austen has described heaven as a place where you would habitually engage in conversation with her. There are Austen societies in England and in the United States. Some readers concern themselves with every detail of her novels and their social settings, down to the cut of dresses and the recipes for the food consumed in them. There is indeed a name for such people, "Janeites." Henry James objected to all this, writing disparagingly of those who, for commercial gain, in his view distorted her actual (and considerable) achievement by inviting readers to think of her as "their 'dear,' our dear, everybody's dear, Jane."[1] Rudyard Kipling, by contrast, wrote a story celebrating a particular group of Janeites – a group of World War I soldiers who kept their sanity intact by engaging in an elaborate ritual of giving the military objects around them names drawn from the persons and places depicted in "Jane's" novels, and testing each other on their details. The palpable realities of her world, its men and women and settings, were apparently sufficient to ward off the horrific realities of trench warfare, if anything could.

The idea that novels contain real people and are told to us directly by their authors is one that teachers of the novel often find themselves combating – usually for good reasons. Readers who think of characters as if they were real people living in the real world have a way of remaking those characters according to the logic of the familiar world they themselves inhabit, which can be a way of short-circuiting a more difficult but in the end more rewarding kind of reading that takes into account historical, cultural, and ideological differences between the present and the past, and is alive to the novelist's craft. Similar problems can arise if we think of a novel as being told by a real-life author. As we have discussed more fully in the introduction, the voice readers of novels are faced with is not that of the author, but that of the narrator, who has been crafted to tell the story in a certain way for certain purposes.

Yet for all of that, Jane Austen's characters do tend to strike readers as very real indeed, and Jane Austen's books seem to be by . . . Jane Austen, a woman who lived in Hampshire at the beginning of the nineteenth century, who is said to have hidden her novels-in-progress if anyone entered the room, and who we know never married. We do think we know Jane, and we do think of her world as real and immediate.

The intuitions of large numbers of people who take pleasure in works of great art should never be discounted, though sometimes they can profit by more careful description than those who feel them would trouble to give them. In Austen's novels, and in the other novels with which we will be concerned, the reader is indeed faced with something real and human from the outset – a real and human voice. This is to say that (as is not always the case with novels, and particularly with twentieth-century novels of the experimental variety) we are faced with a narrator very much modeled on a human scale, who seems (except for her access to her heroine's thoughts) to take in the world as we would do. (One commentator has shown that Austen's novels normally include only characters who live within easy visiting distance of wherever the heroine finds herself at a given moment, and that the narrator only penetrates the minds of characters besides the heroine to reveal information that might be gleaned from external observation by a perceptive observer.)[2] The voice of Austen's narrator seeks to engage us in something akin to a conversation. She wants to amuse, persuade, and move us. With Austen, it is clear enough that the human voice we are hearing is an ideal voice in the precision and discrimination of its language. We cannot quite imagine anyone really speaking that way. But we can just imagine someone thinking with that remarkable clarity. One important reason why we speak so readily of "Jane Austen" is that we want to have a ready way of referring to the remarkable mind behind the voice that tells us her stories. For that mind may be the most important thing about them. It is why the world of her novels seems so "real." Her world seems palpable because, given the underlying network of values that organize it and judge it, it seems in the end completely knowable. We think of it as real because we feel that we can, in principle at least, fully grasp its logic – and more than that, because we are sure that at least one mind, the mind behind the narrator's voice, can do so.

Behind the voice, we sense the existence of a set of standards and values that are, in the end, the most "real" thing about Austen's world. One might reasonably expect Austen's world to be informed by conservative values. She writes about the gentry, a class of well-to-do, genteel people who were neither rich nor titled; she depicts and cares about their privileged mode of life, their social rituals, their houses, their ways. But this may not be quite the whole story, just because of the insistent presence we feel in the narrator's language of a clear and austere set of values. The way of life of the gentry at the opening of the nineteenth century may provide the "social basis" for her novels and even for the ethical discriminations constantly reinforced by the precisions of her language. But Raymond Williams, a distinguished left-wing critic, has suggested that in her novels Austen develops "an everyday, uncompromising morality which is in the end separable from its social basis and which, in other hands, can be turned against it."[3] We will return to the issue of the politics of Austen's novels. For the moment, it will suffice to point out one effect of the powerful ethical underpinnings of her language and the system of values it projects. Behind the real and palpable world of Austen's novels is always another, ideal world against which the real world is measured. We care about Austen's heroines, and we want the best for them. Much of the tension, and pleasure, of an Austen novel stems from our underlying awareness of the ideal world Austen's language projects, and our hope that her heroines will be able to find a place in it as well.[4]

Pride and Prejudice

At times the two worlds seem to meet. As an example of how this can take place, and in preparation for the more extended discussion of *Persuasion* that is the main business of this chapter, we turn to *Pride and Prejudice*. In that novel, blocking figures including obtuse elders and misbehaving siblings stand between the heroine and the man she is destined to marry. One issue is social class: Elizabeth Bennet isn't, in conventional terms, of quite the same class as Darcy, and the escapades of her family (which culminate in the scandalous elopement of Elizabeth's sister Lydia) threaten to rob her, by contagion, of all respectability whatever. A meddling relative of Darcy, Lady Catherine de Bourgh, visits Elizabeth to remind her of all this (and more), asking her at one point if "the shades of Pemberley" (Darcy's country house) are to be "polluted" by such an unsuitable alliance. With a single sentence, Elizabeth brushes away all the complex and (despite the absurd snobbery of the person who voices them) to Austen quite real social considerations Lady Catherine raises: "He is a gentleman; I am a gentleman's daughter; so far we are equal" (ch. 56). To say this is hardly to sing the *Marseillaise*; it is to make reference to an ideal realm in which what it means to be a gentleman and a gentleman's daughter are defined in a way absolute enough to make external complications irrelevant. If you are a true gentleman or a true lady, the assumption seems to be, even disgraceful behavior on the part of your close relatives doesn't affect that. A certain ideal of personal conduct and individual intelligence, arising from education and social position but in the end separable from it, is here turned, as Williams suggests, against anyone (from Lady Catherine to certain kinds of readers, past and present) who would simply reduce the individual to his or her social determinants.

In *Pride and Prejudice*, Austen goes one better than simply making the familiar idealistic assertion that the values of certain exceptional individuals trump the standards of the world that surrounds them. The ideal and real worlds in *Pride and Prejudice* actually coalesce in a scene occurring at that very Pemberley whose "shades" Lady Catherine fears will be polluted, in a way that ultimately defines what it is to be a true gentleman and a true lady, and shows that both Elizabeth and Darcy qualify. Until this point in the novel, Elizabeth and the reader have taken a negative view of Darcy. (So negative has this been on Elizabeth's part, that she has refused an offer of marriage from him.) He has seemed arrogant and rude, full of the "pride" that half names the novel. But when Elizabeth visits his country house (assuming him to be away) while traveling with her uncle and aunt, a dramatic alteration begins. To begin with, the house and its surroundings are in perfect taste, "neither formal, nor falsely adorned" (ch. 43). This is only the beginning. Elizabeth learns from the housekeeper who shows her party around the house that Darcy is quite a different person there from the one she has thought she knew, unwaveringly polite and humane to his servants, a model landlord, affable to the poor, full of filial piety to his dead father, a model and attentive brother to his younger sister. The suggestion emerges that, to be himself and to be understood for what he truly is, Darcy needs to be and to be seen in the proper, the ideal setting.

This underlying assumption is conveyed by the most exquisite novelistic art. Throughout the opening part of the scene, Elizabeth experiences Pemberley in a mode of aesthetic appreciation; this is of course just how one would take in a great country house one is visiting as a tourist. She views the house and its contents as one would a work of art. But this mode of vision keeps passing over into one involving character, ethics, and a judgment on a whole way of life. Elizabeth knows herself to be no connoisseur of art. In reacting to the paintings that adorn Pemberley, she finds herself instead drawn to the portraits of people she knows. A set of miniature paintings on one wall, for instance, surprises her because it contains a miniature of someone Darcy (for good reasons) despises. Why is it there in Darcy's own house? Why hasn't Darcy removed it? The answer is that Darcy's father was fond of the person. The fact that this particular painting has been left on the wall thus has a larger significance: it is a sign of Darcy's filial piety. The aesthetic beauty and orderliness of the house and landscape are similarly shadowed by human, ethical considerations, as the housekeeper tells Elizabeth's party that "there is not one of his tenants or servants but what will give him a good name. Some people call him proud;

but I am sure I never saw any thing like it. To my fancy, it is only because he does not rattle away like other young men" (ch. 43). In the sentences just quoted, we see a typical move on Austen's part, the splitting apart of concepts and words into subtler shades of meaning and possibility, to produce ever finer networks of perceptual and ethical discrimination and intelligence – here, with regard to Darcy's "pride." We are invited to consider whether a certain reticence might be *mistaken* for pride ("he does not rattle away like other young men"). Later in the novel, Elizabeth finds herself explaining her love for Darcy to her father in part by saying of Darcy, "Indeed he has no improper pride" (ch. 59). The suggestion here appears to be that even though pride is traditionally considered a sin (indeed, a cardinal sin), in the proper context and with the proper basis, it can be a good thing. (Pride of ancestry can, for instance, help lead a person to treat his tenants well.) In the scene we are examining, a wonderfully subtle turn on the notion of pride comes in the following unobtrusive bit of description:

> Mr. Gardiner, whose manners were easy and pleasant, encouraged [the housekeeper's] communicativeness, by his questions and remarks; Mrs. Reynolds, either from pride or attachment, had evidently great pleasure in talking of her master and his sister. (ch. 43)

At least two interesting things happen in that one sentence. First, what gets slyly suggested is yet another take on "pride": in Mrs. Reynold's talk of Darcy and his sister, can one really distinguish entirely between pride and attachment – and ought one to do so? Don't the two go together, supporting one another? This in turn suggests that Darcy's own "pride" might, in the proper context, turn out to have its good and even necessary sides and potentialities – which is exactly what turns out to be the case. Second, we as readers enter the circle of those who are contemplating Mrs. Reynolds, assessing her mixture of pride and attachment. We join the group that is touring Pemberley. We too are invited to react in a mode that mixes aesthetic, social, and ethical components. This happens because of a certain softening of focus with regard to "point of view" here. Usually in Austen, we know exactly from whose viewpoint we are seeing things: this control of point of view is one of her strongest and most telling techniques, and it habitually centers in one and only one character at a time. Thus earlier in the scene, when the miniatures are described, it is clear that we are viewing them through Elizabeth's eyes, both physically and evaluatively. Here, however, the point of view is more general: just who is it in the scene to whom it is "evident" that Mrs. Reynolds is taking pleasure, and just who is it who is speculating about her mixture of pride and attachment? Well, the sentence begins with Mr. Gardiner, and so we may be inclined to assign these perceptions to him. But the interest and amusement with which the rest of the party react to her commentary broadens the circle of perception, to include Mr. Gardiner, Elizabeth, the narrator, and ultimately us as readers.

Elizabeth subsequently finds herself faced with a portrait of Darcy, which she views according to the mode of the scene as a whole. When she sees in the portrait "such a smile over the face, as she remembered to have sometimes seen, when he looked at her," we cannot miss the stirrings of desire in her; when she gazes at the portrait "in earnest contemplation," we know she is coming to grips with a "new" Darcy suggested by the context of Pemberley. And then, in a moment of supreme artfulness, when she leaves the house and enters the grounds, the picture comes alive: Darcy, the new and "ideal" Darcy, walks out of the frame and stands before her: "As they walked across the lawn towards the river, Elizabeth turned back to look [at the house] again; her uncle and aunt stopped also, and while the former was conjecturing as to the date of the building, the owner of it himself suddenly came forward from the road, which led behind it to the stables" (ch. 43). The rest of the novel gives Darcy the chance to show that the Darcy revealed by Pemberley is indeed the real Darcy. It is particularly significant that he feels, immediately after what we have called his emergence from the picture frame, an immediate liking and affinity for Elizabeth's aunt and uncle, who as members of the middle, professional class, would be beneath his notice if he had "improper" pride – and who are just the sort of person he did in fact look down upon when he was not in his proper setting, not at Pemberley. It is also true that Darcy warms to Elizabeth's aunt and uncle because he is in love with her and realizes he must change to win her.

We have been laying the groundwork for our consideration of Austen's final novel, *Persuasion*, by identifying, describing, and drawing conclusions about the reader's experience of Austen's narrator. When we read Austen, we have the feeling that we are in contact with a human intelligence of a very high order, an intelligence that can describe and place every person and circumstance it depicts. This is what makes the voice, and the world it depicts, seem so real and authentically human. But the activity of the mind behind the voice we hear is not limited to brilliant description. It extends also to precise evaluation, implied by the highly refined and nuanced shades of meaning inherent in the language by which people and circumstances are described. People are not simply proud: they have various kinds of pride, some of which are improper, others of which may be allied to more (in Austen's precise language) "amiable" qualities. This net of evaluative discriminations is also not an end in itself. The mind behind the voice is engaged in imagining an ideal version of the world it observes and depicts. Such a vision of the ideal is of course "conservative," but (as we might expect from Austen), conservative in a special sense. ("Indeed, she has no improper conservatism," one is tempted to cry.) The visions of the ideal are, to be sure, firmly rooted in what Austen takes to be the social actualities around her. There is absolutely no sense of a visionary alternative to them (as we might find, say, in Austen's rough contemporary William Blake). But though this conservatism is bound up with the status quo, then, it does not simply ratify the status quo. There are few moments in Austen where a setting we might imagine to actually exist in Austen's time and Austen's ideal seem effortlessly to merge, as they do in her depiction of Pemberley. Nowhere is the discrepancy between the two more apparent than in *Persuasion*. But before we pursue this issue, it will be well to take a look at the claims of *Persuasion* as a whole.

Persuasion: Love and Narrative Focus

Persuasion is, first of all, a powerful love story. Among other things, it is a progenitor of what Stanley Cavell has identified as one of the premier genres of the great period of the film studios, the "Hollywood comedy of remarriage."[5] No remarriage, to be sure, occurs in *Persuasion*, but we get the next best thing – the story of a love affair that is broken off, seemingly forever, but that leads (after a great deal of pain) to reunion and marriage. We suspect that one reason why she created this unusual love story is that Austen was on a fundamental level an entirely "professional" author. She knew the novels of her day (what we today might refer to as the "novelistic discourse"), and throughout her career she drew upon but never quite repeated their formulas, or repeated herself. This meant striking out into (and delighting in) new territory, creating ever new permutations of the marriage plot.

Whatever its origin, the affective potential of the kind of story Austen chooses for *Persuasion* is enormous. In *Pride and Prejudice*, Elizabeth advises Darcy to "think of the past only as its remembrance gives you pleasure" (ch. 58), and past mistakes lead easily to present happiness. In *Persuasion*, memories of the past are exceptionally potent and refuse to be so easily forgotten or remolded. The contrast between what Anne Elliot and Wentworth once meant to each other, and his indifference to her throughout much of the novel, provides a sharp backdrop of pain. The pressure of that pain leads Austen to depict moments of perceptual derangement on a very basic level. When Anne finds herself in contact with Wentworth, reality seems to swim before her: she is uncertain of just what is happening, physically; the voices of others become a mere buzz.

Problems of perception have in Austen's earlier novels involved problems of "perceptiveness"; they have meant misassessing a situation or a person, failing to use one's head. In *Persuasion*, by contrast, one character receives a blow to the head that alters her personality, and the very act of perceiving the world is registered at a basic level, several steps beneath the typical Austen concern with effective mental judgment. Beneath this expansion of view lies an acknowledgment of the power of memory and the reality of loss. The irreversibility of Anne's loss of Wentworth seems, through much of the early part of the novel, indisputable, as Wentworth courts other women before Anne's eyes, in a parade of indifference. Wary readers will recognize that it *is* a parade, or at least suspect that it is. But by keeping the narrative focused through Anne, Austen's narrator keeps us guessing.

We are, to be sure, not always in Anne's mind, and we do not always see things through her eyes. There is a moment, early on, for instance, when we are allowed to enter Wentworth's mind, a moment that will repay careful and extended analysis because of what it reveals about the novel and our relationship to it as we read. Anne's sister has (unkindly) reported to her that Wentworth had said that when he re-met her, Anne seemed to him "so altered that he should not have known [her] again." Anne reacts, as one might expect, with mortification and pain:

> "So altered that he should not have known her again!" These were words which could not but dwell with her. Yet she soon began to rejoice that she had heard them. They were of sobering tendency; they allayed agitation; they composed, and consequently must make her happier.

The passage continues in this way:

> Frederick Wentworth had used such words, or something like them, but without an idea that they would be carried round to her. He had thought her wretchedly altered, and, in the first moment of appeal, had spoken as he felt. He had not forgiven Anne Elliot. She had used him ill; deserted and disappointed him; and worse, she had shewn a feebleness of character in doing so, which his own decided, confident temper could not endure. She had given him up to oblige others. It had been the effect of over-persuasion. It had been weakness and timidity.
>
> He had been most warmly attached to her, and had never seen a woman since whom he thought her equal; but, except from some natural sensation of curiosity, he had no desire of meeting her again. Her power with him was gone for ever.

> It was now his object to marry. He was rich, and being turned on shore, fully intended to settle as soon as he could be properly tempted; actually looking round, ready to fall in love with all the speed which a clear head and quick taste could allow. He had a heart for either of the miss Musgroves, if they could catch it; a heart, in short, for any pleasing young woman who came in his way, excepting Anne Elliot. This was his only secret exception, when he said to his sister, in answer to her suppositions, "Yes, here I am, Sophia, quite ready to make a foolish match" . . . Anne Elliot was not out of his thoughts, when he more seriously described the woman he should wish to meet with. "A strong mind, with sweetness of manner," made the first and the last of the description. (ch. 7)

When we encounter this sequence of paragraphs, we have become so accustomed to experiencing the world of the novel with Anne as its narrative focus that some readers mistake all of it as a record of Anne's thoughts – even the part that depicts Wentworth's internal thoughts. (These they take to be what Anne imagines Wentworth must have thought to himself.) This is a testimony, not so much to the inattentiveness of such readers, as to how fully Austen has immersed us in Anne's consciousness, making us share her pain at hearing Wentworth's remark so deeply that our identification with her emotional perspective can be hard to shake. But of course by the end of the passage there really should be no doubt whatever that we are reading a transcript of Wentworth's thoughts and speech, not of Anne's mental recreation of what he must have been thinking. Otherwise, we would have to suppose that Anne is able to recreate in her mind, not only Wentworth's thoughts about her, but his subsequent conversation with his sister! We will add that Wentworth's thoughts are rendered, as Anne's are often rendered, through the use of "free indirect discourse," an important technique explained in the appendix to this book. Readers who learn to identify free indirect discourse will, among many other things, be less likely to mistake the passage for a transcription of Anne's thoughts, not Wentworth's.

The question remains of why Austen should, exceptionally, break away from Anne as narrative focus, not merely to the extent of adding a comment by the narrator, but to the extent of reproducing Wentworth's thoughts "from the inside." Why does Wentworth become the narrative focus at this point? The answer is multi-layered. On one level, we as readers need to be absolutely sure about Wentworth's attitude. We must also be certain about just what in fact did occur between Anne and Wentworth in the past. Austen doesn't want us to begin imagining, for example, that Anne has come to exaggerate their mutual depth of feeling. On a deeper level, Austen has a delicate task to perform throughout the novel. We as readers need to feel with and through Anne: we must share her pain at Wentworth's indifference, so that the contrast will allow us to share her joy all the more when the walls between them fall. But it will not do for us to become completely identified with Anne, particularly when she finds things most hopeless. Our continued interest in the novel depends upon having a sense that change is possible, and some of the pleasure of the novel results precisely from moments when we can see farther than Anne can, despite her intelligence. When we see farther than Anne, we draw close to the consciousness we most admire as we read – the consciousness of the narrator. In this passage, we enter the mode of privileged knowing with respect both to Anne and to Wentworth. A careful reader realizes from the very vehemence of Wentworth's thoughts, that for all his studied indifference, Anne Eliot remains the pivot of his thoughts. (This is what makes the declaration, "Anne Elliot was not out of his thoughts, when he more seriously described the woman he should wish to meet with," so delicious on a second reading of the novel.) This recognition, however deeply it may be buried in our consciousness as we read, gives us enough hope to make us wish to continue reading and allows us to predict, in general terms, the novel's happy outcome. When that outcome arrives, our pleasure is the greater, because it seems both deeply right and entirely plausible, something we have hoped for but also expected all along.

The Letter Scene

The reversal we have been taught to expect, by such means as this rare excursion into Wentworth's mind, occurs most richly in the novel's most celebrated scene, in which Wentworth writes a love letter to Anne based on a conversation between her and one of his friends he half overhears as he sits in a room where they are talking. One of Austen's subtlest readers has recounted how, as a girl, she would sometimes simply read the letter scene over and over, and other times skim through the book just so that she could re-experience the scene when she came to it.[6] The impassioned words of Wentworth's letter certainly deserve such a response. So does the chance the scene affords for Anne to give her views on woman's constancy, in a context where she will not be ignored (as she has been for so many years in her own family circle) but instead will receive the fullest possible attention by two estimable hearers, one of whom (Harville) simply admires her for what she is, while the other (Wentworth) is hanging on her every word because he is deeply in love with her.

The scene also provides a meditation on the uses of fiction itself. The issue of the relationship between the general and the particular fascinated Austen throughout her career, and the idea that there could be an easy fit between general pronouncements and specific situations always excited her suspicion and often amused her – reactions unsurprising in one with her keen powers of nuance and discrimination. (Perhaps the best-known use of the potential gap between the general statements and specific situations underlies the comic opening line of *Pride and Prejudice*, "It is a truth universally acknowledged, that a single man in possession of a good fortune, must be in want of a wife.") The "letter" chapter in *Persuasion* opens with Mrs. Musgrove loudly proclaiming her general opinion about long engagements, a subject painfully applicable to two quieter people in the room, Anne and Wentworth, though in ways Mrs. Musgrove could never imagine. Anne soon finds herself making generalizations about male and female constancy, but in terms that (though she cannot quite admit this to herself) are directed both to the person with whom she is conversing and also to Wentworth, who is in a position to overhear her. What Mrs. Musgrove has to say, and for that matter what Anne has to say, may or may not be true as generalities; it is actually hard to imagine how, as generalities, they could be either true or false in any absolute sense, since they cover so much ground and therefore must admit to so many exceptions. But if properly understood and if put in a suitably concrete and specific framework, what both say, and particularly what Anne says, can indeed offer crucially valid insights to the right listener. Anne's insistence that women can be constant in love even when the situation appears hopeless in fact means everything to Wentworth at this particular moment. Her claim that women experience separation differently from men ("we live at home, quiet, confined, and our feelings prey upon us") and even more the "faltering" acknowledgment that "woman's feelings" would be too great a burden for an active man to bear, also convey something Wentworth needs to hear: just how painful this separation has been for Anne (ch. 23).

This interchange seems, among other things, a figure for Austen's own relationship to her readers. Austen offers us truths of a kind, but we must be listening for them and must know how to take them. If, like Wentworth, we are sufficiently interested and sufficiently perceptive, we can become part of a charmed circle where admiration, respect, and even love circulate, because we know how to attend to the pictures Austen paints, and how to apply the general truths of her fiction to our own lives and desires. It is certainly worth attending to the dialogue we have been examining, not only for its covert message to Wentworth, but also for the movement of the argument itself, which conveys a great deal about both what divides men from women and what unites them. Initially Harville and Anne cannot reach agreement on the relative merits of men and women, both because their experiences are so different and because the culture at large encourages a dismissive view of women's constancy. But when the abstract argument breaks down, the two find common ground in sharing their own feelings, and in doing so they create a small community of shared values whose emotional charge can extend to draw in Wentworth as well. Communities of feeling are important in *Persuasion*, as they will be in *Mary Barton*, *Bleak House*, and *Middlemarch*.

Still, there certainly are barriers between Anne and Wentworth in this most intimate of scenes. The layers of indirection, and particularly the frustrating impossibility for Anne simply to tell Wentworth that she still loves him, create a vivid reminder of how difficult it is for people to be simply themselves in any social setting. It is significant that the one exception to this rule in *Persuasion*, the one character who is simply and perpetually himself, Admiral Croft, is at once amusing and lovable, but also clearly not the stuff of which the novel's hero or heroine could possibly be made. In Austen, the rooms in which we live are always full of other people, and only the comically solipsistic can evade this condition of life.

Coping with the Social

On one level, to be sure, the necessity for indirection in the "letter" scene merely adds to our pleasure, following the general principle (applicable in fiction and in life) that a difficulty overcome produces an additional quantum of pleasure. On another level, however, the sense of social constraint underlines the fact that in *Persuasion*, Austen tests the limits and problems both of individual experience (for example, in the reduction of some of Anne's perceptions to jumbles and buzzes) and of social experience. There is something that, in a less deliriously happy context, would ring of hostility toward society in general in the narrator's announcement that when, shortly after this scene, Anne and Wentworth meet on the street and have the chance to engage in a full and frank expression of their feeling toward one another, they do so "heedless of every group around them, seeing neither sauntering [!] politicians, bustling house-keepers, flirting girls, nor nursery-maids and children" (ch. 23). The next step, to overt hostility, is fully taken at the end of Dickens's *Little Dorrit*, when we are informed that the hero and heroine "went quietly down into the roaring streets, inseparable and blessed; and as they passed along in sunshine and in shade, the noisy and the eager, and the arrogant and the froward and the vain, fretted, and chafed, and made their usual uproar." A very different mind from Austen's lies behind *that* voice.

In some nineteenth-century novels, female characters cope with social and familial injustice and constraint simply by remaining unaware of it: they "rise above" such things. (This is certainly a tendency in Dickens.) Another alternative is rebellion, such as we find in *Jane Eyre*. Austen's heroines take a different path. Elizabeth Bennet is entirely aware of the impropriety of her family's behavior and of her father's neglect in failing to correct it, and she also knows what these things may cost her and her sister Jane. She nonetheless employs wit and irony to keep these matters from dampening her spirits. The difference between her use of wit and irony as a coping mechanism and her father's is a topic which, if carefully explored, will shed a good deal of light not just on the meaning of *Pride and Prejudice* but on Austen's sense of the dangers of her own narrative mode, since the Austen narrator makes extensive use of an irony that at first glance can seem identical to that of Mr. Bennet.

Anne Elliot, too, is entirely aware of the extent to which she is slighted by her family and hemmed in by her social situation. She knows very well that her father's slight regard for her is unfair and that his overvaluation of her sister is groundless, the simple expression of his own dull egotism. She also realizes that their arrogant stupidity (she would not allow herself to call it that) may lead to trouble for them all. By the same token, she is aware that, when she visits Uppercross full of her own deep concerns about her imminent uprooting from Kellynch, the Musgroves simply ignore her pain, remaining immersed in their habitual round of pleasures and petty annoyances. But she nevertheless finds her own mental world rich enough to allow her to register such facts without allowing them to overwhelm her. Faced with the Musgroves' self-absorption, she decides, with a certain amusement, that to be of any use at all in the situation, it will be "highly incumbent on her to clothe her imagination, her memory, and all her ideas in as much of Uppercross as possible" (ch. 6). (The qualifying phrase "as possible" is important: it suggests that for her, unlike a similar character in Dickens, total self-abnegation will be neither possible nor desirable.) Earlier, the narrator has told us that Anne

> always contemplated [the Musgrove sisters] as some of the happiest creatures of her acquaintance; but still, saved as we all are by some comfortable feeling of superiority from wishing the possibility of exchange, she would not have given up her own more elegant and cultivated mind for all their enjoyments; and envied them nothing but that seemingly perfect good understanding and agreement together, that good-humoured mutual affection, of which she had known so little herself with either of her sisters. (ch. 5)

There is of course potential irony in speaking of the "comfortable" feeling of superiority we all have about ourselves, but in this case, the comfort Anne feels is justified and commendable. Darcy, we recall, is said by his housekeeper to have "no improper pride." Assigning the proper value to her own mind helps

Anne to assume a useful place in a social unit that is unable to appreciate her at her true worth, without undue resentment and without making herself a blind slave to the situation.

Persuasion and Renewal

The love story in *Persuasion* is superbly managed, with a rare power that arises most immediately from Anne's earlier pain. Some of the power of the novel's ending, however, draws upon sources that lie very deep in our literary, cultural, and even religious backgrounds, sources that Shakespeare evoked in his late plays, above all *The Winter's Tale*. In that play, a woman who was thought to be dead for many years suddenly and miraculously returns to life, as what appears to be a statue of her moves, descends from its pedestal, and reveals the living woman. It needs hardly be said how many rituals draw on the human need for renewal and rebirth. We can trace the beginnings of a pattern of renewal early in *Persuasion*, in the opening chapter and in the midst of some very incongruous material. After the devastating portrait of Sir Walter Elliot's delight in reading the *Baronetage*, and a brief description of his wife's death, we are given the following explanation of why that father did not marry his wife's best friend, Lady Russell:

> Be it known then, that Sir Walter, like a good father, (having met with one or two private disappointments in very unreasonable applications) prided himself on remaining single for his dear daughter's sake. For one daughter, his eldest, he would really have given up any thing, which he had not been very much tempted to do. Elizabeth had succeeded, at sixteen, to all that was possible, of her mother's rights and consequence; and being very handsome, and very like himself, her influence had always been great, and they had gone on together most happily. His two other children were of very inferior value. Mary had acquired a little artificial importance, by becoming Mrs. Charles Musgrove; but Anne, with an elegance of mind and sweetness of character, which must have placed her high with any people of real understanding, was nobody with either father or sister: her word had no weight; her convenience was always to give way; – she was only Anne.
>
> To Lady Russell, indeed, she was a most dear and highly valued goddaughter, favourite and friend. Lady Russell loved them all; but it was only in Anne that she could fancy the mother to revive again.
>
> A few years before, Anne Elliot had been a very pretty girl, but her bloom had vanished early; and as even in its height, her father had found little to admire in her, (so totally different were her delicate features and mild dark eyes from his own); there could be nothing in them now that she was faded and thin, to

excite his esteem. He had never indulged much hope, he had now none, of ever reading her name in any other page of his favourite work. All equality of alliance must rest with Elizabeth; for Mary had merely connected herself with an old country family of respectability and large fortune, and had therefore *given* all honour, and received none: Elizabeth would, one day or other, marry suitably. (ch. 1)

This passage encapsulates much of the method of the novel, particularly in its manipulation of voice. In the opening section, the narrator's satirical, almost scornful "Be it known" modulates in the course of a few sentences into a voice that sounds very much like Sir Walter's, declaring that his other two children were "of very inferior value." Then the two voices are played off against one another in the following sentence, with Sir Walter's tones predominating in "she was only Anne" – an assessment that condemns him out of his own mouth. After all this unpleasantness (for here even the narrator is, in her own refined way, harsh to the point of unpleasantness), the following, quiet paragraph comes as a lovely oasis, mimicking in its own formal qualities the virtues we are already beginning to assign to Anne, and raising the quiet but persistent theme of rebirth with the words "it was only in Anne that she could fancy the mother to revive again." The reader who attends to similar hints as the novel proceeds will be well repaid. Among the most exquisite of them is one that pits Anne's own elegiac and despairing sense of her loss of Wentworth against nature's own irresistible power of renewal. As she walks among the hedgerows, suffering from Wentworth's attentions to Louisa Musgrove, Anne tries to divert herself by recalling sad poems of autumn; but in the midst of this, we are reminded that the landscape is real and alive, for in their walk Anne's party passes through "large enclosures, where the ploughs at work, and the fresh-made paths spoke [that is, revealed the presence of] the farmer, counteracting the sweets of poetical despondence, and meaning to have spring again" (ch. 10). A further, more lighthearted reference occurs when Anne's "musings of high-wrought love and eternal constancy" are said to have been nearly sufficient "to spread purification and perfume all the way" as she walks in Bath (ch. 21). And there are others.

One of the cleverest ways in which the theme of rebirth and renewal is forwarded involves Anne's own physical appearance. The long passage quoted above gives the initial impression that, when the novel opens, Anne's youthful looks have vanished because of suffering at breaking off her engagement with Wentworth and also because of the passage of time. ("A few years before, Anne Elliot had been a very pretty girl, but her bloom had vanished early; and as even in its height, her father had found little to admire in her, (so totally different were her delicate features and mild dark eyes from his own); there could be nothing in them now that she was faded and thin, to excite his esteem.") But voice and narrative focus are again crucial here. By the end of the passage, we have passed from the narrator's voice and viewpoint to Sir Walter's ("*her father* had found little to admire in her"). This has the effect of leaving open the question of just how much her "looks" have really deteriorated, and how permanently. We are left with enough of a sense of loss to make renewal seem desirable; we do not have a sense of loss so dramatic that it would require an actual miracle (hardly allowable in a realist novel!) to be reversed. This double vision creates an illogical but powerful effect, one denied to visual media such as film. A film would have to show us exactly how Anne actually looks at the opening of the action; it could not rest in fertile ambiguity.

The possibility of renewal brings us to the issue with which this chapter began, Austen's vision of the ideal and how it is embodied in her novels. Earlier we claimed that Austen's ethical discrimination, most concretely apparent in the precision of the narrator's language, projects an ideal world that shadows and judges the world her characters inhabit. In *Pride and Prejudice*, real and ideal worlds seem to meet, at least for a moment, embodied in Pemberley. The situation is very different in *Persuasion*. Here, the country house that dominates the early section of the novel, Kellynch-hall, is nearly bankrupt in a quite literal sense – and so are the values of most of those who inhabit it. The lord of the manor is vain and silly, in a way that endangers his tenants as well as his one deserving daughter. His oldest daughter is as shallow, hard, and materialistic as he is, and as ridden by a ridiculous and superficial pride of caste; his younger daughter is less contemptible, but no less egotistical, and her husband and his landed relatives are too ineffectual to be the basis for change. Only Anne and Lady Russell depart from this most unattractive norm, and Lady Russell herself is, besides being rather slow of mind, hardly exempt from overvaluing birth. *Persuasion* offers us no Pemberley, no imagined merging of the real and the ideal in a house inhabited by the representatives of landed society. We do, however, discover something resembling such a merging elsewhere – in the lodgings of Captain Harville, where Anne finds herself "lost in the pleasanter feelings which sprang from the sight of all the ingenious contrivances and nice arrangements of Captain Harville, to turn the actual space to the best possible account." When she leaves the house, she feels sure that she has "left great happiness behind" (ch. 11).

The power of naval officers and their wives to embody the estimable is further exemplified by the Crofts, who are able to make something even of Kellynch-hall. Admiral Croft removes the full-length looking glasses in which Sir Walter admired himself. ("Oh Lord! there was no getting away from one-self," the admiral remarks, ch. 13.) The ability of the admiral and his wife to transform their surroundings for the better is prefigured by Mrs. Croft's insistence that women can travel in comfort on a ship of war, whatever genteel prejudice might think of the matter: "I know of nothing superior to the accommodations of a man of war" (ch. 8), she tells the Musgroves. The Crofts' mode of going about the countryside also contrasts amusingly with the stately journeys made by Sir Walter, who would rather abandon Kellynch-hall than diminish the number of horses pulling his carriage. We see the Crofts, instead, out for a ramble in a one-horse cart, with the admiral's driving continually putting them in danger of tipping over, and his wife saving them from disaster by "coolly giving the reins a better direction herself" and "afterwards judiciously putting out her hand" (ch. 10).

Yet for all their enterprise and common sense, there is no real sense that the Crofts will somehow breathe new life into country house society. They are, after all, tenants. It is sometimes claimed that *Persuasion* depicts an actual transfer to power from an older, debilitated aristocracy to "new men" like Admiral Croft. This claim cannot really be sustained.[7] Among other things, no such transformation occurred in England during the nineteenth century; the upper class has long been adept at avoiding being supplanted precisely by bringing new men and new money into their orbit, by (as we would now say) "co-opting" them. Partly as a result, there had been no French Revolution in England. But this is not to say that there is nothing revolutionary about the sentiments behind *Persuasion*. What we see, unmistakably, is a more negative judgment of the powers that be than in any other Austen novel (save, perhaps, *Sense and Sensibility*), coupled with at least the beginnings of a vision of how things might and ought to be different. As with personal renewal, the focus rests on Anne and what she values. It seems to involve, somehow, the navy, or at least some of the qualities Austen finds in the navy. Anne discovers in its officers (when she meets them on shore) human warmth, matter-of-fact frankness, freedom from a worship of class, energy, a sense of public duty (mixed, to be sure, with a frank desire to make money), and (somewhat surprisingly) a strong value for domesticity. The novel ends with a salute to naval officers as members of "that profession which is, if possible, more distinguished in its domestic virtues than in its national importance" (ch. 24). Austen's imagination, like that of many nineteenth-century realist novelists, is "conservative" in that it imagines human possibility in terms of existing institutions or modifications thereof. The fit, and lack of fit, between Austen's wish to find an embodiment of the ideal, and the British navy (even as she depicts it – and especially if one considers what she does not depict of its membership and activities) shows how strong is the desire to escape the negative aspects of Kellynch-hall.

The hope for renewal also appears to depend on a significant measure of solidity and independence among women, though in ways that modern readers may not immediately recognize (and may not find satisfactory when they do recognize them). *Persuasion* conveys a sharp sense of the injustice of women's position in society. (Here again, it is of course well to remember the limits of what counts as "society" in Austen.) This sense focuses most sharply on the figure of Mrs. Smith. Austen stresses her conversion from socially oriented frivolity to thoughtfulness, her basic decency, and her extraordinary natural good humor in the face of suffering and adversity. All play their part in mounting a protest against the legal situation of women which has victimized her. To see such a person denied what ought to be her legal rights simply because of the selfish indifference of a man like Mr. Elliot (appropriately enough, the heir apparent of Kellynch-hall) creates in the reader outrage at the legal and economic nonentity of women in Austen's world. (Mrs. Smith's physical frailty reminds us, too, of something Austen was also quite clear about, namely that a person can literally die, as nearly happens in *Mansfield Park*, from being in economic straits.) But it is only when we see Mrs. Smith assume a complicity in the process that would marry off Anne Elliot, for whom she has sincere feelings of friendship, to the same Mr. Elliot who has treated her with such immoral neglect that we feel fully how intolerable it is that this woman, or any woman, should feel the need to play such an ugly role as a matter of economic survival.

For *Persuasion* is a novel in which female ties, and their lack, vitally matter. Lady Russell is a woman of little imagination, yet even she can imagine Anne filling the place in a female circle Anne's mother's death has left vacant ("it was only in Anne that she could fancy the mother to revive again"). Lady Russell is certainly to blame as the person who centrally persuades Anne to break her engagement with Wentworth in the first place. Yet, in the most surprising moment in the novel, Anne tells Wentworth, after they find themselves engaged again, that she was absolutely right to follow Lady Russell's advice:

> I have been thinking over the past, and trying impartially to judge of the right and wrong, I mean with regard to myself; and I must believe that I was right, much as I suffered from it, that I was perfectly right in being guided by the friend whom you will love better than you do now. To me, she was in the place of a parent. Do not mistake me, however. I am not saying that she did not err in her advice. It was, perhaps, one of those cases in which advice is good or bad only as the event decides; and for myself, I certainly never should, in any circumstance of tolerable similarity, give such advice. But I mean, that I was right in submitting to her, and that if I had done otherwise, I should have suffered more in continuing the engagement than I did even in giving it up, because I should have suffered in my conscience. I have now, as far as such a sentiment is allowable in human nature, nothing to reproach myself with; and if I mistake not, a strong sense of duty is no bad part of a woman's portion. (ch. 23)

This is a remarkable speech for many reasons. We might have expected Anne to triumphantly declare her freedom from her erring mentor, to congratulate herself at having grown beyond her. It is typical of Austen that an adequate response to the situation Anne finds herself in involves, not simple rejection or rebellion, but the making of fine and difficult distinctions (such as the one in *Pride and Prejudice* between proper and improper pride). One of the fine subtle things about this speech is its resistance to a certain kind of girlish giving in to the still dashing and handsome Wentworth: Anne tells him, to his face, that she was not simply right, but "perfectly right" to give him up – and also that he "will" learn to love Lady Russell better than he now does. There are, it seems, other ties between human beings than the romantic love men and women feel for each other, and these include the claims of a certain faithfulness to a female line of solidarity, the one that Lady Russell imagines, truly, that Anne will renew, though Anne does this in a way and with a difference Lady Russell herself could not imagine.

Persuasion is a remarkable novel in which there occurs a significant revision of some of Austen's deepest concerns. In her other novels, perceptions and ideas often are in need of realignment; here, the very stuff of perception comes into view and into question, with Anne's experiences of buzzes and blurs, and personal experience is probed to a new depth, as we share Anne's pain, and then her joy. The issue of a renewal of social values, too, takes on new dimensions in *Persuasion*, with the country house left behind. Pemberley as an embodiment of value is supplanted by a group of naval officers and their wives, and in the background of the domestic scene they create, we feel the stirring of mythic rebirth, as a heroine awakens to a new and fuller life and forges a triumphant connection with her past and what had seemed happiness lost forever.

Chapter 2

Waverley

History has not been kind to Sir Walter Scott. In his own day, he was the most famous and influential British novelist alive. In our day, he is the least read major novelist of the nineteenth century. The book before you begins with Austen and not Scott, partly under the assumption that Austen will be a more familiar and more immediately enjoyable author for most of its readers. Yet Scott's influence on British fiction and European culture was far greater than that of Austen. Writing the history of the British novel without attending to the example and achievement of his works leads to myopia and distortion. And for those who know them well (a company including George Eliot), Scott's novels can be a source of great pleasure and insight. The aims and methods of Scott's novels are liable to misunderstandings of various kinds, and so this chapter opens with an extended discussion of how his attempt to capture key elements of historical process affects the kind of fiction he writes, particularly with regard to narrative voice and characterization. It then considers the many levels on which *Waverley* explores the Jacobite Rebellion of 1745, and what that exploration implies about the human costs of the coming of modernity. The chapter concludes by considering some important objections postcolonial critics have raised with regard to Scott's project.

Approaching Scott: History and Character

The issues that matter most to Scott in the Waverley novels have been central concerns for thinking people since the coming of modernity. He does not explore them by creating the precise mapping of values through shades of linguistic meaning we find in Austen. Instead, he depicts a medley of different languages, arising sometimes from different cultures, sometimes from different strata of the same culture. But he does this as part of an exploration of values just as serious as Austen's, though it involves different issues, above all the question of how it is that societies move forward in time, and at what human cost. His novels have much to teach us about the uses of tradition and the power of ideology, and about the claims of different cultures and the possibility of their coexistence. Scott brings the British novel alive to what it means to live in history.

Scott was the right person at the right time to discover history for the novel (and also for historiography – a host of eminent nineteenth-century historians owed a significant debt to him). The British novel itself arose as part of the transition from traditional to modern society, and nowhere was the reality of that transition more palpable than in Scotland. In 1745 (the year in which *Waverley* is set) a traditional clan society whose roots extended deep into the past existed just across the Highland line from the city of Edinburgh, which was a vital center of progressive European Enlightenment culture; by Scott's own time, traditional Highland society had been destroyed, but was remembered clearly enough to be recoverable. Such dramatic juxtapositions were not lost on Scott, and his fiction brought them and their significance to life for his contemporaries throughout Europe and America.

Our main business is not with Scott's extraordinary influence, but with his fiction. How should we approach his novels? On the simplest level, to enjoy reading Scott, we must enjoy his genial, shrewd, and sometimes very funny narrator. (Scott's humor has been neglected. It is pervasive and can take some surprising turns: it can even descend to slapstick in the drinking scene early in *Waverley* involving Waverley, Bradwardine, and several of Bradwardine's neighbors.) When you begin reading *Waverley*, you find yourself listening to a genial and amusing narrator who, in the process of telling you why he chose the novel's title, describes several kinds of novels he has chosen not to write. There follow four chapters of leisurely preliminaries before the main story of the novel begins with Edward Waverley's journey to Scotland. (In the collected edition of the novels Scott published toward the end of his life, he extends the preliminaries even further, with a lengthy introduction.) Why does Scott choose to begin his first novel in this fashion? One reason for creating a leisurely narrative pace and strong narrative voice is that work needs to be done in the novel which the story and its characters cannot accomplish by themselves. Early in the novel, the chapter entitled "A Stag-Hunt and its Consequences" begins as follows:

Shall this be a long or a short chapter? – This is a question in which you, gentle reader, have no vote . . . Let me therefore consider. It is true that the annals and documents in my hands say little of this Highland chase; but then I can find copious materials for description elsewhere. This is old Lindsay of Pitscottie ready at my elbow, with his Athole hunting . . . (ch. 2)

What the narrator is doing here is to remind you of the peculiar status of the fiction you are reading. Though the novel is about the Jacobite Rebellion of 1745, and though the clans did gather their forces in that Rebellion, the stag-hunt Scott describes did not quite occur during the Forty-Five as he describes it (a note informs us that something like it occurred in the Jacobite Rebellion of 1715) – yet such hunts did occur in the Highlands, and they left records, on which he is drawing for the chapter. So that, after all, the scene has a basis in history and can tell us about history. The need to stake out and clarify the claims of a new kind of fiction also lead Scott's narrator in the opening chapter to specify so elaborately what sort of fiction this novel will *not* be – that it will not be a Gothic novel as written by Radcliffe, or a novel of genteel society. In his attempt to nudge the reader toward a sense of what kind of novel this *will* be, Scott does not attempt a direct definition, but instead works by what we might call successive approximation. The reader will notice that our own approach to Scott is like his approach to introducing his new kind of fiction. We haven't plunged straight into *Waverley* itself, but instead are taking the time to help our readers approach Scott's kind of fiction in a fruitful way.

Thus the narrator boldly announces in the first chapter that this will be a novel "more a description of men than manners" (ch. 1) and tells us that, beneath the differing manners of different historical periods, human beings are really alike. Yet in the final chapter (the title of which says that *it* should have been the preface), the narrator states that "for the purpose of preserving some idea of the ancient manners [of the Highlands] of which I have witnessed the almost total extinction, I have embodied in imaginary scenes, and ascribed to fictitious characters, a part of the incidents which I . . . received from those who were actors in them" (ch. 72). Beneath what looks like a simple contradiction – are "manners" important in the novel or aren't they? – lies the attempt to re-define the role "manners" play for human beings in history and should play in the novel. In the first chapter, Scott is reassuring us that his novel won't be about external costumes and conventions (the "manners" involved, for instance, in knowing which fork to use). It will involve human issues that matter. By the end of the novel, he assumes that the novel itself will have taught us that the "manners" he has in fact portrayed with relish throughout involve much more than social superficialities. As a result, he is now in a position to stress that these "externals" are actually part of a larger, more complex picture. The customary, traditional behavior of societies, past and present, is full of human meaning, because it reveals human values. By the end of the novel, Scott hopes, we as readers will realize that he has revealed to us the experience of authentically human characters who are enmeshed in history, whose humanity is bound up with their place in the historical stream.

Our relationship with Scott's narrator also has an effect on our relationship with the characters in the novel. In this regard, Scott is working very much in the tradition of the eighteenth-century novelist Henry Fielding. Samuel Johnson once compared Fielding unfavorably with Samuel Richardson on the score of characterization, suggesting that Fielding is superficial, Richardson profound. Fielding, according to Johnson, depicts only the outside of characters: he is like a person who can tell the time of day from a clock, but nothing more. Richardson, by contrast, gets inside his characters: he is like a person who can take off the face-plate of a clock and show you how the thing works.[1] Henry James made a similar point about Fielding nearly two hundred years later, but added that though the hero in *Tom Jones* doesn't seem to have "a grain of imagination," he does have "so much 'life' that it amounts . . . almost to his having a mind." James added that Fielding himself, who is "handsomely possessed of a mind . . . has such an amplitude of reflexion for him and round him that we see [Tom Jones] through the mellow air of Fielding's fine old moralism, fine old humour and fine old style, which somehow really enlarge, make every one and every thing important."[2] James's stress on the "mind" of the Fielding narrator applies far beyond Fielding: it is of the greatest importance for understanding the realist novel. It clearly illuminates the narrative practice of Scott (though some might doubt that his prose is informed by a "fine old style"). Our sense of a lively depth of character in a novel need not arise solely from our experience of its characters; it can arise from an ongoing conversation between ourselves and the narrator, in which the characters are embedded and from which they draw vitality and depth.

Scott of course did not have a chance to respond to James's comments, since he died eleven years before James was born. But he did respond to Johnson's simile of the watch, in a way that is highly revealing of his own artistic priorities:

Dissenting as we do from the conclusions to be deduced from Dr. Johnson's simile, we would rather so modify it as to describe both authors as excellent mechanics; the time-pieces of Richardson showing a great deal of the internal works by which the index is regulated; while those of Fielding merely point to the hour of the day, being all that most men desire to know. Or, to take a more manageable comparison, the analogy betwixt the writings of Fielding and Richardson resembles that which free, bold, and true sketches bear to paintings that have been very minutely laboured, and which, amid their excellence, still exhibit some of the heaviness that almost always attends the highest degree of finishing.[3]

It is amusing to see how quietly and neatly Scott reverses Johnson's evaluation by his shift of simile. In Scott's hands, Fielding's fiction becomes bold and free, Richardson heavy and labored. Scott's modest, unobtrusive dexterity is as telling as the substance of what he has to say. We hear a flexible, good-humored, conversational intelligence that hardly needs to engage in a noisy refutation of the redoubtable Dr. Johnson, but at the same time invites us (if such a thing is to our taste) to pause and admire an adroit turning of the tables on a critical adversary. This is very much the mode of Scott's narrator in the novels.

For all its modest surface, Scott's subversion of the "watch" comparison has its own depth. For those who take the trouble to pursue its implications, it suggests that Fielding knows just as much about "the heart" as Richardson does – unlike Richardson, he just doesn't feel the need to go on and on about "the heart," and most readers don't want him to, anyway. But for those readers who are interested in such things, an anatomy of "the heart" is there for the asking: if we lift the face-plate of Fielding's watches, we will find that the works underneath them have an admirable intricacy and are in perfect order. Whether or not this is true of Fielding's fiction, it is true of Scott's. His sense of character is unerringly shrewd: again and again, if we pause to ask ourselves why his characters do what they do, we find that subtle calculations underlie Scott's seemingly simple depiction of them.

For an example, we can turn to a passing comment, early in *Waverley*, explaining why the Baron of Bradwardine, contrary to the customs of the day, allowed Edward Waverley to spend so much unchaperoned time with his daughter. Why didn't he realize that this continued "intimacy" would put Rose in "danger" of falling in love? The narrator explains that the Baron was oblivious to this "danger" because he

---

was greatly too much abstracted in his studies, and wrapped up in his own dignity, to dream of his daughter's incurring it. The daughters of the house of Bradwardine were, in his opinion, like those of the house of Bourbon or Austria, placed high above the clouds of passion which might obfuscate the intellects of meaner females; they moved in another sphere, were governed by other feelings, and amenable to other rules, than those of idle and fantastic affection. In short, he shut his eyes so resolutely to the natural consequences of Edward's intimacy with Miss Bradwardine, that the whole neighbourhood concluded that he had opened them to the advantage of a match between his daughter and the wealthy young Englishman, and pronounced him much less a fool than he had generally shown himself in cases where his own interest was concerned. (ch. 14)

This is a sly passage. The Baron's blend of self-absorption and naïveté about matters of the heart is amusingly noted: we feel that the claims of youth will surely win out against the likes of *him*, and that they should. Yet we can't help liking the Baron's unworldliness in comparison with the cynical opportunism of his neighbors. It's really quite amusing to discover how far from the truth their knowing, automatic assessment of the situation is. And yet – might there not be something to their views, though on a level they wouldn't understand? Can the Baron really be *that* blind? Waverley is after all the heir of an old and wealthy friend, the Baron likes him, and the Baron knows that his daughter will be left impoverished when he dies. At the end of the novel, when Waverley asks for Rose's hand, the Baron declares that "if I had been to search the world, I would have made my choice here" (ch. 67). It is of course inconceivable that he deliberately plots to throw his daughter and Waverley together, but isn't there a chance that desire is having its way with him on a level of which he is not consciously aware? If so, then we begin to hear an additional, more subtle wink and nod in the narrator's voice as he offers the explanation we have been considering. To be sure, Scott doesn't insist on such things. The possibility is there, but only for those who choose to follow up on it. It is worth adding that a recognition that our desires tend to find their fulfillment despite our conscious ideologies appears repeatedly in Scott; it is in his eyes a crucial mechanism that allows human beings to survive in periods of historical change, when fidelity to their official beliefs might seem to demand suicidal resistance.

Listening attentively to the voice of Scott's narrator can add depth to our sense of his characters. Still, his characterization does have its limits. What, in the end, are we to make of Waverley as a hero? He is clearly no Heathcliff. The view that Scott's heroes are pale and uninteresting was voiced by some of their earliest readers, and it deserves to be considered. Later in the century, Henry James suggests along these lines that in Scott's novels the "centre of the subject is empty and the development pushed off, all round, toward the frame – which is, so to speak, beautifully rich and curious."[4] What would happen if we put some pressure on James's simile, as Scott does with Johnson's? The type of painting James seems to be thinking of is the portrait of an individual. But what if the subject Scott wishes to paint is not an individual human being, but instead (to borrow a term from the world of computers) the way individuals interface with society and history? What if he wishes to reveal human nature, not from the skin in, but from the skin out? Then what James calls the "frame" (which would include what in a conventional portrait would be the background of the painting as well as the actual physical frame surrounding the painting as a whole) might be more important than the individual.

Indeed the individual might simply provide a sense of scale for the picture's true subject. (One thinks of the shadowy figures who are depicted as looking at a landscape or seascape in the paintings of Scott's contemporary, Kaspar David Friedrich.) Scott's heroes, heroines, and love stories are indeed in some respects conventional, but it may be that their very conventionality allows them to serve as windows through which the reader is led to perceive the world in ways that are anything but conventional. A Heathcliff might not serve Scott's needs. Greater stress on the individual singularity, rebelliousness, and inner growth on the part of the protagonist might turn our attention entirely toward inner passions and away from the larger social and historical contexts that produce cultural uniqueness, political rebellion, and historical change.

So it is with Scott's depiction of the historical personages represented in his pages. In *Waverley* the historical figure known as Bonnie Prince Charlie, the "Young Pretender" to the throne of England, appears as a character. One might suppose that such a famous figure would enter the novel quickly and dominate it. He doesn't. The great Marxist critic Georg Lukács has explained why. Scott does not believe that the course of history is driven or ruled by famous individuals (or any other individuals), and he does not wish to reduce historical process to the dimensions of the (often trivial) inner lives of such figures. History explains them; they do not explain history. They emerge for a moment when larger historical forces require their services. As a result, Scott first introduces us to the trends and social groups that really call the tune. Only when he has done so (in *Waverley*, 250 pages into the novel!) does he allow the likes of Bonnie Prince Charlie to enter the picture.[5] By the same token, Scott does not follow the course of the Jacobite Rebellion as an official historian might: he prefers to include only the incidents required to give us a sense of what the rebellion was like, to explain its initial success and ultimate failure, and to assess its significance. Some critics have supposed that, by featuring minor battles instead of major, and particularly by leaving out the decisive battle of Culloden, Scott inadvertently reveals that all historical narratives are "arbitrary" in what they choose to tell us. Nothing could be farther from the truth. What Scott reveals is that you can grasp the essentials of a historical movement by looking at seemingly minor aspects of it. He doesn't want to distract the reader with "big" events, any more than he wants to center his novel on "big" historical figures.

By the same token, the protagonist of a Scott novel is there primarily to serve as our delegate in the novel, our window into the world of the past. This is one reason why his inner life is kept out of the way, and why his romantic life is kept simple, almost schematic, though their handling is informed by the shrewdness about human motivations we have already noted. (In Waverley's case, this shrewdness includes, among other things, an amused understanding of the mentality of a certain kind of adolescent male, who requires that his love-object induce in him a degree of anxious adoration whose intensity makes him feel important in his own eyes.) Waverley's "personal" character-istics sometimes make sense only as they embellish the larger historical story Scott is telling. At the high point of the Jacobite Rebellion, Waverley suddenly displays a remarkable flow of spirits and conversation that lead the Pretender to call him "one of the most fascinating young men whom I have ever seen" (ch. 43) – a description that would not, before this moment or after, occur to the reader. When the rebellion has failed, Waverley feels "entitled to say firmly, though perhaps with a sigh, that the romance of his life was ended, and that its real history had now commenced" (ch. 60). The fleeting appear-ance of such characteristics and thoughts is perfectly appropriate for the kind of novel Scott is writing, but it helps to make our involvement in Waverley significantly different from our involvement in Anne Elliot.

Waverley and Other Worlds

Waverley is the first novel Scott published. He turned to novel-writing in his forties, after an enormously successful career as a writer of long poems that touch on Scottish history (but not with the depth and richness his novels do), realizing that the rise of Byron's poetry meant the eclipse of his. He published his novels anonymously. (Why he did so is something we will never know for certain; the subject is fascinating, but we lack time to explore it here.) The title pages of his novels were signed simply with the phrase, "by the Author of Waverley": this is why his novels as a whole came to be known as the Waverley Novels. In what follows, we will consider the various levels on which *Waverley* enriches its depiction of what the Jacobite Rebellion of 1745 (known for short as the "Forty-Five") meant to Scotland, and of what it reveals about the com-ing of modernity for all of us. It is important to emphasize that the historical analysis we will be offering here flows primarily from Scott's pages, which sup-ply their own "background"; enjoying Scott requires attentive reading, but does *not* require large amounts of prior knowledge.

On one level, *Waverley* introduces us to a society that Scott expects us to find interesting just because it is not ours – an expectation which was richly fulfilled so far as his contemporaries were concerned. To enjoy a novel like *Waverley*, we need to be curious about different groups of people and differ-ent locales – we need to take pleasure in the depiction of Highlanders and Jacobites, and of Scottish and English aristocrats and peasants at a certain period of history and the landscape that surrounds them. The pleasure offered here does not involve mere exoticism or escapism. A delight in sheer cultural difference is part of the mix, but only part, because Scott also offers quite a deep analysis of why these people are as they are, how different parts of their historical surroundings and antecedents have combined to form them, and what their chances for survival might be as history progresses. There is much more involved here than "local color."

Waverley, the rich, inexperienced Englishman who visits the Highlands, is in this regard as in others our representative in the novel. (It is worth remembering that Scott knew as he wrote *Waverley* that the majority of his audience would be English, not Scottish; indeed the novel is in part an apologia for Scotland offered to English readers.) When Waverley goes to visit the Bradwardines at the opening of the novel, he is introduced to an intriguing transitional moment in the history of a certain segment of Scottish society, and through him, so are we. The decaying manor house of the Baron reminds Waverley of something from a Spenserian romance; the dirt and poverty of the village outside its gates raise less dreamy associations. Yet both result from the same political and economic causes, the narrator lets us know: the Baron has been reduced to an amusing eccentric and his house is falling into picturesque decay (which, however picturesque, *is* decay) because as a Jacobite, he has been impoverished and kept out of the mainstream of political power and economic prosperity. His village suffers along with him. The human costs involved are noted unsparingly, and in the process a subtle hint is planted that the destruction of the Jacobite cause could only improve the situation of the villagers (as indeed it seems to have done by the end of the novel): "It seemed, upon the whole," the narrator concludes after depicting the village, "as if poverty, and indolence, its too frequent companion, were combining to depress the natural genius and acquired information of a hardy, intelligent, and reflecting peasantry" (ch. 8). Yet the historical moment which has produced this result is not without its charms. A few pages later, we, like Waverley, are expected to be amazed that the gentle Rose Bradwardine has actually witnessed events he had only read about in romances, precisely because she is part of a "backward" society.

This aspect of the novel reaches something of a climax when Waverley enters the Highlands. Here the immediate literary past poses certain problems, and raises certain opportunities, for Scott. His readers would have been familiar with depictions of exotic, violent, "primitive" people from the Gothic novels of such authors as Ann Radcliffe, who regularly offered her readers word-paintings of craggy scenery, replete with picturesque peasants and terrifying "banditti." Scott draws on this tradition. The moment when Waverley looks up from the bottom of a Highland gorge to see Flora MacIvor on a thin bridge far above him, for instance, transposes a scene from the sixth chapter of Radcliffe's

The Italian. But in *Waverley*, Scott modifies this sort of Gothicism to suit his historicist purposes. In the early chapters, he sets up a rhythm where the literary sublime tumbles into the ridiculous but then recovers, only to point the way to a truer cultural sublime. When Waverley finds himself in the midst of Highland scenery, as part of an expedition charged with recovering some cattle stolen from Bradwardine during a raid, he is enthralled:

> He had now time to give himself up to the full romance of his situation. Here he sate on the banks of an unknown lake, under the guidance of a wild native, whose language was unknown to him, on a visit to the den of some renowned outlaw, a second Robin Hood perhaps . . . and that at deep midnight, through scenes of difficulty and toil, separated from his attendant, left by his guide. – What a variety of incidents for the exercise of a romantic imagination, and all enhanced by the solemn feeling of uncertainty, at least, if not of danger? The only circumstance which assorted ill with the rest, was the cause of his journey – the Baron's milk-cows! This degrading incident he kept in the background. (ch. 16)

The same pattern is repeated a few pages later, with a more pointed reference to Radcliffe (who regularly invokes the painter Salvator Rosa in such formulae as "It was a scene that Salvator would have painted"), when Waverley enters the robbers' hideout, a huge Highland cavern. His imagination races as he anticipates meeting their chief: "The profession which he followed – the wilderness in which he dwelt – the wild warrior-forms that surrounded him, were all calculated to inspire terror. From such accompaniments, Waverley prepared himself to meet a stern, gigantic, ferocious figure, such as Salvator would have chosen to be the central object of a group of banditti." As it turns out, however, the bandit chief is in fact "the very reverse of all these. He was thin in person and low in stature, with light sandy-coloured hair, and small features," and so on (ch. 16).

All of this makes for some engaging comedy at the expense of Waverley and his overheated imagination, but it has a more serious purpose. As he lets us know in the novel's opening chapter, Scott intends to write a new kind of fiction, not to replicate Radcliffe's. He draws on her kind of fiction for imaginative excitement, but he wants to attach that excitement to what he takes to be the truly impressive aspect of the Highlands. Despite his genuine enthusiasm for Highland scenery (which he had made famous in his poems, inadvertently creating a tourist industry in the process), he wants to persuade us that the true Highland sublime involves not mountains and waterfalls, but human beings, and that this sublimity is based on actual historical fact, not on literary tradition or the overheated imagination of an avid reader like Waverley. When we enter Fergus MacIvor's feasting hall, we find ourselves in the presence of what is truly remarkable (and tragically doomed) about the Highlands. In the figures ranged down Fergus's long tables, which extend all the way down his banqueting hall and out into the sunlight beyond, we see a living example of what is known as "organic" society, a society in which people feel intense bonds of kinship (what makes a clan a clan is the fiction that all its members are descended from a single person) and occupy an almost infinite set of hierarchical ranks, not a few broad social classes pitted against one another. Everyone in the room is in a determinate relationship with everyone else, and all accept their places within the larger whole. They are parts of a single social organism, one that is remarkably unlike the one we ourselves, as moderns, inhabit. A prime purpose of *Waverley* is to remind us that (in Scott's view at least) such things have been, and are (at least in "Great Britain") no longer. When Fergus gives away a gold cup to his bard, after the bard has refreshed the memory and vitality of his clan by singing a song that links their coming part in the Jacobite Rebellion with the deeds of their distant ancestors, he himself might almost be one of those ancestors. For that matter, he might almost be Hrothgar, throwing gold chains to his thanes during a feast in *Beowulf*.

Almost, but not quite. For the historical exhibit Scott presents includes the perception that, as the narrator tells us, had Fergus MacIvor lived sixty years earlier or sixty years later, he would not have been the same man (ch. 19). Because of his family's participation in an earlier Jacobite rebellion, he was raised in exile at the court of the Stuart Pretender in France, not with his clan. Fergus is passionately attached to his clan, but he is no longer quite one of them, no longer an organic sharer in their mentality. And so, as the other members of the clan are whipped into near frenzy by the bard's song, Fergus sits there, relatively unmoved. He is already, without realizing it, more fit for the new world he is trying to resist than for the old one he is trying to restore. Only when the Jacobite hopes are dashed does he revert to a more traditional mentality. He then has a vision of the spirit that traditionally foretells the death of the chief of his clan, and he accepts its validity. He can rejoin the clan mentality only on his way to death.

Historical Loss and Survival

Here we encounter a second level on which Scott's novel operates. Scott does not wish simply to introduce us to a vanished kind of society; he provides us with the means of understanding why that society was doomed. For readers unfamiliar with the tract of history Scott is covering here, a very brief and schematic account may be helpful. At the beginning of the seventeenth century, a Stuart king of Scotland also became king of England (though both nations remained separate political entities). At the end of that century, the Stuarts were replaced by a series of other rulers (culminating in the Hanoverian dynasty, which under the changed name of "Windsor" persists today). In part to prevent the return of the Stuarts, England and Scotland were politically merged (as a result of pressure from England) in the early eighteenth century to become "Great Britain," a single kingdom. The Stuarts nevertheless attempted to regain the throne by fomenting a series of Jacobite uprisings, which typically began in the Scottish Highlands. (They were called "Jacobite" rebellions because the Stuart pretender to the throne they sought to restore was named James, or "Jacobus" in Latin.) The largest of these occurred in 1715 ("the Fifteen"), ending in a stalemate and Stuart withdrawal; the second major uprising, the Jacobite Rebellion of 1745 ("the Forty-Five"), is the subject of *Waverley*. From the point of view of those who were at the cusp of political and economic power, the Stuarts represented retrogression on a number of levels. They were associated with the Divine Right of Kings and thus royal absolutism, instead of with constitutional monarchy influenced (perhaps even controlled) by those representing the interests of economic expansion and modernization.

The Forty-Five, like any civil war, was serious and deadly, but it also had an authentically romantic side. Prince Charles ("Bonnie Prince Charlie") began the uprising by landing in the Highlands with only a handful of men, risking his fate on the generosity of the Highland clans. Some, but by no means all, rallied to his cause, and with the capture of the city of Edinburgh (but not of its castle), things looked bright. But after reaching Derby in England, the Jacobites turned back and were eventually defeated at Culloden in Scotland. Prince Charles then returned to France, after months of adventure replete with hairbreadth escapes, romantic disguises, and extraordinary examples of clan loyalty in hiding him from his pursuers.

But for all its glamour, the Forty-Five was doomed from the start. It is not only or mainly that Bonnie Prince Charlie failed to force the hand of the French, who he expected would send him reinforcements once he had begun the rebellion. On the military side of things, the very conditions of his early successes were those that led to his ultimate failure. His forces were light and mobile; this allowed them some quick initial victories but meant that when the slower but massive English army finally got itself going, it would crush them. He was able to assemble his forces quickly because of clan loyalty, but that loyalty belonged more to the clan leaders than to him, and the very dynamic of cohesion for individual clans itself predicted strife between them, not to mention strife with Lowland Jacobites.

We have just been giving what may seem a history lesson, but it proceeds not from the writings of historians but from the pages of Scott. The analysis we have provided of why the Forty-Five failed exists in the pages of *Waverley*, for readers willing to attend to such things. Notice for instance the care with which Scott depicts the inherent instability of the Jacobite forces (see particularly chapter 58, entitled "The Confusion of King Agramant's Camp"). As we shall see, Scott's view of the Forty-Five and its significance is controversial, as the view of anyone about any historical event must be. What matters, however, is not whether he got its meaning "right," but whether he presents the Forty-Five in a way that is sufficiently substantial and complex to make it live for readers and to raise issues (and objections) that matter.

Scott's evaluation, implicit and explicit, of the significance of the failure of the Forty-Five offers a third level on which *Waverley* operates. Scott does not merely wish to bring to imaginative life a political cause and a form of society that have vanished, and to explain how and why that loss occurred. He also invites us to adopt a certain attitude toward that loss. Briefly put, Scott (or more properly, the novel's implied author – see the Introduction to this book) wishes us to experience and celebrate all that is heroic about the Jacobite cause and the older way of life it is made to symbolize, but in the end to accept its passing as inevitable and in some ways a good thing. Though the past may be an exciting place to visit, we wouldn't want to live there.

A good deal of the structure and conduct of *Waverley* derives from a wish to forward this view, which we may call the "official" doctrine of the novel. The simplest device involves our identification with Waverley himself, an identification grounded in the way in which he provides a window or lens for us to experience the novel. In operation here is what we might call the "default" expectation we have about protagonists in novels, which is either that they will meet some sort of grand end or that they will survive. Waverley is obviously not cut out for a heroic demise; we therefore come to hope for his survival. But it becomes increasingly clear that he cannot survive in the world of heroic strife (represented by Fergus MacIvor) and unyielding idealism (represented by Flora MacIvor) associated with the Jacobite Rebellion. This is one reason why Scott makes Waverley unobtrusively more "modern" than the other characters. Flora MacIvor suggests his incipient modernity when she remarks that "high and perilous enterprise is not Waverley's forte. He would never have been his celebrated ancestor Sir Nigel [a war hero of an earlier age], but only Sir Nigel's eulogist and poet." She adds that he will "be at home . . . and in his place" in the "quiet circle of domestic happiness, lettered indolence, and elegant enjoyments" of the English estate he will inherit, and predicts that when he returns there, he will

> refit the old library in the most exquisite Gothic taste, and garnish its shelves with the rarest and most valuable volumes; and he will draw plans and land-scapes, and write verses, and rear temples, and dig grottoes; – and he will stand in a clear summer night in the colonnade before the hall, and gaze on the deer as they stray in the moonlight, or lie shadowed by the boughs of the huge old fantastic oaks; – and he will repeat verses to his beautiful wife, who will hang upon his arm; – and he will be a happy man. (ch. 52)

Donald Davie observed some time ago that this description is anachronistic: Flora describing a typical late-eighteenth-century "man of feeling" before the type had emerged.[6] This unobtrusive anachronism reinforces our sense that Waverley belongs to the future, not the past – to the elegance and safety of modernity, not the heroism and danger of earlier eras. As readers, we want Waverley to survive, and so we acquiesce in the historical process that dooms the more colorful past, because it allows his survival (and leads to our own secure existence in the modern world).

In depicting Waverley's first experience of battle, Scott reinforces the feeling that Waverley simply does not belong with the past the Jacobites represent, by drawing on the rhythm of romantic expectation followed by realistic dis-illusion we noted earlier. When Waverley observes the Jacobite troops assem-bling from afar as he hurries to catch up with them (his tardiness is itself a telling detail), he is at first impressed by their picturesque appearance, but "a nearer view . . . rather diminished the effect impressed on the mind by the more distant appearance of the army" (ch. 44). And during the battle itself, his dis-illusionment takes on a nightmarish quality, when he hears the voice of his English former commander giving order to the troops that oppose the Jacobites:

> It was at that instant, that, looking around him, he saw the wild dress and appear-ance of his Highland associates, heard their whispers in an uncouth and unknown language, looked upon his own dress, so unlike that which he had worn from his infancy, and wished to awake from what seemed at the moment a dream, strange, horrible, and unnatural. (ch. 46)

The novel's denouement gives him the chance to awake, to his and our relief.

Class allegiances promote the same end. When Waverley is separated from the Jacobite army in retreat, he first goes into hiding with some peasants in the Lake District. But when a false report leads him to make his way in disguise to London in the hopes of saving his father and his uncle from government reprisals, and he finds himself hiding instead in the house of a member of the upper classes, he is "delighted at being restored, though but for a moment, to the society of his own rank, from which he had been for some time excluded" (ch. 62). Only by rejoining the modern world and the winning side can he continue to enjoy such company.

Flora MacIvor gives the description we earlier cited of what will make Waverley a "happy man" during a conversation with Rose Bradwardine, knowing that Rose is just the person to make him happy. Rose agrees. When Flora says that Waverley "will repeat verses to his beautiful wife, who will hang upon his arm; – and he will be a happy man," Rose thinks to herself, "And she will be a happy woman" (ch. 52). She adds a sigh, because at this point she does not suppose Waverley will ever be hers (and neither does he). But fate, history, and Scott are wiser than both of them. Edward eventually realizes that Rose, and not the heroic Flora, is the wife for him. The marriage between Waverley and Rose symbolizes a new, mutually beneficial union between Scotland and England. By the same token, when Waverley's money repairs and restores to Baron Bradwardine his mansion, Tully-Veolan, which had been damaged during the uprising, we are invited to feel that much that is valuable about the old order may survive its passing – and to assume that the native intelligence of those living in the village outside Bradwardine's gates will no longer be "depressed," as Scotland rejoins the historical and economic mainstream and prospers. The reconciliation between England and Scotland, figured by the marriage of Waverley and Rose and the restoration of the Baron's mansion are, the novel's official doctrine would have us believe, the best possible outcome to the Jacobite Rebellion, because it will move Scotland into modernity.

Yet things are not quite so simple as that, either for Scott or for the reader. Consider the restoration of Tully-Veolan. It is simply too good to be true. We learn that the restoration falls short of perfection twice in a single paragraph: we are told, first, that "all seemed *as much as possible* restored to the state in which [Bradwardine] had left it when he assumed arms some months before" and then, a few lines later, that everything had been done to return the house and gardens to their former "character" and "to remove *as far as possible*, all appearance of the *ravage* they had sustained" (ch. 71; our emphasis). And even the imperfect degree of restoration that is possible – including as it does every Bradwardine bear, and even the Baron's favorite drinking cup! – seems, as they say, "over the top." It is evident that we have entered into the realm of fantasy and wish-fulfillment here (every single bear?). We must also note a gap in what has been saved from the ravages of history. The Scottish Lowlands and England have been symbolically reunited and refreshed in the marriage and the restoration of Tully-Veolan, but the Highlands are not part of this happy scene. Fergus MacIvor is dead; Evan Dhu is dead; Calum Beg is dead; Flora is on her way to a convent. The Highlands appear in the novel's finale only in a "spirited" painting, safely framed on the wall of the Baron's dining room, which gives an idealized picture of Fergus, his clan, and Waverley. The weapons Waverley received from Prince Charles are there too, instruments of war no longer, museum exhibits instead. In fact, at the historical moment when the novel imagines Bradwardine to be restored to his mansion and Waverley absolved of any guilt for his part in treason and rebellion, the Highland clans were suffering from the brutal military repression that earned the Duke of Cumberland the nickname of "butcher Cumberland."

Waverley and Colonialism

Some have found the omission in *Waverley* of any direct depiction of these horrors an example of political betrayal and artistic dishonesty. Waverley may have promised to Fergus that he will act as a protector of his clan, and the novel may assure us that Waverley "afterwards so amply redeemed" this promise "that his memory still lives in these glens by the name of the Friend of the Sons of Ivor" (ch. 69). But these gestures are taken to be disingenuous evasions of a grim historical reality that Scott, in his enthusiasm for promoting the solidarity of "Great Britain," chooses to ignore. Such objections have a particular force today. At a moment in history when Scotland has reclaimed part of its political independence, it is only natural that readers should question Scott's part in promoting an acquiescence in its earlier loss.

Postcolonial critics have extended such charges (which are in fact old ones) to issues that are even broader and more fundamental. One branch of this criticism draws on the important work of Edward Said, who argues in *Orientalism* that over the course of hundreds of years, Western writers succeeded in creating an "orientalizing" discourse that led their cultures to conceive of the region of the world they called the "orient" in terms that justified and promoted imperialist aggression. In such a discourse, cultural difference always turns out to mean cultural inferiority, whatever the conscious intention of those who create it: the nature of the lens they are using can produce no other result. Since Scott made cultural and historical difference available to the novel, it seems only reasonable to ask if the vision he promotes does not share the qualities Said identifies as characteristic of orientalism. Some critics think that he does. They see in his treatment of the Highlanders nothing but an ultimate condescension and denigration, in which geographical difference is automatically translated into cultural inferiority. Scott's nostalgia for certain aspects of the past they consider simply a cover, whether or not he knows it, for a vision that seeks to promote the interests of a "British" upper class that is reaping, and will continue to reap, the benefits of British imperial rule, not only in Scotland (where the English are sometimes said to have engaged in "internal colonialism") but around the globe.[7]

The issues such a critique raises are awesome in their magnitude and importance as well as highly controversial, and they extend far beyond the works of Scott or any other novelist. In dealing with them, it is important that certain distinctions be made. Some critics seem to believe that novels have intrinsic ideological properties that determine how they will be read: the notion that a cultural discourse (such as the orientalizing discourse) will *determine* in and of itself how an object is viewed is congruent with such an assumption. From our point of view, however, this assumption is mistaken. There are always two parties to any cultural transmission, and the receiver's power must not be discounted. Scott was, clearly enough, highly conservative in his views: he felt it a good thing that people should know their social places, as they do in his vision of "organic" societies. Yet it is a matter of record that some working-class readers have found reading Scott an empowering experience.[8] The model in which cultural objects can, in the aggregate, form coercive lenses best fits modern, media-dominated society, in which subjects are bombarded with images of the world that do, indeed, often tend toward one unfortunate ideological end. But Stuart Hall seems absolutely right to remind us that even in such a situation, much depends upon how different ideological messages are articulated with one another, and with the minds of those who receive them.[9] The ability to place bits of ideology in larger, revealing contexts is the reason, after all, why cultural critics can imagine that they have discovered a coercive lens at work, but not fall under the spell of that lens themselves.

We believe that, for those who concern themselves with novels, the most fruitful question to ask is how such works *can* be read and *might* be read – what kinds of articulations they might promote. If we are not looking for a univalent, coercive ideological lens that "really" underlies a given text, we may find that, on an ideological level, it points in various or even contradictory directions. This would certainly seem to be the case with Scott. Robert C. Gordon wrote, many years ago, of the "basic energizing dissatisfaction that lies behind the Waverley Novels."[10] That Scott felt from deeply divided allegiances has been clear to readers ever since the Waverley Novels first appeared. He simultaneously accepts and deplores the passing of the old ways and the loss of Scottish independence chronicled and seemingly ratified in *Waverley*. With the forward-looking ending of *Waverley* we may juxtapose an incident that occurred several years before the publication of *Waverley* when, walking down the hill from the medieval part of Edinburgh to the elegantly laid-out, eighteenth-century New Town, Scott exclaimed to Francis Jeffrey, with tears in his eyes, that the changes in the Scottish legal system Jeffrey favored would "little by little . . .

destroy and undermine, until nothing of what makes Scotland Scotland shall remain."[11] Ambivalence about the coming of modernity colors all of Scott's novels and provides grist for the mills of those whose political views differ from his own. So, for that matter, does Scott's narrative stance itself, for his narrator invites us to look, if we choose, beneath the face of the apparently simple and straightforward clock-face he has crafted to discover an intricate, subtle, and discordant mechanism beneath it.

Chapter 3

Wuthering Heights

To encounter *Wuthering Heights* after reading Austen and Scott is to feel that one has entered a radically different – and profoundly challenging – fictional world. The novel is awash in powerful, disturbing emotions. The level of physical and psychological violence is high, and is often directed at relatively powerless figures like children and animals. Even affective qualities usually seen as positive – romantic love, parental solicitude, the loyalty of servants – are pushed or twisted to reveal destructive undersides. More importantly, the novel lacks many of the stabilizing features we take for granted in fiction of this period: a reliable narrative voice (or an obviously and predictably unreliable one), a clearly sympathetic central character, a consistent pattern of value judgments – even, given the novel's ambiguous treatment of ghosts and spirits, a stable material reality. Its central characters appear to be driven by deep psychological forces no one in the novel fully understands, though both they and the narrators sometimes think they do. Its social world seems weirdly *sui generis* and self-contained, but its core conflicts are structured with a kind of emblematic starkness, making it both tempting and difficult to connect the story to broader social issues.

Yet this is not to say that the novel is flawed or incoherent. Its characters are vivid and compelling figures, whose stories have haunted and obsessed generations of readers. Though the narrative's multiple back-and-forth jumps across the years may be confusing on a first reading, the movements of characters across time and space are actually laid out with great precision (though it was some time before critics noticed this; today, most editions intended for students are published with a clarifying chronology of the novel's main events). The descriptions of Wuthering Heights, Thrushcross Grange, and their environs are beautifully evocative. They envelope the story and central characters in a dense web of metaphorical associations, and they are also vivid enough in their own right to have played a major role in transforming the Yorkshire moors into "Brontë country."[1]

Scott's and Austen's novels may legitimately provoke debate about the ultimate nature and force of their ideological commitments, about whether it is more fruitful for us to read them "against the grain" or with it, but this presupposes (reasonably enough) that there is a visible "grain" in their fiction to begin with. It is difficult, by contrast, to imagine how one would begin to go about reading *Wuthering Heights* "against the grain": critical debate is more likely to divide on the question of where (if anywhere) "the grain" *is*, and what it looks like. *Wuthering Heights* has generated a broader range of radically incompatible readings than any novel we will discuss here. It is small wonder, therefore, that Victorian novel-readers and critics, accustomed to having their sympathies and sentiments directed with a gentle but firm hand, found *Wuthering Heights* too disturbing for unqualified praise, even when they found it also too powerful to be dismissed as a mere failure. It alone of the novels we discuss in this book was not a success in its own day. It was not widely read until Charlotte Brontë's more popular work, and later Elizabeth Gaskell's popular biography of her, began to create an audience for all things Brontëan, and even then it was usually seen as a deeply flawed if impressive work. Only in the twentieth century did the novel acquire the status of an acknowledged literary masterpiece.

It is tempting, then, to class Emily Brontë altogether outside of the tradition of nineteenth-century British novelists – as a belated Romantic poet pushed by circumstances into writing prose fiction; as a brilliant if unwitting precursor of post-Freudian modernism; or as a kind of literary Noble Savage, mercifully cut off from the repressive influences of Victorian society to nourish her wild spirit on the desolate natural beauty of the Yorkshire moors.[2] All of these approaches have their charms, as well as merits, but we will not do more than note them here. For all its strangeness, *Wuthering Heights* belongs in the tradition of realist fiction, and it is engaged, however obliquely, with many of the same issues. It is also, as we shall see, deeply concerned with the dynamics and implications of reading, hearing, and telling stories. Our discussion of the novel will thus be dwelling at length on the narrators and narrative frame of the novel, not because we consider them more important than the story itself, but because the very compelling qualities of that story make them easy to pass over. No reader of *Wuthering Heights* needs to be reminded that Cathy and Heathcliff are important, but they may well need to be encouraged to focus their attention on the complexities of the roles played by Lockwood and Nelly.

Wuthering Heights lacks the wise, reassuring, authorial narrative voice of an Austen or Scott novel, which offers us a clear center of value while judiciously exploring and weighing alternatives to it. Instead, we have two distinct personalities as narrators, Lockwood and Nelly Dean, providing two layers of mediation between the private and mysterious story at the core of the novel on the one hand and a public audience on the other. Lockwood is the outer layer: all of our information in the novel comes to us from him, but relatively little of this represents his own direct experience. The bulk of the narrative he tells purports to be a more or less verbatim account of the story Nelly tells him. Much of what Nelly tells does derive from her own direct experience, though she is not, at least ostensibly, at the center of the story. But she in turn frequently recounts stories told to her by other characters, which themselves report dialogue with or speeches by others. Narratives nest within narratives like a set of Russian dolls.

Neither the employment of first person (or "homodiegetic") narrators nor the creation of a fictional "frame" narrative to introduce the central story are particularly unusual in themselves. Both fictional autobiographies, like Defoe's *Moll Flanders* and *Robinson Crusoe*, and more cursory frame narratives of the "here's an interesting story I encountered on my travels" variety are common enough in the century leading up to Brontë's novel (the latter device is often used by Scott, particularly for his short stories). What is distinctive in *Wuthering Heights* is the complexity of the narrative framing and the complications of perspective it introduces into the novel. Both narrators emerge as distinct characters with their own investments in the stories they are telling: for Nelly especially, who has been intimately involved with the main characters throughout her life, this potentially raises questions about the ways in which personal interests and commitments may be shaping her presentation of the story. Lockwood more closely approximates the position of the typical frame narrator, who offers the reader a way into the story but generally fades from view once it is underway, but his position too is complicated by the repeated possibility of his becoming more intimately involved in the story he hears.

To begin at the beginning of the novel – with Lockwood's blundering entrance into the ugly domestic scene at Wuthering Heights – is to begin actually very late in the chronology of the story that will make up *Wuthering Heights*, but also on the outside of its nesting sequence of stories. Lockwood is a total outsider to this scene. He comes in much like the reader of the period – primed by, on the one hand, the Romantic, especially Byronic, popularization of dark, self-tortured misanthropes (and perhaps by an interest in "local color" that Scott's fiction helped to create), and on the other by a set of social codes and practices akin to those that inform Austen's novels. Both prove painfully inadequate to responding to the scene at hand. Lockwood's fatuous social niceties fall comically flat, and his desire to identify with a Byronized Heathcliff is thwarted by the sheer ugliness of the latter's behavior to his household and guest. From here, Lockwood crosses boundary after boundary – the fortress-like house itself, the locked room, the enclosed bed, the book and its diary-like marginalia – to find himself suddenly, and terrifyingly, confronting the heart of the house and story of Wuthering Heights in his two dreams.

Lockwood's dreams, and the scenes that lead up to and follow them, offer a kind of overture to the novel as a whole. Significantly, the dreams are set off by Lockwood's *reading*, first of the diary rebellious young Cathy has kept in the margins of her religious books, and then of the printed text of one of those books, the "pious discourse" of Jabes Brandersham on "the First of the Seventy-first, or "the unforgiveable sin."[3] The dreams reverse this order, the first being based on the printed text and the second on the diary. The first dream's conflict is founded on a problem of interpretation: is the "unforgive-able sin" the preacher's perversely literal and cruelly punitive reading of the Gospel passage, or is it actually Lockwood's resistance to his interminable sermon? The dream thus neatly sets up the ambivalent status of moral and religious authority in the novel – with its radically incompatible value systems literally coming to blows in the general melee at the chapel with which it closes – while also floating the idea of an "unforgiveable sin" at the core of the story: the question of who has sinned – Cathy? Heathcliff? – and against what – Christian morality? The truth of their love? – will haunt the novel. Lockwood's resistance to the religious authority associated with Joseph and Brandersham sets the stage for his engagement with the diarist Cathy's rebellion, and this engagement is then literalized in the second dream, as the "childish hand" of the diaries becomes the "little, ice-cold hand" of the ghostly child, literally grip-ping her reader. But this form of contact proves too disturbingly direct, and Lockwood rejects it with a scene of violent cruelty that – dream or no dream – rivals anything we will meet in the novel, scraping the child's wrist over the broken glass of the window until the blood "soaks the bedclothes." He is also then quick to assign to Catherine the burden of unforgiveable sin, calling her "a wicked little soul" whose twenty years' wandering must be "a just punish-ment for her mortal transgressions." As in his earlier encounter with Heathcliff, Lockwood finds that the transgressive thrill of identifying himself with dark and rebellious figures has the potential to take him further than he is com-fortable going.

Lockwood retreats to the safe distance of Thrushcross Grange, and of Nelly's mediation as narrator. His role then becomes much like ours: he is in a sense subject to the story, caught up in it, but he also sets the terms on which he encounters it, ordering Nelly to stay up late telling it when he cannot sleep, forbidding her to abridge it, and, when he feels ready, passing judgments on its contents – almost as if Nelly were a book at his disposal.

Nelly's role as an audience and conduit for the story is radically different. In the course of the story she tells, she is constantly having to interpret, take sides, make judgments, and act upon them – she lacks the luxury of waiting to see how "the story" will turn out. Her interpretations are hence "partial" in all senses of the term. They are also consequential, and hence risk-taking: Nelly's judgments and choices often have dramatic, and sometimes disastrous, effects. The actions she takes on the strength of them not only change what happens, they also change the interpretations on which they were initially based. Hence she withholds Catherine's illness from Edgar in the belief that it is minor and wholly under Catherine's control – that is, based on a certain "reading" of Catherine – but is then forced to acknowledge its seriousness as she sees the disastrous result of her own actions. More interestingly, she acquires a fondness for Heathcliff after nursing him through a dangerous illness, not because the illness has revealed anything loveable about him – she claims that "hardness, not gentleness, made him give little trouble" (ch. 4) – but simply because she *has* nursed him, the act itself giving her an almost involuntary investment in his well-being. That investment in turn makes her more attuned to the ways Heathcliff is being ill-used, more inclined to interpret him as a victim deserving sympathy rather than simply as an irritating or dangerous presence.

Nelly's partiality is as crucial to the experience of reading *Wuthering Heights* as Lockwood's distanced, aestheticized desire for a coherent and entertaining story. Though Nelly clearly has her long-term sympathies – with Edgar and the younger Catherine, for example – there is hardly a character in the story with whom she does not side at one point or another, in opposition to other characters who themselves previously or later hold her loyalty. Our own sympathies may not always align with hers, but her ability to evoke pathos on their behalf helps to sustain the ambiguity and complexity of the novel's conflicts while intensifying the reader's engagement with them. Nelly's shifting partialities invite us to care deeply about the well-being of particular characters at particular points without ever quite allowing us simply to organize our understanding of the story around the perspective and desires of any one character.[4] Nelly does of course pass judgments, but they are not as important to her, ultimately, as the affective ties she develops at different times to nearly all the characters in the novel. She knows, for example, that Heathcliff's actions since Catherine's death are evil – so insistently and unapologetically evil, at times, that she is driven to wonder if he is fully human – but that does not stop her from fussing anxiously over his health when, late in the story, he stops eating and takes to wandering in wet weather.

The contrast between Lockwood's and Nelly's orientations toward the narrative is played out sharply in their exchanges about the younger Catherine. Nelly expects her narrative to generate a level of engagement with its protagonists which will inevitably generate a concrete and active concern with Catherine's well-being:

Last winter, I did not think, at another twelve months end, I should be amusing a stranger to the family with relating them! Yet, who knows how long you'll be a stranger? You're too young to rest always contented, living by yourself; and I some way fancy no one could see Catherine Linton and not love her. You smile; but why do you look so lively and interested, when I talk about her? and why have you asked me to hang her picture over your fireplace? and why – (ch. 25)

Lockwood cuts her off: he has no intention, he says, of "venturing his tranquility" – that is, taking emotional risks – by getting involved with Catherine, and he quickly replaces himself in the role of an audience more interested in narrative trajectories than in the current living reality of the protagonists: "Go on. Was Catherine obedient to her father's commands?" (ch. 25).

We might then see Lockwood and Nelly as offering two contrasting models of what it means to read novels, and especially realist novels. Lockwood displays a readerly willingness to identify provisionally with characters and to engage himself imaginatively in the overall shape and movement of the narrative for as long as these are pleasurable, but he backs quickly away from anything that might threaten the security of his role as audience: he is a distanced, aestheticizing and totalizing reader, a kind of connoisseur of the novel as art form. Nelly, by contrast, could be taken as representing the reader who immerses him- or herself in the story "as if" it were real life: such a reader is partial, committed, and consequential, risking engagement, identification, even fantasies of intervention.

Wuthering Heights may seem, on the face of it, like an odd place to locate an interest in "committed and consequential" reading. Novels like *Mary Barton* and *Bleak House* are far more overt in asking their readers to move directly from immersion in their fictional worlds to concrete real-world action, and they are also fairly explicit about what that action would look like. In *Wuthering Heights*, in the most literal sense we as readers never have the option that Lockwood rejects, of becoming actively involved in the world of the novel. Nelly may seem too embedded in the story's strangely alien world to provide a model of reading for *us* to approach it. Lockwood himself, in conversation with Nelly, stresses the degree to which the protagonists of her story, and Nelly herself, are qualitatively *different* from you and me:

They *do* live more in earnest, more in themselves, and less in surface change, and frivolous external things. . . . One state resembles setting a hungry man down to a single dish, on which he may concentrate his entire appetite and do it justice; the other, introducing him to a table laid out by French cooks: he can perhaps extract as much enjoyment from the whole; but each part is a mere atom in his regard and remembrance. (ch. 7)

Nelly herself, he says, has "thought a great deal more than the generality of servants think. You have been compelled to cultivate your reflective faculties for want of occasions for frittering your life away in silly trifles."

But Nelly offers an instructive dissenting view. "Oh! here we are the same as anywhere else, when you get to know us," she responds, and as for herself:

> I certainly esteem myself a steady, reasonable kind of body, not exactly from living among the hills and seeing one set of faces, and one series of actions, from years end to years end; but I have undergone sharp discipline, which has taught me wisdom; and then, I have read more than you would fancy, Mr. Lockwood. You could not open a book in this library that I have not looked into, and got something out of also. (ch. 7)

While Lockwood (characteristically) attributes both Nelly's qualities as a storyteller and the power of the story itself to the one thing that most clearly separates them from him – and from us – that is, their immersion in a tiny, isolated Yorkshire community, Nelly herself locates her abilities in precisely what links her to us most closely: her pleasure in reading. Her reply to Lockwood implicitly equates direct experience – the "sharp discipline" that has "taught her wisdom" – with textual experience – the library books that she has also "got something out of." She thus dissolves the boundaries between textual inside and outside, audience and participant, that Lockwood so strenuously maintains.

In offering these contrasting models of reading, we do not mean to suggest that Brontë demands or promotes one over the other. In this as in so many ways, *Wuthering Heights* offers a balanced opposition of forces, so that the choice to privilege one over the other perhaps says as much about our own predilections as readers as it does about the novel itself. But the practice of academic literary criticism tends to valorize the Lockwoodian approach while often casting the alternative as merely naïve. In that context, it is worth reminding ourselves to be open to the ways realist novelists seek to *do* things to and with their readers.

In turning now from the narrative framing to the story of *Wuthering Heights*, we will not attempt to offer either a single coherent reading or a comprehensive overview of critical approaches to the novel. Instead we offer a topical approach that looks at key loci of ambivalence or conflict within the novel and in approaches to it.

Heathcliff

The story at the core of *Wuthering Heights* is to a large degree the story of Heathcliff: his status, character, and actions generate the conflicts that drive the narrative forward. The story begins with his arrival at Wuthering Heights, which immediately begins disrupting and reconfiguring relationships within the household. His flight makes possible the uneasy stasis of Catherine's marriage to Edgar, which is again disrupted by his return. Subsequent developments are almost entirely driven directly or indirectly by his actions, and the story reaches its resolution shortly after, and largely as a result of, his death.

Does this make Heathcliff the protagonist of the novel? Heathcliff arrives at Wuthering Heights, like many a nineteenth-century protagonist, as an orphan of unknown parentage. The pathos of his subsequent mistreatment by Hindley, together with his passionate devotion to Cathy and his anguish at their separation, make it tempting to cast him as the emotional center of the novel, as many readers do.

Yet Heathcliff is an elusive center. His inner life, insofar as we get it, seems to be organized solely around the twin poles of hatred of Hindley and love of Catherine, and even there, the tension between these impulses is rarely articulated except in externalized forms (such as, late in the novel, through the hints that Cathy's ghost is distracting him from his destructive plans toward the remains of her family). Unlike his literary fellow-orphans of the nineteenth century, Heathcliff never (as far as we see) experiences an inner crisis of social identity, never finds or even seeks his true parents. While he returns to Wuthering Heights having evidently managed to lift himself from his degraded and uneducated status and acquire sufficient fortune to call himself a gentleman, how he does so – or even whether by admirable or sinister means – remains a complete mystery. After Cathy's death, the determined malevolence and extreme physical and emotional cruelty of his behavior, though offset by his occasional moving soliloquy about the anguish of his continuing love, tend to cast him into the role of a villainous obstacle to the happiness of more engaging characters. In other words, if certain features of the plot and affective structure of the novel cast Heathcliff as a protagonist and a psychologized subject, others place him more in the role of an allegorical figure, an almost impersonal disruptive force which enables narrative by creating conflicts for other characters   rather like the role disease plays in *Bleak House*, war in *Vanity Fair*, or historical change in *Waverley*.

Viewed in the latter light, Heathcliff acquires over the course of the novel a variety of associations and potential identities that also suggest some of the ways this seemingly hermetic story can be linked to a larger social history. Having been found starving and abandoned on the streets of Liverpool, he is associated most clearly with the impoverished urban underclass who were at this time the subject of both philanthropic concern and considerable political unease on the part of the middle and upper classes.[5] This ambivalence toward the poor as at once an object of sympathy and a revolutionary threat is reflected in the difficulty, based on evidence from the text, of tracing Heathcliff's later malign impact on the two families clearly either to Mr. Earnshaw's initial charitable act of rescuing, nurturing, and educating the abandoned child as his own (the idea that Heathcliff was always inherently dangerous: a "little dark thing, harbored by a good man to his bane," ch. 34), or only to the psychic damage induced by Hindley's later violent efforts to put him "back" in his "proper" place as an uneducated and degraded servant.

Upon his return to the neighborhood, Heathcliff takes on the role of another cultural threat to the social position and security of the old landed gentry: the noveau-riche capitalist, who has the veneer of wealth to pass for a "gentleman" but has made his money God-knows-how, and now threatens to ruin older landed families by drawing them into "speculation" (as Heathcliff ruins Hindley by gambling), or by luring their daughters into disastrous marriages.

Heathcliff is also cast as a racial other, on the strength of his dark complexion and his origin in Liverpool, a major port, as when Mr. Linton refers to him as "a little Lascar or [Native] American or Spanish stowaway." For the Lintons, defining Heathcliff as a colonial racial inferior is part of the project of maintaining the purity of their own local stock, as they take it upon themselves to "rescue" Cathy from Heathcliff's influence. The tactic proves moderately successful, not only on Cathy, who is (at least partially) seduced by the charms of being treated and dressed as a "lady," but on Heathcliff, who begins to see himself as Edgar's inferior in terms that neatly conflate racial, social, and economic categories: "I wish I had light hair and fair skin, and was dressed and behaved as well, and had a chance of being as rich as he will be!" he tells Nelly (ch. 7). But the comfort Nelly offers him in return shows some of the ways Britain's colonial involvements also worked to destabilize that neat conflation:

You're fit for a prince in disguise. Who knows but your father was Emperor of China, and your mother an Indian queen, each of them able to buy up, with one week's income, Wuthering Heights and Thrushcross Grange together? And you were kidnapped by wicked sailors, and brought to England. Were I in your place, I would frame high notions of my birth; and the thoughts of what I was should give me courage and dignity to support the oppressions of a little farmer! (ch. 7)

Just as noveau-riche manufacturers threatened class boundaries, so the vast fortunes made possible by colonial enterprises – which could dwarf the resources of local rural gentry, converting the heir of an ancient landed family into a mere "little farmer" – were perceived as coming alongside an uncomfortable degree of racial mixing: one thinks of the "mulatto" heiress Miss Schwarz in *Vanity Fair*, or the dark-complexioned "Creole" heiress Bertha Mason in *Jane Eyre*.

In all these respects, then, Heathcliff reflects a disturbing fluidity of social and racial identity, which is seen to threaten the purity and worth of the older landed families. Yet on his adoption by Mr. Earnshaw, Heathcliff, we are told, acquired his name from an Earnshaw son who died in infancy, and he quickly takes that son's place in the older Earnshaw's heart. Cathy, a home-grown Earnshaw, has so much in common with him that they seem to each other like two parts of the same self. And the havoc Heathcliff later wreaks on the family can be read as little more than a reflection of the cruelty initially visited upon him by another native-born Earnshaw, Hindley. If Heathcliff represents the people the rural gentry define themselves in opposition to, he also shows the degree to which those qualities cast out as other to the self may turn out to be an integral part of it, and can turn upon it with a vengeance when denied. In light of this pattern, Terry Eagleton suggests that Heathcliff may actually be meant to be Irish. Much of the urban underclass around Liverpool was Irish, and stereotypes of Irishness at the time exaggerated their physical differences from the English "race" and associated them with the inferior "dark" races. The Act of Union in 1799 had ostensibly made Ireland "one" with Britain, just as Heathcliff is adopted into the role of an Earnshaw son, but in practice Ireland was an exploited and often rebellious colony. The identification gains added force from the fact that the Brontës themselves were of Irish extraction. Rev. Patrick Brontë, Emily's father, was born in Ireland as Patrick Brunty, and the alteration in his name was made precisely to obscure this less-than-desirable origin. The identification of Heathcliff as Irish then, though unsupported by any concrete evidence in the novel, has the advantage of neatly encapsulating his status as simultaneously a threatening, alien Other and a repressed part of the self.

In keeping with his association with various forms of Otherness, Heathcliff is also, as his name implies, closely associated with nature, especially with its more uncontrollable forces, with animals, and with the supernatural beings that are the folk remnants of pre-Christian personifications of natural forces: changelings, goblins, and vampires, even the Devil himself. These associations align Heathcliff in opposition not just specifically to one class of society, but more broadly to what we might term "the social" or "civilization" in general.

Cathy, Heathcliff, and the Idea of Love

At the core of the story, and certainly of its continuing hold on readers, is the intense bond between Cathy and Heathcliff. *Wuthering Heights* is most popularly read as a "tragic love story": a fable of a transcultural, transhistorical True Love that by its nature transcends and dissolves social boundaries. In this reading, Cathy is generally seen as betraying the fundamental "natural" truth of their love ("I *am* Heathcliff") in the favor of the more superficial appeals of social propriety and personal ambition in her marriage to Edgar. Heathcliff is cast as the tragic victim of this betrayal, or (depending on the reader's sympathies) as himself later enacting a similar betrayal in the name of petty revenge, material greed, and the trappings of patriarchal power. After a sufficient period of suffering, the lovers are reunited after death, their spirits freed from the trivial social bonds that held them apart.

There is a great deal to be said for this reading (not least of which is that it is probably the one Heathcliff himself would offer). But to engage with the novel critically in its historical context, we need to be more precise about what gets subsumed under the category of "love" in this and other novels. The "marriage plot" – the story of a rocky courtship closing with a happy marriage – is almost ubiquitous in fiction of this period; even novels whose main focus is elsewhere will usually have at least one courtship subplot, and end with a happy marriage (as do all the novels we discuss here). Love stories, whether happy or tragic, have always had their appeal, but there is an obsessiveness to the focus on courtship and marriage in this period which suggests that more is at stake. As indeed it is. Marriage for the middle and upper classes at this time remained an institution with important social and economic functions that made it appear necessary to circumscribe young people's choices of partners, but popular sentiment increasingly dictated that marriages should first and foremost be for love. The reasons for this are complex, and we can only touch on them here.[6] In social terms, the valorization of marriage for love could help to justify marriages that crossed social boundaries in productive ways, uniting the energies and wealth of the rising bourgeoisie to the status, social connections, and political power of the gentry, while obscuring the uncomfortably mercenary aspects of that union. But the same valorization risked promoting mere misalliances if young people allowed themselves to be swayed by superficial or inappropriate attractions. At the same time, there is a broader movement of culture in which romantic love comes to absorb much of the longing for connection and meaning that had previously found its outlet in religious faith or in the sense of occupying one's proper place within an organic society: "Ah love, let us be true to one another," writes Matthew Arnold in

"Dover Beach," "for the world . . . /Hath really neither joy, nor love, nor light, /Nor certitude, nor peace, nor help for pain."

Consequently, fiction of the period carries on a vital and finely nuanced debate about the nature of romantic love: its mental, emotional, and physical content, and its moral and social value. In the quest for "true" love – love which leads both to personal spiritual fulfillment and to a socially productive marriage – what role is played, on the one hand, by conscious and voluntary forces like intellectual and moral judgment, self-knowledge, and self-control, and on the other by unconscious and involuntary forms of attraction or attachment, including sexual desire? In the happy unions that end so many novels of this period – such as that of the younger generation in this novel – these elements do not need to be sorted and weighed against each other, because they all neatly coincide. In unhappy or failed romances, though, or in marriages which are represented as somehow inadequate, we see this debate taking shape.

So, in *Pride and Prejudice*, Elizabeth's highly self-conscious (though not entirely voluntary) transition from intense dislike to genuine love for Darcy has the largely rational "foundation" of "gratitude and esteem," and is reinforced by her recognition that their marriage would be "to the advantage of both" in terms of their characters. This union, which could "teach the admiring multitude what connubial felicity really [is]," is contrasted both with Charlotte's coldly mercenary marriage to Mr. Collins and with Lydia's unreflectively libidinal elopement with Wickham. Even in *Persuasion*, where the involuntary depth and endurance of the love between Anne and Wentworth are clearly highly valued, the value of their love is inseparable from its embeddedness in and expression through social acts and identities. Though the narrator's claim that their love came about only because circumstances threw them together at a time when "he had nothing to do, and she had practically nobody to love" is comic, it is also largely true – probably any two reasonably attractive people thrown into these circumstances would have fallen in love. The love of these two particular people is lifted above the uninteresting mass of such localized, circumstantial attractions – like those between Charles Hayter and Henrietta, or Benwick and Louisa – by degree rather than by kind, and its degree is in turn based on excellencies of temperament, morals, and intellect that are reflected in, and to some degree produced by, the social particularities of their lives. Romantic love will, we are assured, lift Anne out of the superficialities and false values of her home environment into truer, more fundamental ones – but only because she has already lifted herself out of them, through the sweet temperament and moral and intellectual self-cultivation that *made* her so enduringly loveable to Wentworth in the first place.

In Cathy's oscillation between Edgar and Heathcliff, Brontë splits apart the version of "love" that brings about such socially useful marriages from the "love" that offers spiritual fulfillment and completion of the self. Cathy's rationale for marrying Edgar is a kind of shallow parody of the ingredients for Austen's "connubial felicity": she loves him, she claims, because he is handsome, has a nice personality, is rich, and loves her – and because he happens to be the only eligible bachelor in the neighborhood. But such love, she suggests, remains as contingent as its origins: "My love for Linton is like the foliage in the woods. Time will change it, I'm well aware, as winter changes the trees." Her love for Heathcliff is not only more permanent – "resembl[ing] the eternal rocks beneath" – it offers a spiritual fulfillment that even the prospect of heaven lacks for her:

> Surely you and everybody have a notion that there is, or should be, an existence of your own beyond you. What were the use of my creation if I were entirely contained here? My great miseries in this world have been Heathcliff's miseries, and I watched and felt each from the beginning; my great thought in living is himself. If all else perished, and *he* remained, I should continue to be; and, if all else remained, and he were annihilated, the Universe would turn to a mighty stranger. . . . Nelly, I *am* Heathcliff.

Nelly, who usually acts as the voice of conventional morality in the novel, finds this splitting apart either incomprehensible or immoral, underlining (like Cathy's dream of being unhappy in heaven) the novel's clash of incommensurate value systems: "'If I can make any sense of your nonsense, Miss,' I said, 'it only goes to convince me that you are ignorant of the duties you undertake in marrying; or else that you are a wicked, unprincipled girl'" (ch. 9).

It is easy to feel that Nelly is missing the point here, and that the love Cathy so eloquently declares is more real and more valuable than the socially sanctioned dutiful affection Nelly evokes as the proper grounds for marriage. But in the course of the novel, Brontë strips from the bond between Cathy and Heathcliff nearly every feature we normally associate with "love," such as affection, esteem, or even a modicum of concern for each other's feelings and well-being. Cathy can insist that she "loves" Heathcliff despite describing him to Isabella as "an unreclaimed creature, without refinement, without cultivation" who is "quite capable of marrying your fortune" out of sheer "avarice" and then "crush[ing] you, like a sparrow's egg, if he found you a troublesome charge" (ch. 10). Heathcliff returns her devotion (if it can be called that) despite the conviction that she has treated him "infernally" and that she wants to "torture [him] to death for [her] amusement" (ch. 11). Can we really call this bond by the same name as whatever brings Darcy and Elizabeth, or Anne and Wentworth, together?

In other ways too, the relationship as it is described in the novel makes an uneasy fit with familiar models of romantic love or even sexual attraction: the mutual bond they both look back on and aspire to reanimate was formed as playmates in early childhood – the problem, at adolescence, of translating this bond into socially recognizable forms of "romance" is arguably just what tears them apart.[7] Furthermore, their repeated assertions of the absolute unity between them obscure the degree to which their actions suggest a more unequal, and unsavory, play of power-relations: from childhood onward, Cathy often shows off or brags about her ability to command and control Heathcliff. He does not claim a remotely equivalent power to control her actions, but he does resist her commands, and even seeks revenge on her for failing to respond to his desires. Certainly Cathy's confidence that Heathcliff would, for her sake, abstain from hurting anyone she loves proves painfully misplaced.

This is not necessarily to say that Cathy and Heathcliff don't "really" love each other – not only do they both experience their feelings for each other in those terms, but other characters generally do also. Isabella's crush on Heathcliff derives from her recognition of the intensity of his devotion to Cathy, a devotion she fantasizes about being the object of. Readers of the novel often find themselves in the same boat. We might say that Brontë brings into focus for us the darker side of "love" – the aggression inherent in the desire to possess another, the fear and anger generated by the acknowledgment of needing another to complete the self. These are qualities that remain largely hidden in Austen, though we glimpse them, perhaps, in the stormy beginning of Darcy's courtship of Elizabeth, or in Wentworth's unjust resentment of Anne's rejection. But the stark contrast between Brontë's and Austen's versions of love should also remind us that the idea that there is a single, universally recognizable "true love" that automatically transcends and dissolves all social categories is likely to obscure more than it illuminates about the treatment of love and courtship in nineteenth-century novels.

Thrushcross Grange

The force that comes between Cathy and Heathcliff comes from Thrushcross Grange. There Cathy meets the Lintons, and comes to absorb the values according to which marriage to Heathcliff would be "degrading." From the time Thrushcross Grange and the Lintons are first introduced into the story – when Heathcliff and Cathy peer through the lighted window of the Grange – the two houses are set in complex opposition to each other. Here is what Heathcliff sees:

we saw – ah! it was beautiful – a splendid place carpeted with crimson, and crimson-covered chairs and tables, and a pure white ceiling bordered by gold, a shower of glass-drops hanging in silver chains from the centre, and shimmering with little soft tapers. . . . Edgar and his sister had it entirely to themselves; shouldn't they have been happy? We should have thought ourselves in heaven! And now, guess what your good little children were doing? Isabella . . . lay screaming at the far end of the room . . . Edgar stood on the hearth weeping silently, and in the middle of the table sat a little dog shaking its paw and yelping, which, from their mutual accusations, we understood they had nearly pulled in two between them. (ch. 6)

Compare this to Lockwood's opening view of Wuthering Heights:

One step brought us into the family sitting-room. . . . They call it here "the house" pre-eminently. It includes kitchen and parlour, generally. . . . One end . . . reflected splendidly both light and heat from ranks of immense pewter dishes, interspersed with silver jugs and tankards, towering row after row, in a vast oak dresser, to the very roof. The latter had never been underdrawn: its entire anatomy lay bare to an inquiring eye, except where a frame of wood laden with oatcakes, and clusters of legs of beef, mutton, and ham, concealed it. Above the chimney were sundry villainous old guns, and a couple of horse-pistols, and, by way of ornament, three gaudily-painted canisters disposed along its ledge. The floor was of smooth, white stone; the chairs, high-backed, primitive structures, painted green, one or two heavy black ones lurking in the shade. (ch. 1)

Both houses give an initial impression of plenty and prosperity, but in Wuthering Heights the "anatomy" of this prosperity is "laid bare" as both the structure of the house and the products of the farming labor going on within and around it are exposed to view. Utility and decoration are combined in the polished jugs and tankards and painted canisters. The potential for violence, in the form of "villainous old guns," also remains in plain view. Though we are told that "the house" is no longer where cooking is done, its beams are still used to store food. At Thrushcross Grange, this "anatomy" is obscured by luxurious decorations: the crimson carpet and upholstery, crystal chandeliers, and gilt and white ceiling. The room is entirely a space for leisure, comfort, and the display of wealth, with the productive labor of the household exiled to servants' quarters. But within this space, all is not well: surrounded by material comforts and expensive commodities, Edgar and Isabella are alienated from each other. In fighting over the right to hold the dog, they have converted it into another commodity, and nearly destroyed it in the process – as Isabella will later fight Cathy for Heathcliff, as Edgar will fight Heathcliff for Cathy.

This initial contrast is carried out and developed through the rest of the novel. Wuthering Heights remains a place where productive labor is more exposed to view; the lines between laborers and employers, servants and family, are correspondingly more fluid, as servants play a vital and powerful role within the family, and individual characters (Heathcliff, Hareton, the younger Cathy, Nelly) move from one role to the other, and back again, in contrast to the relative fixity and determined enforcement of class distinctions at the Grange. The Grange is not only where the first Cathy learns – and learns to care – that marriage to Heathcliff would "degrade" her, here too she learns to "play the mistress" at home more generally, ordering the servants around and treating them, as Nelly resentfully puts it, "like slaves."

The Heights is also more exposed to nature, and is consequently associated with physical health and vitality, while the Grange, situated within the tamed and bounded nature of a walled park, nurtures the uniformly weak and sickly Lintons. But for all that, as the guns hint, the Heights is also the site of most of the violence and cruelty in the novel – often hellishly so. If it feels closer to the raw vitality of nature, its inhabitants appear to have a correspondingly more tenuous hold on civilization, and even their own humanity. It is often associated with darkness and bad weather, while the Grange is generally portrayed in light, sunshine, and warmth. The veneer of civilization at the Grange may cover some darker impulses, but it *does* cover them, though at a price. Both Isabella and Edgar Linton find themselves drawn to the rude energy of the Heights, even (perhaps especially) when it shows itself in violence. They long to absorb it into their own comfortably civilized world, only to find themselves destroyed by it. But with the marriage of Hareton and Cathy, the Grange at least appears to triumph.

Nelly

If we approach Nelly's role in purely functional terms – i.e., given a commitment to plausible first person narration, how can Brontë convincingly get us privileged access to a variety of perspectives on such a strange and deeply private story? – Nelly's role as a trusted and loyal servant who has grown up in intimate connection with the family seems beautifully crafted for the task at hand. But the same qualities that help to make her convincing in that role also invite us to consider her as a character in her own right. Nelly's position in the family bears some intriguing resemblances to Heathcliff's. Like him, she is expected to move from a sibling-like role as playmate of the Earnshaw children to the inferior status of a servant. Like him, she has had a particularly close childhood bond with one member of the family – Hindley, who is her own age – but has then seen him grow apart from her and marry a more refined but sickly member of his own class. It is no surprise, then, that the young Nelly should have resented Heathcliff's intrusion into the household: as Hindley's ally, she would resent his displacement as the favored son; as a child of the household expected to mature into servitude in it, she may have resented even more this street urchin's apparent elevation into the status of her "masters." Nelly seems most sympathetic toward Heathcliff when he comes to share her ambiguously inferior position in the household, and the readiness with which she tells Heathcliff how he might use his imagination to place himself above "the oppressions of a little farmer" suggests she is not averse to such expedients herself.

Nelly also clearly resents the older Cathy for personal reasons – for abusing her role as "mistress," for separating her from her beloved foster-child Hareton by insisting on bringing Nelly with her to Thrushcross Grange on her marriage, and for disturbing the peace at the Grange by expecting the family to welcome Heathcliff's presence. At various key points in the narrative, Nelly's decisions about sharing or hiding information prove crucial to the plot, often in negative ways, so that it is possible, with a stretch, to attribute a great deal of the suffering of the novel to her malign influence. To do so, though, is also to participate in the Earnshaw and Linton habit of scapegoating Nelly for situations in which she actually has little power, and holding her to contradictory standards as both confidant and underling – for example, Nelly is castigated at different points by the same people both for "carrying tales" and for not carrying them. Small wonder she is often motivated by the fear of "losing her place."

The Younger Generation

When readers refer to *Wuthering Heights* as a great love story, it is generally not the happy love of Hareton and the younger Cathy they are thinking of, and film versions frequently omit the younger generation altogether. But the younger generation's story takes up nearly half the novel, and it at least attempts to resolve some of the conflicts that destroyed their elders. If the (presumed) union of Cathy's and Heathcliff's spirits after death heals the spiritual wound of their love, the struggles, trials, and final union of their heirs could be said to heal its social damage.

Linton Heathcliff, young Catherine Linton, and Hareton Earnshaw clearly reproduce elements of the original Earnshaw/Heathcliff/Linton triangle, but in ways that mingle its terms ambiguously. Linton Heathcliff, the unattractive product of an unlikely union, is both, as Heathcliff's son, the agent for Heathcliff's revenge on the Linton family, and, as a Linton himself, the object of it. With his death, Heathcliff's literal genetic stake in the younger generation is effaced, but the two who remain are arguably better candidates for the spiritual reproduction, and happy social resolution, of Cathy and Heathcliff's love. Hareton Earnshaw is another object of Heathcliff's revenge, this time on Hindley, but Heathcliff's (perceived) success in reproducing in Hareton his own experience of "degradation" in turn creates a powerful sense of identification with, and even affection for, his younger counterpart. In this sense, Hareton is more truly Heathcliff's heir than Linton is. (From another perspective, though, Hareton's experience can be taken as a repudiation of Heathcliff's belief that others are to blame for his own malevolence: Heathcliff does not, after all, succeed in twisting Hareton's character to the degree he felt his own was twisted. As he himself acknowledges, Hareton is made of better stuff: he is "gold put to the use of paving stones.") Young Cathy, at least in Nelly's view, is herself a union of the best qualities of Earnshaws and Lintons, uniting her mother's "high spirit" and "capacity for intense attachments" with the Linton mildness: "she had a gentle voice, and pensive expression: her anger was never furious; her love never fierce; it was deep and tender" (ch. 18). Their love, then, seems to promise all that was denied in Cathy and Heathcliff's separation, and it is tempting to attribute Heathcliff's final abandonment of his project of destroying their lives (despite his own denials) to his recognition of this fact.

But the second love is qualitatively different from the first in more than its happy conclusion, becoming much more like a conventional marriage-plot narrative. Like Wentworth and Anne, Hareton and young Cathy fall in love because he has nothing to do and she almost nobody to love. Ironically, the main result of Heathcliff's intervention in their lives is to convert their union from a predictable and uninteresting alliance between the scions of two local landed families to a love match triumphing over heavy social odds: Hareton is *both* the ancient heir of the Earnshaws (his name is carved over the door with the date, 1500) and an uneducated servant of coarse habits and no social aspirations. Cathy is *both* the well-bred, well-educated, petted, and privileged daughter of the wealthiest local family and a penniless dependent in the rugged household of Wuthering Heights, obliged to earn her keep by performing the work of a female servant without pay. In keeping with the greater conventionality of their love story, the couple will move to the Grange on their marriage.

Thrushcross Grange, then, is the future of Wuthering Heights, and Heathcliff is all that must be cast out to attain it. This should remind us of the pattern in Scott's novels, in which the representatives of the future (the novelist's present) have a certain drab ordinariness along with their comfort and security, in contrast to the romantic intensity that accompanies the violence of the past. In Scott's novels, some traces of the romance of the past – especially its association with passionate attachments to people and ideals – are retained to brighten and uplift the drab commercialism of the present, often in the form of innocuous anachronisms within characters, settings, and local communities, and, more importantly, in the form of stories – a process to which Scott is himself contributing. In *Wuthering Heights*, the seeming erasure of Heathcliff's influence from the social world of the novel is accompanied by his and Cathy's entry into local folklore as ghosts – and, of course, into Nelly's own storytelling.

Conclusion

Is Heathcliff's energy ultimately absorbed and reintegrated with the social world of the novel? Or does its conclusion represent his final defeat and exile from that world, and the collapse of all his efforts to impact it permanently? Do Hareton and young Cathy attain the romantic fulfillment Cathy and Heathcliff were denied, or is their love only a pale, unsatisfying imitation of their elders' undying passion? Is the young couple's abandonment of Wuthering Heights the sign that they have ceded to the alienated class-bound values associated with Thrushcross Grange? Or does the fact that we leave them happily rambling the moors together, undaunted by rumors of ghosts, mean that they have succeeded in uniting the Heights' closeness to Nature with the civilized decency of the Grange? Should we see something sinister in the fact that Nelly, who has clearly helped to engineer their union, is also now handling their finances as well as the management of the household? Or should we see her happy centrality in the household as a recovery of the mother-figures who have been lost or absent throughout the novel, and the ambiguity of her role as mother, employee, and household manager all rolled into one as an encouraging resolution of some of the novel's class, familial, and gender conflicts? We can, and should, argue fruitfully about these questions. To answer any of them decisively is to test the depth of one's own investment in the novel's conflicting fantasies of escape from, or reconciliation with, the multiple restraints of selfhood that enable a stable social world.

Chapter 4

Jane Eyre

Jane Eyre is one of the most enduringly readable novels of the nineteenth century. It was a huge hit in its own day, spawning dozens of imitations – to the point where one reviewer complained about the glut of "plain" heroines in fiction. It was also, though, widely censured for "immorality" and rebellious tendencies: even Gaskell, Brontë's friend and eventual biographer, forbade her teenage daughters to read it. With the rise of feminist literary criticism in the 1970s, *Jane Eyre*'s defiant heroine-narrator quickly made it the feminist Victorian novel *par excellence*: it provided the title and the most exemplary text for Gilbert and Gubar's groundbreaking study, *The Madwoman in the Attic*, and Victorianist critics of all theoretical schools have continued to cut their teeth upon it. At the same time, its rather Gothic tale of stormy romance between a vulnerable and unprotected young woman and an attractive but dangerous man with a dark secret is exemplary in another sense, providing the plot template for a large proportion of popular romance novels today. This range of audience appeal is the mark of Brontë's success in holding in tension, and at least appearing to resolve, the opposing forces of docility and rebellion, self-control and self-expression, personal ambition and all-consuming love. Much of this chapter will map these tensions and their implications, but first, as is our wont, we will consider the narrative voice.

The Narrator

Jane Eyre's first person narrator, with her striking blend of emotional immediacy and self-conscious artistic control, is central to the novel's success in winning readers' sympathetic engagement with its unconventional heroine, and the novel's formal influence on subsequent fiction, though less widely noted, may be as significant as its thematic engagements. Consider the opening:

> There was no possibility of taking a walk that day. We had been wandering, indeed, in the leafless shrubbery an hour in the morning; but since dinner (Mrs. Reed, when there was no company, dined early) the cold winter wind had brought with it clouds so sombre, and a rain so penetrating, that further out-door exercise was now out of the question. I was glad of it. (ch. 1)

This opening plunges us immediately, without explanation or introduction, into the uncomfortable world of Jane's childhood. The reference to "that day" (what day?) and to Mrs. Reed and later her children, give the impression that we are jumping into a narrative already underway, that we are assumed to know who the speaker is, who the Reeds are, why this day matters. As the opening chapter proceeds, we are able to fill in some of these details by inference or direct explanation, but immersion comes first.

It is now a matter of convention for novels to begin this way, by immersing us directly in a scene, a conversation, a dramatic action, before stepping back to orient us, directly or indirectly, with background information about characters, setting, and situation. But in 1848, an opening so completely devoid of *any* gesture of introduction or orientation was far more unusual. This was particularly true for a story narrated by a woman.[1] Since virtuous ladies, fictional or actual, were supposed to shun attention or publicity of any kind – the reason Austen, like many of her female contemporaries, published her fiction as "by a Lady" rather than under her own name – such narratives would conventionally begin with some form of explanation and exculpation for the narrator's presumption and seeming immodesty in intruding her private story upon the reading public, typically by suggesting that it might be of value as a cautionary tale, a religious inspiration, or a source of insight into larger social issues. The narrator of *Jane Eyre* offers none of these. Instead she simply plunges us into the midst of her world, compelling our attention on her own terms.

This immersion of the reader in Jane's experience is the keynote of the narrative method of *Jane Eyre*. Though the narrator occasionally steps in with knowledge or judgments acquired after the period she describes, for the most part she restricts herself to describing events very much as Jane experienced them at the time. We get to know Jane, in other words, predominantly by sharing the way she experiences the world, rather than by learning *about* her. Here, for example, is a passage telling of the aftermath of young Jane's illicit night-time excursion to visit her sick friend, Helen Burns:

> When I awoke it was day: an unusual movement roused me; I looked up; I was
> in somebody's arms; the nurse held me; she was carrying me through the pas-
> sage back to the dormitory. I was not reprimanded for leaving my bed; people
> had something else to think about: no explanation was afforded then to my many
> questions; but a day or two afterwards I learned that Miss Temple, on return-
> ing to her own room at dawn, had found me laid in a little crib; my face against
> Helen Burns's shoulder, my arms round her neck. I was asleep, and Helen was
> – dead. (ch. 9)

Here, the progression of clauses and sentences closely tracks the experience of
the awakening child, with physical sensations (daylight, movement) gradually
resolving themselves into more and more particular awareness of her circumstances, and then into curiosity about them, a curiosity whose satisfaction
has been carefully deferred "a day or two" for young Jane and is deferred in
turn for the reader, with the further addition of a dash, to the very end of the
paragraph.

This emphasis emerges too, in Brontë's method for evoking the tenor of
Jane's everyday experience. The opening chapters have numerous instances
of what Genette terms the *iterative* – actions narrated once but understood
to have happened many times – and these are most often implied through
the description of the habitual feelings they evoke. Thus, while the opening
episode represents a crisis point in Jane's time at Gateshead – her explosion
into open rebellion after years of quiet endurance – the account of Jane's
feelings and actions around this crisis simultaneously, and with admirable
narrative economy, builds up a detailed portrait of Jane's everyday life until
that point. So, Jane "never liked long walks" because she dreads "the coming
home in the raw twilight, with nipped fingers and toes, and a heart saddened
by the chidings of Bessie, the nurse"; when John intrudes on her solitude in
the window seat, she tells us that because of his bullying, "every nerve I had
feared him," to the point where "there were moments when I was bewildered
by the terror he inspired." Her explosion of rage is dampened later in the red
room by her "habitual mood of humiliation and self-doubt." And perhaps
nothing evokes the emotional experience of a routinely abused child like the
"soothing conviction of protection and security" she feels whenever she
"knew there was a stranger in the room" (ch. 3).

Later in the novel, at moments of particular intensity (though, interestingly,
not of trauma), the narrator takes the reader's immersion a step farther by
shifting into present tense narration. Here is Jane returning to Thornfield after
her visit to her dying Aunt Reed, shortly before she and Rochester will declare
their love:

> They are making hay, too, in Thornfield meadows: or rather, the labourers are just quitting their work, and returning home with their rakes on their shoulders: now, at the hour I arrive. I have but a field or two to traverse, and then I shall cross the road and reach the gates. How full the hedges are of roses! But I have no time to gather any; I want to be at the house. I pass a tall briar, shooting leafy and flowery branches across the path; I see the narrow stile with stone steps; and I see – Mr. Rochester sitting there, a book and a pencil in his hand: he is writing.
>
> Well, he is not a ghost; yet every nerve I have is unstrung: for a moment I am beyond my own mastery. What does it mean? I did not think I should tremble in this way when I saw him – or lose my voice or the power of motion in his presence. I will go back as soon as I can stir: I need not make an absolute fool of myself. I know another way to the house. It does not signify if I knew twenty ways; for he has seen me. (ch. 22)

Here the narrative tracks more complex moment-to-moment shifts in Jane's thoughts and awareness, shifting rapidly among external perceptions (the haying, the roses, Mr. Rochester sitting), involuntary feelings ("every nerve I have is unstrung"), reflections on those feelings ("I did not think I should tremble this way"), and rapid changes of plans ("I shall cross the road . . . I know another way to the house . . . It does not signify if I know twenty ways"). At moments like this, the narration comes close to what we now term "stream of consciousness."

Throughout the novel, then, Jane's personhood is an intensely *felt* experience. We know her feelings – of security, longing, terror, rage, relief – long before she is presented to us as a narrative object; even physical self-description is deferred until relatively late, though other characters' appearances are described from Jane's viewpoint, sometimes in great detail. The sense of immediacy created by these techniques has been compared to the effect of epistolary fiction, most particularly to what Samuel Richardson termed the "lively *present-tense* manner" of his novels, in which beleaguered heroines often appear to be transcribing events as fast as they occur. But in *Jane Eyre* the mature voice of the retrospective narrator is still present, and over the course of the novel she is vested with quasi-authorial status. She is explicitly represented as *writing* the story of her own life, *retrospectively* (from a distance of "I will not say how many years," ch. 1), and for a *public* audience, whom she occasionally addresses directly, most famously in her defiant "Anyone may blame me who likes" and the final "Reader, I married him." (Compare this to Nelly Dean, whose story focuses on others, is delivered orally to a private audience in response to a personal request, and is for the most part narrated before and in ignorance of the story's eventual conclusion.)

Significantly, the narrator is also represented as making self-consciously *aesthetic* choices about what to include or exclude in her narrative. "This is not to be a regular autobiography," she writes at the opening of one chapter: "I am only bound to invoke memory where I know her responses will possess some degree of interest; therefore I now pass a space of eight years almost in silence" (ch. 10). A chapter later, she is equating her autobiographical project with a novel: "A new chapter in a novel is something like a new scene in a play; and when I draw up the curtain this time, reader, you must fancy you see a room in the George Inn at Millcote, with such large figured papering on the walls as inn rooms have; such a carpet, such furniture, [etc.]" (ch. 11). Juxtaposing references to the narrative as an "autobiography" and as a "novel" might induce the kinds of ontological queasiness about the narrator's relationship to her tale that some readers experience with the narrator of *Vanity Fair*. What they suggest, though, is that Jane as narrator is understood to be self-consciously using the materials of her life to create a work that possesses a "degree of interest" of the sort people expect from novels. Thus, just as the actual author of *Jane Eyre* is creating a novel in the form of an autobiography, so its narrator represents herself explicitly as writing an autobiography in the form of a novel. Brontë, in other words, is not trying to create a naïve or unreliable narrative voice, like that of an epistolary novel, which is more limited in its knowledge, understanding, or literary aims, than she is herself; she takes pains to give her first person narrator "credit" for the rhetorical artistry of the story. In this context, the felt intensity of these scenes of memory becomes a signal not only of how deep Jane's feelings were at the time, and how important these particular memories are to her, but of her own skillfulness in re-evoking them for herself and for the reader.

Feeling with Jane makes us less likely to step back and judge her – important, because Jane is actually very far from the kind of heroine Victorian audiences could be counted on to approve. Not only is she not pretty, she is also not particularly modest – she clearly believes her intellectual and creative powers make her superior to most of her associates – nor is she notably pious, sweet natured, or deferential to men or social authorities. Instead, she is honest, principled, intelligent, creative, often witty, but most of all, passionate. It is her capacity for passion and her ability as narrator to evoke the experience of varied and sometimes conflicting passions that, more than anything else, grounds her claim on the reader's attention and sympathy. In this, Brontë shows her affinities with Romantic poets, while challenging the Romantic tendency to see both passion and creative genius as predominantly masculine attributes. But passionate feeling is a double-edged force in the novel: as the red room episode suggests, the very force of Jane's thwarted desires threatens to isolate her from the human society that offers her the only hope of fulfilling them. Hence the novel's fairytale-like story of wish-fulfillment runs parallel with a *Bildungsroman* in which development is tracked by the capacity for increasingly vigorous self-suppression.

As in *Wuthering Heights*, then, psychological intensity and complexity are crucial to the novel's artistic success, but it is worth noting that in *Jane Eyre* that complexity is almost entirely focused on Jane herself, only rarely extending tentatively outward, to Helen Burns, St. John Rivers, or, especially, to Rochester. One corollary of this focus is that characters tend to become increasingly flat and stereotypical the further they are removed from Jane's immediate concerns (minor characters in *Wuthering Heights*, by contrast, tend to become more enigmatic with distance) and negative figures like the Reeds, Mr. Brocklehurst, and Blanche Ingram are reduced to mere caricatures. Brontë also routinely falls back on familiar, and often virulent, national and racial stereotypes, most obviously in the linkage of Bertha Mason's "bestial" tendencies toward sexual immorality and violence with her mixed-race, "Creole" origins (with Mrs. Reed and her son and Blanche Ingram also being descriptively linked to Bertha's dark complexion and Africanized features). This reliance on negative racial, class, and national stereotypes is also evident in Rochester's thumbnail sketches of his French, German, and Italian mistresses (ch. 27), in the association of Rochester himself with the figure of the "Oriental despot" both thematically and physically,[2] in depictions of English aristocrats as languid and washed-out, and in the implicit linkage of St. John Rivers' marble-like Northern European good looks with his despotic coldness.[3] By drawing upon widely held cultural preconceptions about race, class, and national character, Brontë subtly reinforces Jane's intellectual and moral superiority to those whom the accidents of birth or colonial wealth place above her socially.

In recent years, *Jane Eyre* has been justifiably criticized for its reliance on these stereotypes – even by the standards of the period they are rarely employed quite so uncritically and uncharitably as here. Their use in the novel, we would stress, is part of a larger pattern of flattening out the social world beyond the circle of Jane's own immediate concerns. *Jane Eyre*, in other words, is simply not the place to look for compelling social portraiture or profound insight into social relations – any more than, say, Scott is the place to look for compelling psychological depth. (For a writer who can bring the two into relation with each other, we will have to wait for George Eliot.) Instead, both plot and characters frequently slide into a quasi-allegorical mode, standing as representatives of psychological or social hurdles Jane faces in her struggle to reconcile her own desires and capacities with the demands and restrictions her social world places on a middle-class woman deprived of the social capital of the day: money, beauty, and powerful family connections. At the same time, though, this layering of national and international allegory in the treatment of plot and individual characters allows the novel to participate in a broader English cultural project of national self-legitimation, ultimately casting *Jane Eyre* as the only proper "heir" of England's cultural and material wealth, a process we will discuss in more detail in the section on Bertha Mason.

The Narrative

The plot of *Jane Eyre* might be classed as a *Bildungsroman* (novel of education) cross-bred with a romance or courtship novel, with some Gothic twists thrown in. As feminist critics have often noted, it is an uneasy mix. The *Bildungsroman* is a traditionally male genre, tracing the education and development of a hero from childhood, through a variety of trials and adventures (usually including a contrasting pair of love affairs), to his establishment in a secure adult role. The story might well end in marriage, but this is the reward, rather than the goal, of successful development. In the courtship novel, focused on the experience of a young woman, marriage is the primary goal. Convention, both social and literary, dictated that a woman would find her identity in the man she married, just as legally her personhood was subsumed into his. The education and development of the heroine, if it occurred at all, would most often come at the hands of her future husband, and would succeed when it brought her to the point of acknowledging his worth (think of *Pride and Prejudice* or *Emma*). *Jane Eyre* could be said to participate in this courtship pattern, in the sense that the romance with Rochester, whom Jane persists in calling her "master," dominates the novel emotionally as well as in sheer length, with the Thornfield section being far and away the longest in the novel. But this section is framed by extended stretches of narrative that fall outside the love plot: the Gateshead and Lowood sections that treat Jane's childhood and education before her arrival at Thornfield, and the Marsh End section in which she must rebuild her life after the traumatic break from Rochester. Together these make up nearly half the novel, and they trace the heroine's progress through distinct phases of personal development – with each evocatively named location being associated with its own particular set of challenges and lessons – to the mature, responsible, and independent adult, who *chooses* union with Rochester (who has himself had to undergo some rather drastic education in the meantime) rather than being swept up into it.

Childhood

The young girl who explodes into rage at the beginning of *Jane Eyre*, and then wrestles for years with the internal and external repercussions of her act, is an entirely new and different kind of literary child in English fiction. Dickens had already broken new ground in the literary representation of childhood, in *Oliver Twist*, by making a child the protagonist of an entire novel. But young Jane is far more psychologically complex, and less sentimental, than the pathetically mistreated and angelic children who for years had been evoking sympathetic tears from Dickens's readers. (That Dickens recognized the effectiveness of Brontë's method is evident in the first novel he wrote after the publication of *Jane Eyre*, *David Copperfield*, which also adopts an auto-biographical narrator and, in the account of David's childhood, closely mirrors the plot and emotional effects of the childhood portion of *Jane Eyre*.) Jane's first words in the novel, "What does Bessie say I have done?" question the grounds for Mrs. Reed's criticism of her "disposition," and her first significant act is a violent "revolt" against her physically abusive cousin. The pathos here, crucially, is located not just in the treatment itself, but Jane's own violent and confusing reactions to it. Jane's rage, here and subsequently, takes her by surprise: throughout this section of the novel, the language stresses the involuntariness of her acts of defiance: "I received him in frantic sort. I don't very well know what I did with my hands" (ch. 1); "I was a trifle beside myself; or rather *out* of myself, as the French say" (ch. 2); "I cried out suddenly and without at all deliberating my words," "something spoke out of me over which I had no control" (ch. 4), and so on. Young Jane is frightened by this capacity for rebellion breaking through her "habitual mood of humi-liation, self-doubt, forlorn depression," fearing that it may confirm her elders' assessment of her as "wicked," and recognizing that the small local victories it brings her will do nothing to assuage her powerful longing for love and approval:

A child cannot quarrel with her elders, as I had done; cannot give its furious feelings uncontrolled play, as I had given mine; without experiencing afterwards the pang of remorse and the chill of reaction. A ridge of lighted heath, alive, glancing, devouring, would have been a meet emblem of my mind when I accused and menaced Mrs. Reed: the same ridge, black and blasted after the flames are dead, would have represented as meetly my subsequent condition, when half an hour's silence and reflection had shewn me the madness of my conduct, and the dreariness of my hated and hating position. (ch. 4)

Viewed in purely practical terms, Jane's rebellion is actually moderately successful: as a consequence of it, Bessie, the only person in the household Jane loves, becomes more demonstratively affectionate; Mr. Lloyd takes her side, recommending her removal from the house under the guise of medical advice; Mrs. Reed isolates Jane from her children, freeing her from John's tortures, and appears to back down when Jane later attacks her verbally. And though Mrs. Reed may intend exile to Lowood to be a humiliating punishment, the school actually offers a crucial step forward for Jane.

From the perspective of Jane's emotional life, though, what is significant about the opening episode is its profound psychic trauma, a trauma which "gave my nerves a shock, of which I feel the reverberation to this day." The trauma is connected with her incarceration in the "red-room," the bedchamber of her late uncle, as punishment for her desperate physical attack on her bullying cousin, but the sources of trauma here are intriguingly dispersed among several qualitatively different causes: Jane's own loss of control over herself; her absolute rejection by Mrs. Reed in the face of her frantically urgent plea for mercy; and her superstitious fear of Mr. Reed's ghost – a fear heightened, interestingly, by her awareness that he loved her, and hence that his resentment of her own mistreatment by the family may actually be making him uneasy in his grave. All these share in common the fear of being shut off, cast out, from human society, but they locate the agency for it variously: in a loss of control over the self that makes one unfit for human society; in rejection by others; or in a love that transgresses ordinary human boundaries. Added to this are the symbolic implications of the red room itself. The red decor recalls the "red moreen curtains" within which Jane enclosed herself in the first chapter to form a haven where she could be alone with her books and the imaginative reveries they provoke; the isolation of the red room, then, might be read as the logical extension of this withdrawal into herself. The color red, of course, evokes the rage that is the more immediate cause of her imprisonment, but the red and "fawn" decor also evokes flesh, which in combination with the imagined ghost of Mr. Reed and the ghostly paleness of Jane's own reflection in the mirror suggests womb-and-tomb (or womb-as-tomb?) associations, so that the red room scene may be read as Jane's confrontation, at the threshold of adolescence, with the "trauma" of her own female embodiment. With its complex and obscure roots, then, the red room trauma haunts the remainder of the novel, reappearing whenever Jane risks losing control of herself, going "mad" with rage or fear or desire. It re-emerges most forcefully with the portrayal of Bertha Mason, herself permanently astray from reality, grotesquely embodied, enraged, and incarcerated, as a kind of dark alter-ego to Jane.

In the tension between passion and control, Gateshead presents both in their starkest and most negative forms. Control is violent, purely external, and indifferent to the better qualities of Jane's character; it offers no reward, only further exactions, for acceding to its claims. But the alternative is a kind of blank internal rage that is as blind to the particularities of the self's desires and capacities as her oppressors are. Jane leaves Gateshead longing for love and approval, but longing also for what Lowood will abundantly provide: training in self-control. She brings with her Gateshead's only (unwonted) gift: a richly developed inner world of imagination.

The rule-bound, regimented, and factory-like Lowood school is a classic disciplinary institution of the kind Foucault famously analyzed in *Discipline and Punish*: every moment and detail of its pupils' lives is intended to further the aim of producing a uniformly "hardy, patient, self-denying" product. For young Jane, though, this is precisely its virtue. The school holds the promise of being a place where both expectations and the means of meeting them are clear: it offers Jane the substantial advantages of congenial companionship with peers, stable and consistent standards of behavior, the opportunity to excel intellectually, and at least a couple of admirable role models. The problem with Lowood before its reform is less with its rigor than with the incoherence and inadequate reach of its disciplinary program: insufficient food and clothing produce the "distracting irritations" of hunger and chilblains, disrupting studies, as well as the abuse of younger girls by the elder ones, and Mr. Brocklehurst's hypocritical attention to the students' "outside" appearance only drives the "inside . . . further beyond his interference than he imagines"; finally, the epidemic of typhus brought on by poor diet and "neglected colds" leaves "the few who continued well" with "almost unlimited license" as any pretence of education is abandoned. With these failings corrected, Lowood becomes "a truly useful and noble institution," and Jane is able, for a time at least, to fully internalize its values, achieving the "better regulated feeling" and "allegiance to duty and order" that make her appear to others and to herself "a disciplined and subdued character."

But focusing on Jane's "development" in this way also points up another key difference with the male *Bildungsroman*: the fact that, for a Victorian woman, development into a socially acceptable adult was as much a matter of denying or stunting talents and capacities as of discovering and developing them. In contrast to the typical cant of the day, *Jane Eyre* is unusually explicit about the painfulness of this process of self-stunting, and the comparative slightness of its rewards. From early on at Lowood, Jane senses that her quest for acceptance and love may require her to damage herself: "Look here," she confesses to Helen, "to gain some real affection from you, or Miss Temple, or any other whom I truly love, I would willingly submit to have the bone of my arm broken, or to let a bull toss me, or to stand behind a kicking horse, and let it dash its hoof at my chest" (ch. 8). Throughout the novel subsequently the narrator again and again describes the experience of self-suppression in violent terms: from the restlessness that "agitated me to pain" at Thornfield, to the requirement that she "cut off her right hand" in leaving Rochester, to the struggle to please St. John that "racked her hourly" (ch. 34) and threatens to enclose her in an "iron shroud."

Lowood is also the site of young Jane's tentative reconciliation with Christianity, through her friendship with Helen Burns, who both explains Christian values and models them through her endurance of undeserved humiliation and oppression and her acceptance of death. The Christ-like imagery surrounding Helen helps constitute her friendship as a conversion experience for Jane, moving her from her childhood focus on self-preservation and revenge to a capacity for forgiveness and self-denial. Her internalization of these values is underlined at key points in the plot: in her forgiveness of Mrs. Reed even in the face of the latter's continued resentment; in her painful decision to leave Rochester in obedience to "God's law"; and finally in her (conditional) willingness to join St. John Rivers' missionary expedition even knowing that it is likely to lead to her early death. But Jane's adoption of Helen's values never quite extends to Helen's patient tolerance of abuse: Jane continues to stand up for herself against oppression, even when, as with St. John, it comes in the form of genuine devotion to God's service, and she is careful to distinguish between obedience to God and obedience to his self-proclaimed messengers on earth. Hence St. John's effort to claim Jane for his religious ambitions is paralleled to Rochester's attempt to appropriate her for his own amoral revitalization, and Jane responds to both with similar declarations of autonomy, insisting to Rochester that "I care for myself" and to St. John that "God did not give me my life to throw it away."

Love

Having contrasted the treatments of romantic love in Austen's fiction and *Wuthering Heights*, it is worth thinking about how the portrayal of love in *Jane Eyre* compares with both. The love between Jane and Rochester draws on many of the same general features of romantic passion as Cathy's and Heathcliff's: their love is portrayed as fated; it is repeatedly associated with supernatural forces, both metaphorically through the frequent comparisons of Jane and Rochester to fairies, elves, brownies, or goblins and through the intrusion in the plot of omens, prophetic dreams, supernatural "calls," and the like. Their passion does not so much cross social boundaries as claim to dissolve them altogether: the narrator says that she "naturally and inevitably loved" him despite the "ocean" that "wealth, caste, and custom" put between them (though the novel's emphasis on Jane's exemplary Englishness, in contrast to Rochester's previous wife and mistresses, in fact puts them squarely on the same island). Rochester himself is an obviously Byronic hero: dark, dangerous, tormented by a bad conscience, and self-exiled from a shallow, materialistic social world that has signally failed to do justice to his ideals and talents. The near-deadly anguish both Jane and Rochester experience on their separation links them to all the undying passions of the romance novels Victorian parents were so worried about their daughters reading. If anything, Charlotte Brontë's portrayal of this passion seems more unambiguously celebratory, or at least less conspicuously double-edged, than her sister's: the anti-social implications of passion, the power-plays and covert aggression are there, but in themselves they seem to pose no significant obstacles to mutual affection and happiness – indeed, they add spice to the relationship.

But significantly, Jane and Rochester's romance also incorporates some of the more self-conscious elements of Austenian love, most particularly in its emphasis on intellect and character as the foundations of "true" love, an emphasis heightened by Brontë's portrayal of both characters as physically unattractive. The challenge posed by Jane's quiet defiance of his orders may provide the seed of Rochester's interest in her, but that interest takes root in his perception of her character and talents, particularly as these are exhibited in her unconventional drawings, with the hints of intellectual and creative depth they offer. And Jane's declaration of her love for him stresses the same qualities: she has been happy at Thornfield, she says, because "I have not been buried with inferior minds, and excluded from every glimpse of communion with what is bright, and energetic, and high. I have talked, face to face, with what I reverence; with what I delight in, – with an original, a vigorous, an expanded mind" (ch. 23). After their marriage, the mark of their happiness is that they "talk, I believe, all day long" (ch. 38). Though Rochester's and Jane's assessments of each others' characters place a much higher value on creative originality than Austen would – again a mark of Brontë's Romantic leanings – her emphasis on intellectual cultivation, an "expanded mind," as one of the foundations of enduring love would be right at home in an Austen novel.

Just as the *Bildungsroman* takes its hero through a contrasting pair of love affairs, juxtaposing degrading and uplifting love, so the courtship novel frequently offers its heroine a contrasting pair of suitors, in this case often contrasting the false and the genuine as a test of the heroine's marital discernment (Wickham and Darcy, Mr. Elliot and Captain Wentworth). The pairing of St. John and Rochester offers an interesting twist on this pattern, since by any external judgment St. John would appear to be the better suitor: better principled as well as better looking. Both St. John and Rochester seek, in their different ways, to appropriate Jane and control her for their own purposes, but the contrast with St. John's purely pragmatic desire to put Jane's capacities to work for his cause serves to emphasize the genuine respect and love for Jane's unique personhood that underlies Rochester's desire for her.

But if St. John is clearly the wrong suitor, it is also important that he *is* a suitor: that Jane has options. The Marsh End segment of the novel establishes Jane's emotional and practical independence of Rochester's love even before the chance discovery of her inheritance supplies her at one stroke with loving relations and financial autonomy. At the same time, as we shall see, it plays an important role in the novel's engagement with English colonialism and its implications for national identity.

Bertha

The hidden madwoman of Thornfield is a classic Gothic plot device: Rochester's hideous secret; the demonic horror that haunts Thornfield at night, and of course, the obstacle to a too-easy happy ending for our heroine and hero. What gives the figure such power, though, is the numerous ways Brontë parallels or associates Bertha with Jane herself. Jane most often hears "Grace Poole's laugh" when she herself has been driven to walk the roof by her own sense of restless entrapment. Her first view of her, significantly, is in a mirror, and dressed in the wedding veil that was to be Jane's own. And Bertha proves the rightful possessor of the social identity Jane had expected to take on herself – that of "Mrs. Rochester." As we suggested earlier, Bertha also embodies many of the qualities Jane had had projected onto her, or herself feared becoming, at Gateshead: not only is she uncontrolled and violent, like Jane in her attack on John Reed, but she is also dangerously cunning, a quality the Reed household also attributed to Jane, who was, according to the maid, Abbot, "an under-handed little thing . . . sullen and sneaking."

Given the novel's emphasis on repression – and on the sheer force of the passions it keeps in check – it makes sense to read Bertha as a personification of all that Jane represses: the rage that overwhelms her at Gateshead, her frustration at the confinement of ordinary women's lives, her baulked desires. For Gilbert and Gubar, "maddened doubles" like Bertha express and act out the rage that their more proper counterparts – and authors – cannot: Bertha, after all, is the agent who finally punishes Rochester for his betrayal of Jane, and by maiming and blinding him helps shift the balance of power in Jane's ultimate marriage to him. At the same time, Bertha is a figure for Jane's *fear* of her own rage, and of the ambition that feeds it.

But the emphasis on Bertha's Caribbean and racially ambiguous origin, and the circumstances of Rochester's marriage to her, suggests that she is also the site of deep-rooted cultural anxieties about the colonial Other, and about the violent and exploitative roots of colonial wealth, particularly in the use of slave labor on the sugar plantations of the West Indies. Slavery had been abolished in British colonies since 1833, thirteen years before *Jane Eyre* was written – a subject of prominent national self-congratulation in Britain. But Rochester's marriage to the daughter of "a West India planter and merchant" (ch. 27) is set fourteen years prior to his meeting with Jane at Thornfield, which is in turn many years removed from the unspecified present point from which the narrator actually writes. So the whole of Rochester's four years of married life in Jamaica would have taken place in the context of the slavery system, and Bertha's thirty thousand pound dowry – the fortune for which the marriage was arranged in the first place – would have derived directly from the exploitation of slaves on her father's sugar plantations.

Chronology aside, there are good reasons to suspect that slavery haunts the novel through the figure of Bertha. The marriage, in what was by then a familiar arrangement in fiction and fact both, trades the Rochesters' aristocratic bloodline and English social standing for a share of a colonial wealth whose precise origins might not bear too much examination. The sordidly venal quality of the transaction in this case is highlighted by the fact that the bargain is sealed by the parents without the couple's knowledge and before they have even met, and that Rochester's father takes pains to verify the reality of the fortune while making no effort to investigate the character of the bride or her family, which turns out to be "notorious." Rochester is cast as the object of exchange here – though it is worth remembering that this is his own self-exculpatory account – and the Masons want to "secure" him because he "was of a good race" – a turn of phrase more suggestive of literal breeding than of abstract social connections. Shipped off to Jamaica like a prize bull ordered in to upgrade genetically faulty local stock, then carefully maneuvered and manipulated into the sexual response his purchasers require, Rochester finds himself in a position disturbingly akin to that of the human chattels his in-laws presumably also buy and exploit.

Within the marriage, the positions and responses of Rochester and Bertha evoke the moral and psychological horrors of both enslavement and slave ownership in ambiguously shifting ways. Rochester quickly discovers in his new wife powerful "vices" that "only cruelty would check, and I would not use cruelty," language that evokes the experience of many newly installed English owners of West Indian estates who discovered to their dismay that cruelty to slaves was a seemingly indispensable feature of profitable plantation management. Bertha's character conflates the subhuman qualities imputed to African slaves to justify their enslavement – a "pygmy intellect" combined with "giant propensities" for vice, and hypersexualized drives – with the despotic tendencies called forth in their overseers, such as a "violent and unreasonable temper," a penchant for "absurd, contradictory, exacting orders," and unrestrained sexual self-indulgence. And of course, she is soon reduced to literal captivity and treated as little more than a beast, a status that is implicitly justified by reference to her Africanized physical characteristics. But the social circumstances that prematurely develop Bertha's "madness" also provide the wealth her husband enjoys. Rochester's horror at finding himself indissolubly allied to a waking nightmare of degradation and violence in Jamaica might thus be read as a figure for broader English anxieties about the conditions and implications of their colonial projects.

Jane, characteristically, is both overtly contrasted and covertly associated with the qualities Bertha represents. While Bertha is racially ambiguous, large, dark, and sexually alluring, Jane is English, pale, diminutive, and plain. While Bertha is self-indulgent and corrupted by the despotism of wealth, Jane is rigidly self-controlled and supports herself by her own labors to install English virtues in a rising generation of young women. But by the end of the novel, Jane too brings an inherited fortune to Rochester, the origin of which is a kind of revised and sanitized echo of Bertha's: while Mason is a "planter and merchant," Jane's uncle Eyre is merely a "merchant," doing business on another tropical Atlantic island, Madeira, which is not a British colony and does not have sugar plantations or slaves. But Eyre also turns out to be "the Funchal correspondent" of the Masons – a business connection by which Rochester's impending bigamous marriage is revealed and thwarted. The size of Jane's inheritance – twenty thousand pounds – recalls the thirty thousand of Bertha's dowry, but Jane explicitly declines the opportunity to use it to purchase a higher social position for herself, reducing it by division with her cousins to the less socially conspicuous sum of five thousand. This also allows her to emancipate her two female cousins from the "yoke" of "slaving amongst strangers" as governesses, enabling them to live in "equality and fraternization" with her (ch. 33). Their brother St. John, meanwhile, is freed by his share to pursue his longstanding dream of devoting his life to missionary work in India.

The virtuously mercantile Mr. Eyre, then, provides a bridge between the exploitative and dehumanizing profit-based colonialism associated with Jamaican plantations and the self-sacrificial "civilizing" mission that would increasingly be used to justify British rule in India while masking its more exploitative aims. While the atmosphere of despotic self-indulgence in Jamaica prematurely develops Bertha's worst qualities, the Christian mission, we are assured, will more positively absorb and redirect St. John's own considerable inclinations toward despotism and exploitation. But note that this positive transformation only happens *through* Jane: John Eyre himself, still bound by an older generation's quarrel – and probably, like Rochester's father, hoping to improve the family's social status through a more focused concentration of wealth – leaves nothing to the Rivers branch of the family. Money they had hoped might come to them by dynastic right thus comes instead as a free gift from Jane, a result of both her innate sense of justice and, more powerfully, her longing to create a functional family for herself out of people she had come to love and admire long before she learned they shared her blood.

We suggested earlier that the novel's employment of national and racial stereotypes functions in part to subtly cast Jane Eyre as the proper "heir" of English cultural values. In national as well as personal terms, Bertha acts as a nightmare version of the English self, whose demonization and eventual self-destruction serves to exorcise deep-seated anxieties about the terms of English national identity. By contrast with Bertha, Jane sanitizes foreign-earned wealth by recentering Englishness on a domestic "fraternity" and equality that is intellectually open to the rest of the world – Jane first comes upon the Rivers sisters as they teach themselves German – and, through St. John, self-sacrificially willing to export its best talents and highest values to benighted Others. At the same time, St. John's denial of domestic affection in his rejection of Rosamond Oliver's love, his self-righteous narcissism in casting himself as the privileged interpreter of Providence's intentions toward those around him, and his capacity for emotional abusiveness, all subtly undercut this apparently positive redirection and revaluing of English imperialism. The reader can scarcely envy the Indians subjected to this man's missionary zeal, a point recognized at the time by those contemporary readers of the novel who complained that it unjustly disparaged Indian missionaries.

Conclusion

Jane Eyre was written to sell. Its hero reforms, its heroine marries happily, and all conflicts are apparently reconciled in the ending, with even the sternly judgmental St. John lending an implied sanction to the relationship with his correspondence at the novel's close. However constrained Jane may have felt up until now by social expectations of women, or by the ease with which men as different as St. John and Rochester justify appropriating and subordinating women to their own needs, her marriage now, it is suggested, satisfies all longings. But concerned as it is with originary traumas, buried secrets, and the eruption into conscious perception of inexplicable forces of need or desire (often in the form of quasi-supernatural interventions), *Jane Eyre*, even more than most nineteenth-century novels, thematizes tensions between surface and depth, the apparent and the hidden. Depth is often the source of value – passion, creativity – that sets the heroine apart from her shallower contemporaries, but it also represents a threat through the eruption of uncontrolled subterranean depths: the passion that adds depth and complexity shades into the chaos of rage, fear, and desire that animates mere beasts or monsters. Consequently, the novel invites readings that set a latent, hidden content at odds with its surface assertions. Perhaps Jane is not as happy as she wishes to seem, one such reading might assert – note, for example, that Ferndean, the couple's final home, is the same unhealthily situated place Rochester was too conscientious to exile Bertha to. Troubling details in the novel's conclusion, in other words, hint at the kinds of resistance to conventional plots for women – both fictional and actual – that Brontë more amply and defiantly explored in her earlier and later fiction. We needn't fully take the hint here – i.e., conclude that the ending contains a secret message that Jane's marriage is really stifling – but neither should we dismiss it altogether. Thomas Carlyle, in his influential 1831 philosophical novel *Sartor Resartus*, had famously observed that "the Fraction of Life can be increased in value not so much by increasing your Numerator as by lessening your Denominator."[4] Jane would seem to have taken this advice very much to heart – as when, at Lowood, she resolutely exchanges her longing for "Liberty" for the more obtainable prospect of "a new servitude" – but she also fights fiercely and without apology for such happiness as she does find legitimately within her grasp. Jane's final happiness, in other words, is hard-won, and won through battles fought as much with herself, to control and moderate her own desires, as with the world around her, to meet them. The tension between these two kinds of struggles, and the extraordinary psychological vividness with which they are conveyed through Brontë's innovative narrative style, have everything to do with the novel's continuing power to delight and impress its readers.

Chapter 5

Vanity Fair

Vanity Fair has certainly been Thackeray's most popular novel, and we believe that its combination of rich detail and a strong overarching structure makes it his best. Its gallery of characters is deservedly famous. Above all, there is Becky Sharp. Those who read the novel in their youth may forget everything else about it (though we hope they will not), but they are unlikely to forget the scheming, resilient, self-serving, endlessly energetic and resourceful Becky. In what follows, we will dwell on the novel's thematic structure and above all on its narration, because we believe that the wealth and variety of character and incident in the novel will speak for themselves. Not wishing to get into the business of explaining jokes, we will also neglect the comedy everywhere present in what is at base a very serious novel.

The Vanity of Human Wishes

Vanity Fair may seem a sprawling novel, but it is in fact carefully constructed to demonstrate the theme stated in its final sentences: "Ah! *Vanitas Vanitatum*! Which of us is happy in this world? Which of us has his desire? or, having it, is satisfied?" (ch. 67).[1] Thackeray enacts this theme by following the careers of the two contrasting female characters who leave Miss Pinkerton's academy together at the novel's opening. With Becky Sharp, the emphasis lies most obviously on not gaining one's desires: she seems on the verge of achieving everything she wants, only to see it all slip away when her husband discovers her with Lord Steyne. But there are hints that Becky would not remain satisfied for very long even if she had succeeded with Steyne. Amelia Sedley, on whom the other storyline centers, certainly discovers that even fulfilled desire can fail to satisfy. She marries a man unworthy of her, devotes much of her life to idolizing her false memory of him after his death, and only at the very end of the novel appreciates William Dobbin, a man who is in every respect her former husband's superior. Of all the characters, only Dobbin seems to achieve a recognition of the underlying dynamic at work here. He remains hopelessly in love with Amelia throughout most of the novel, but when he finally breaks momentarily free from that love, he sums up his experience as follows:

> It was myself I deluded, and persisted in cajoling: had she been worthy of the love I gave her, she would have returned it long ago. It was a fond mistake. Isn't the whole course of life made up of such? and suppose I had won her, should I not have been disenchanted the day after my victory? Why pine, or be ashamed of my defeat? (ch. 67)

Yet when Amelia asks him to return to her, he does so immediately. In later years, after their marriage, she realizes, "with a sigh," that he has come to love their daughter more than he does her, even though "he never said a word to Amelia that was not kind and gentle; or thought of a want of hers that he did not try to gratify" (ch. 67). The words we have just quoted come directly before the final words of the novel, which ask us: "Which of us is happy in this world? Which of us has his desire? or, having it, is satisfied?" What Amelia most wants at novel's end is that Dobbin will love her best, and that is a wish Dobbin, though he takes pleasure in attempting to gratify her every desire, simply cannot fulfill.

The fecundity with which Thackeray illustrates this overarching theme of the novel is remarkable. So is the depth of his implicit analysis of human desire. One example is the novel's account of how Dobbin became attached to George Osborne at the boarding school they both attended. The incident that precipitated their friendship was this. Dobbin, who was slightly older than George, had spent his time at the school as an academic failure and the butt of ridicule because his father was a grocer, not a "gentleman." One afternoon, however, he observed young Osborne being bullied by the school's most glamorous and prestigious student, a boy named Cuff. Dobbin demanded that Cuff desist; a fight resulted; and Dobbin won. His situation in the school, socially and academically, changed overnight because of the prestige and increased self-respect he gained from this victory, and he became the devoted friend of George Osborne.

The key moment in this sequence of events occurs when Dobbin decides to stand up to Cuff. What motivates him? The narrator tells us with disarming candor, "I can't tell what his motive was. . . . Perhaps Dobbin's foolish soul revolted against that exercise of tyranny: or perhaps he had a hankering feeling of revenge in his mind and longed to measure himself against that splendid bully and tyrant who had all the glory, pride, pomp, circumstance, banners flying, drums beating, guards saluting, in his place" (ch. 5). When a narrator announces that he "cannot tell" what motivates one of the characters, readers would do well to focus their attention. In principle, a heterodiegetic narrator (that is, a narrator who tells the story from "outside," who is not one of the characters) *could* tell if he wished. Why should Thackeray's narrator suddenly assume a stance like that of one of the novel's characters, who of course can never be quite sure of just what motivates the other characters? Here, as is often the case, the answer is that the narrator wants us to take responsibility for putting together the pieces of the puzzle, and in the process to attend to its depths. What are the pieces of *this* puzzle?

Here are some of them. When Dobbin rises to Osborne's defense, we know that he has just been reading the *Arabian Nights*. We also know that he had previously defied Cuff when Cuff tried to bully him while he was writing a letter to his mother. (Dobbin reacted with such a "wicked" look that Cuff desisted.) Finally, we know that it was George Osborne who had brought on Dobbin's social disgrace at the school by revealing that his father was a grocer, but that Dobbin "bore little malice: – not at least toward the young and small" (ch. 5). All of these bits of information point in a similar direction: Dobbin is consistently, in one way or another, a defender of what is presented as the innocence of childhood. Reading and imaginative privacy figure prominently in that innocence. The narrator exclaims:

> If people would leave children to themselves [as Dobbin has been left to himself to read the *Arabian Nights*]; if teachers would cease to bully them; if parents would not insist upon directing their thoughts and dominating their feelings – those feelings and thoughts which are a mystery to us all (for how much do you and I know of each other, of our children, of our fathers, of our neighbours? and how far more beautiful and sacred are the thoughts of the poor lad or girl whom you govern likely to be, than those of the dull and world-corrupted person who rules him?) . . . (ch. 5)

Thackeray values the childhood imagination because it allows human beings to engage in stories that escape the dynamic of fruitless desire his novel shows to be the inevitable fate of those who live in the adult world. There is an important sense in which, when Dobbin springs to George Osborne's defense, he is seeking to continue his reading of the *Arabian Nights*: he is writing a chapter in which he himself is the hero. One notes the same stress on childhood imagination and on reading in the narrator's description of how Dobbin transfers to George Osborne the credit for his own transformation after the fight with Cuff:

> Dobbin was much too modest a young fellow to suppose that this happy change in all his circumstances arose from his own generous and manly disposition: he chose from some perverseness to attribute his good fortune to the sole agency and benevolence of little George Osborne, to whom henceforth he vowed such a love and affection as is only felt by children – such an affection as we read in the charming fairy-book Uncouth Orson had for splendid young Valentine his conqueror. (ch. 5)

This is touching and makes us warm to Dobbin, but in the end, the attempt to transfer the imaginary plots of childhood into life in the adult world cannot succeed: it provides no lasting escape from the fate of being doomed either to miss one's goals or to find them empty if one attains them. In the sequel, we see Dobbin center his imagination on another object – Amelia, the young woman he knows is sworn to his best friend. In an attempt to write a happy marriage plot for George and Amelia, he pushes George, who on some level he must know to be unworthy of Amelia and who is incapable of making her happy, into a marriage with her. Doubtless he does this in an attempt to save her happiness, since she is in love with George. But the marriage will also relieve his own feelings by putting a stop to any chance that Amelia might return his own, hopeless love for her. (Dobbin knows that she won't respond in any case, but hope does spring eternal.) This is a sign that even Dobbin has a degree of selfishness, and a demonstration that there is a darker side to the wish to transfer fictional plots to the real world.

The human tendency to fictionalize the real world is pervasive in *Vanity Fair*. One thinks of Jos's interminable (and false) stories of India and Waterloo and of the stories that the tradespeople who foolishly trust Becky and Rawdon allow themselves to construct about how her alleged affair with Lord Steyne will keep her solvent. One might nonetheless expect that at least some of the novel's characters would be immune to fictionalizing. Surely the knowing, manipulative, utterly worldly Becky Sharp must be capable of resisting it? In fact, not even she escapes it. She daydreams about how she could easily be a "good woman" (ch. 41) if she had £5,000 a year (though her swift boredom with respectable life demonstrates this to be false, and no reader wishes her to become a good woman anyway). More dramatically, at the very moment when her husband Rawdon's interruption of her evening assignation with Lord Steyne brings her schemes of advancement to ruin, Rawdon (of all people!) suddenly becomes an object on which her desire and admiration can rest with awe and satisfaction, the hero of an implicit narrative in which the strong and simple prevail. When Rawdon strikes and flings Steyne to the floor, Becky "stood there trembling before him. She admired her husband, strong, brave and victorious" (ch. 53).

And so does the reader. The scene seems to deliver us from the confusion of the world of Vanity Fair, replacing its creeping ethical uncertainty with simple, storybook clarity. When Rawdon strikes down Steyne, we momentarily suppose that all the ambiguities that Becky's career has helped to reveal in society have suddenly been solved. But this too is vanity and illusion – for Becky, for Rawdon, and for us as readers. As soon as the scene ends, the web of moral ambiguity that blunts and trammels desire reasserts itself, as Rawdon's wish for a final duel to the death with Lord Steyne is baffled, and the narrator repeats a question about Becky that no attentive reader can answer with certainty: "Was she guilty?" It isn't simply we do not really know if Becky is guilty or not of sexual transgression with Steyne. As the narrator repeats the question, we come to realize how difficult it is to decide what "guilt" means in the world of Vanity Fair. Are any of the characters less than guilty, in one way or another? Are we as readers entirely innocent for enjoying the spectacle of seeing Becky worship the brute force of her husband? That of course may not be all of the appeal of the scene, but surely it is a part of it. What matters most here is not how such questions are answered, but instead that they arise to cloud the ethical and emotional clarity the scene seemed to allow our desires as readers to rest on.

Thackeray's "Intrusive" Narrator

Vanity Fair, then, demonstrates the vanity of human wishes in a vivid, varied, and memorable way, as its characters pursue their desires only to find them unattainable or disappointing if obtained, and imagine themselves as participants in clear, satisfying stories, only to have those stories cloud. But to narrow our focus to the richly entertaining and instructive careers of the characters would ignore much that is most distinctive about our experience of reading Thackeray's novel. In the scene in which Rawdon throws Steyne to the ground, the narrator seems to recede, even vanish: we have the illusion that the characters are simply there before us. But this *is* an illusion, and one that is not supported by our experience of the novel in general. We do not simply experience scenes in the novel, we experience scenes told by a palpable narrator. And at times, the narrator simply talks with us, with no scene taking place at all.

In all the novels we have considered thus far, to be sure, the narrator plays a crucial role. The reader of Austen is aware of a fine intelligence behind the intricate, systematic web of distinctions informing the narrator's language and illuminating the moral clarity she seeks to instill in us. Our conversation with Scott's narrator is, at least on the surface, simpler and less exacting: he seems part genial host, part orchestrator of a medley of cultural voices. Yet there are levels of slyness and indirection present in his voice that invite us to assess the materials he presents, human and historical, with what can turn out to be a remarkable degree of subtle complexity. With the dramatized narrators of the Brontës, the distance of the narrator from the world of the story diminishes, but the importance of the narrator remains. The multiple narrators in *Wuthering Heights* draw us into the intense, and intensely ambiguous, world of the novel, as they model ways of reading that world, while the autobiographical narration in *Jane Eyre* is crucial in defining the central perspective in the novel as that of Jane herself.

Vanity Fair draws on elements of all these modes of narration, but its center of gravity lies closer to Scott than to Austen or the Brontës. We encounter a considerable narrative intelligence when we read Thackeray, but that intelligence does not crystallize into a web of verbal and social/ethical distinctions with the precision we find in Austen. And though there is some hint of dramatic presence and definition in Thackeray's narrator (who at one point briefly enters the novel's action), he hardly possesses the importance as an actor in the fiction of Lockwood or Nelly Deans or Jane Eyre. Instead, what we have is a more character-like descendant of Scott's companionable, storytelling narrator.

In putting his narrator in the center of the stage, Thackeray is drawing on an important literary tradition that flourished in the century preceding his – the tradition of the eighteenth-century moral essay. (Austen and Scott draw on this tradition also, but not to the extent that he does.) Moral essayists (who included Addison, Steele, Samuel Johnson, and Mackenzie) might be seen as the precursors of opinion and feature columnists in today's newspapers, or of the men and women who deliver their views on all kinds of subjects, from politics to language to street fairs, at the conclusion of Public Broadcasting news programs in the United States. The moral essayists wrote for periodicals, exploring a wide range of subjects that also are central to the novel, then and now – morals, manners, the relationship between the sexes, and the arts. The focus was on private life, not politics. The appeal of the moral essay lies in the wisdom it provides, but also in the mind and personality of the essayist. A number of eighteenth-century novelists incorporated narrators with similar attractions in their works. In *Tom Jones*, Fielding's narrator writes the equivalent of a moral essay to begin each of the books into which the novel is subdivided, and he makes frequent appearances throughout the text as a commentator. We noted in our chapter on Scott that Henry James considered the "mind" of the narrator of *Tom Jones* superior to the minds of any of the novel's characters.

When the narrator of a novel gains the prominence of Fielding's or Thackeray's narrators, certain questions arise. On the simplest level, we must ask whether the judgments expressed by the narrator correspond with those of the author (more properly, the "implied author" – see the Introduction). Beyond that, as with a moral essayist (or anyone we converse with seriously in everyday life), we will want to evaluate the perceptiveness and incisiveness of the mind the narrator projects. A different set of questions is raised by the very existence of such a prominent narrator: on a number of levels, we must wonder just what the relationship of the narrator is to the fiction he or she inhabits. Are we to take the narrator as, essentially, another fictional character? This is easy enough to do in a novel that purports to be a fictional memoir, though even in such a case we need to deal with the difference between what the character knew when he experienced most of the scenes he relates, and what he knows "now" as he relates them. Despite the narrator's sporadic assertions in *Vanity Fair* that he has talked with the novel's characters, and despite his description of how he himself met Amelia, Jos, Dobbin, and young George in Pumpernickel and walked home with them from the theater (ch. 62), *Vanity Fair* hardly strikes readers as a memoir. But if we aren't to take the narrator as a fictional character or an autobiographer, why is he so prominent? Isn't the whole point of novels to create their effects and enact their meanings through the depicted actions of fictional characters? Don't the antics of Thackeray's narrator short-circuit this primary fictional process? Henry James was not alone among early twentieth-century novelists in considering such narrators "intrusive" and demanding that novelists "show" and not "tell."[2] Why attenuate our experience of the world of the fiction, by placing a figure between us and that world?

There would indeed seem to be little point in creating a work of fiction, if it were possible to sum up adequately its meaning and impact in non-fictional words, whether expressed by the narrator or by any other figure (including the literary critic, which is why this book spends much of its time and energy in suggesting different ways in which the novels it discusses might be most fully experienced by the reader). But even the most "intrusive" narrator can play very different roles from that one. Such narrators can function in conjunction and counterpoint to the fiction, to enrich its meaning, not to duplicate it. Thackeray's narrator is not a character in *Vanity Fair*, but is best understood as being at times *like* a character: he seems to have a definite personality, and his viewpoint, like theirs, can become constrained and limited.[3] When so constrained, the narrator often dramatizes a set of reactions to the world of the novel, inviting us to share or contest the feelings he expresses. The narrator thereby leads us to respond to his fiction in a way that is adequate to the human complexities in his novels and the world outside them.

The Narrator in a House of Mourning

The description of the elder Osborne's death provides an example of the careful way in which the narrator's "intrusive" comments are framed to model an attitude toward the world of the fiction which can enrich our view of our own world:

> He was much shaken of late, and aged, and his mind was working inwardly. He had sent for his lawyers, and probably changed something in his will. The medical man who looked in, pronounced him shaky, agitated, and talked of a little blood, and the sea-side; but he took neither of these remedies.
>
> One day when he should have come down to breakfast, his servant missing him, went into his dressing-room, and found him lying at the foot of the dressing-table in a fit. Miss Osborne was apprised; the doctors were sent for: Georgy stopped away from school: the bleeders and cuppers came. Osborne partially regained cognizance; but never could speak again, though he tried dreadfully once or twice, and in four days he died. The doctors went down; the undertaker's men went up the stairs; and all the shutters were shut towards the garden in Russell Square. Bullock rushed from the city in a hurry. "How much money had he left to that boy? – not half, surely? – Surely share and share alike between the three [of old Osborne's possible heirs, one of whom is married to Bullock]?" It was an agitating moment.
>
> What was it that poor old man had tried once or twice in vain to say? I hope it was that he wanted to see Amelia, and be reconciled before he left the world to the dear and faithful wife of his son: it was most likely that; for his will showed that the hatred which he had so long cherished had gone out of his heart. (ch. 61)

It used to be common to speak of the mixture of cynicism and sentimentalism in Thackeray's works, but if we wish to account for the peculiar force of such a passage as this one, such a polarity won't get us very far. Let us consider, first of all, the narrative focus Thackeray employs. Though the narrator has ready access to the mind of Bullock, whose thoughts he reports (and indirectly evaluates) in free indirect discourse, that access does not extend to the mind of Osborne, the principal subject of the scene. For that matter, the narrator lacks certainty even about some of Osborne's actions. Though he knows that Osborne's "mind was working inwardly" (which is something that anyone in the Osborne household might have inferred from his demeanor), he is reduced to guessing (the grounds for the guess appear at the end of the passage) that Osborne "probably changed something in his will," an act Osborne would have performed in the privacy of his study, away from the eyes of the other members of his household. Why does the narrator place himself, with respect to Osborne, but not Bullock, in the situation of one of the novel's characters?

There is, to be sure, nothing startling or new about selective narrowings of narrative focus, in Thackeray or in other authors. We have already examined a minor example in the narrator's comment that he "can't tell" why Dobbin challenged Cuff. What is striking here isn't that the narrator denies himself a knowledge of Osborne's mind and actions; it's the close juxtaposition of his opaque view of Osborne and his transparent view of Bullock. This juxtaposition has its thematic value. Bullock and his concerns are both familiar and trivial. If you know him, you already know what he *would* think at such a moment, in all its breathtakingly single-minded materialism. Bullock cares about the money involved in this death, period – that's why when he hears of the death, he experiences "an affecting moment." (In the dark comedy of this deadpan line, we see Thackeray employing his skills as a literary parodist: in nineteenth-century novels, the sentence "It was an affecting moment" might well appear in the dramatization of a deathbed scene, but grief at the loss of the deceased would be involved, not a calculation of inheritance shares.) Bullock's panic stems from the values of the world of Vanity Fair; it is easy enough to grasp. The situation of a character who is actually facing death, however, is another matter. Death is a mystery that cannot be penetrated as easily as can the mind of Bullock, and thus it is only fitting that Thackeray's narrator should see through Bullock but be limited in his ability to penetrate what old Osborne experiences as he meets death. Beyond that, however, lies an important rhetorical maneuver with regard to the reader. When, faced with Osborne's encounter with death, the narrator limits himself to the knowledge one of the novel's characters would have, we as readers are invited to share that limitation, which is one we would experience when faced with the death of others in our own lives. We may laugh at the Bullocks of the world and imagine we understand them from top to bottom, but in our own lives, we find it harder to laugh at death and impossible to penetrate another's experience of it. Thus we are invited to take the death seriously, to open ourselves to its chilling significance.

After enjoying a moment of ironic amusement at Bullock, the narrator's tone abruptly changes, as he voices a sad, awed wish about what it was that Osborne tried unsuccessfully to say before he died: "I hope it was that he wanted to see Amelia, and be reconciled before he left the world to the dear and faithful wife of his son." From one point of view, it would be hard to imagine a more intrusive comment. ("Don't tell us what you hope; get on with the story" we might be tempted to exclaim.) But given the context Thackeray has created, this "intrusive" comment heightens our involvement with the scene; it does not stand between the scene and us. The narrator is voicing a response to a situation he has shown us that we all face, and he invites us to share that response. He wants us too to share his hope for Osborne, even though we know that such hopes may well be vain, since they are in some measure products of our wish to tell certain kinds of reassuring stories about life. (Here the "fictionalizing" impulse we have discussed with regard to the novel's characters spills over to the narrator and ultimately to us as readers.) We may well doubt that anything quite so coherent and reassuring would actually have passed Osborne's lips, for we have been told that he "tried dreadfully" to speak, and the word "dreadfully" recalls the fear and confusion that accompany bodily dissolution. We hear a certain half-despairing urgency in the narrator's voice, a plea for some sign of human warmth and dignity in the face of the brisk, mechanical apparatus surrounding death: "The doctors went down; the undertaker's men went up the stairs; and all the shutters were shut towards the garden in Russell Square. Bullock rushed from the city in a hurry." Any story, however wishful, is better than *that*. And in the end, the narrator seems to recognize that his reconstruction of Osborne's last words is indeed wishful: the most he can say is that they were "most likely" the ones he supplies. This seemingly simple passage thus carries the theme of the vanity of human wishes into a new key, as the wishes that are likely to be at best incompletely realized turn out to be the narrator's, and ours. In saying that he "hopes" Osborne's last words expressed our common humanity, then, the narrator models for us a decent, somber reaction to the terrors of the human situation. A reaction the narrator more frequently models, when he puts himself in the limited situation of one of the novel's characters, is one of anger at human heartlessness.

The Narrator, Dialogue, and Bakhtin

One way to frame the standard objections to Thackeray's "intrusive" narrator would be to say that when we read novels, we do not expect to be subjected to authoritative monologues. We have been suggesting that Thackeray's narrator instead constantly involves the reader in situations of dialogue. In the scene we have been discussing, it is just when he is at his most personal and intrusive ("I hope that it was that he wanted to see Amelia") that the narrator becomes least authoritative. Instead of issuing edicts from on high about what the novel means, the narrator joins the novel's world and invites us to accompany him. His expression of his own wishes becomes one of many elements and forces that constitute the scene as a whole. We may say that all of these forces become part of a larger dialogue provided by the experience of the novel as a whole.

In speaking of "dialogue" in this fashion, we draw on the thought of the Russian critic Mikhail Bakhtin.[4] According to Bakhtin, dialogue is at the heart of authentic human thought and indeed of language itself. Every word in the language we use bears within it an implicit dialogue, retaining the accents of all those users of the language who have employed it with different accents, for different purposes, and in different contexts. As users of language, we have the choice to employ our words with a maximum or a minimum of sensitivity to their inherently dialogic nature. For some purposes (say, the purposes of science), we are likely to suppress dialogic possibilities. For others, we will be more attentive to them. Bakhtin believes that of all literary genres, the novel is the most richly dialogic. A lyric poem has a single speaker, delivering a single point of view. The novel, at least potentially, is an orchestration of a multitude of voices and resonances. Our claim is that Thackeray's narrator is an agent, not of monologue but of dialogue: even when he speaks in tones that seem flatly authoritative and single-minded, the larger context of the novel is bound to qualify and subtilize whatever he says, putting it in dialogue with other aspects of the fiction as a whole. The narrator's most seemingly authoritative pronouncements fall into a larger, more equivocal novelistic fabric, just as Becky's vision of Rawdon as "strong, brave, and victorious" cannot stand unchallenged for more than the instant in which she experiences it.

Consider, in this regard, a celebrated passage in which the narrator describes Becky's social fall after Rawdon discovers her with Steyne, by comparing Becky to a "syren":

We must pass over a part of Mrs. Rebecca Crawley's biography with that lightness and delicacy which the world demands – the moral world, that has, perhaps, no particular objection to vice, but an insuperable repugnance to hearing vice called by its proper name. . . . In describing this syren, singing and smiling, coaxing and cajoling, the author, with modest pride, asks his readers all round, has he once forgotten the laws of politeness, and showed the monster's hideous tail above water? No! Those who like may peep down under waves that are pretty transparent, and see it writhing and twirling, diabolically hideous and slimy, flapping amongst bones, or curling round corpses; but above the water-line, I ask, has not everything been proper, agreeable, and decorous, and has any the most squeamish immoralist in Vanity Fair a right to cry fie? When, however, the syren disappears and dives below, down among the dead men, the water of course grows turbid over her, and it is labour lost to look into it ever so curiously. They look pretty enough when they sit upon a rock, twanging their harps and combing their hair, and sing, and beckon to you to come and hold the looking-glass; but when they sink into their native element, depend on it those mermaids are about no good, and we had best not examine the fiendish marine cannibals, revelling and feasting on their wretched pickled victims. And so, when Becky is out of the way, be sure that she is not particularly well employed, and that the less that is said about her doings is in fact the better. (ch. 64)

Some have seen this passage as a simple attack on Becky that rests upon a disgust with female sexuality itself (the threatening, slimy part of the mermaid that lies beneath the water). Surely, however, the language of stereotypical misogyny here is inflated to the point of self-parody, with its picture of the mermaids "twanging" on their harps, not to mention the description of their victims as being "pickled." The attack here is not so much on Becky as on "the moral world, that has, perhaps, no particular objection to vice, but an insuperable repugnance to hearing vice called by its proper name." Becky may indeed be immoral in the way in which she treats others (her son, for instance), but this way of imagining her immorality clearly won't do. The fear of women that permeates the descriptive language here is something the narrator (goaded on, one suspects, by Thackeray's frustration with the censorship his age imposed on what could be properly represented in novels) is not so much participated in as revealed by exaggeration. For the narrator, it is absurd to narrow the notion of what is "immoral" to sexual matters, and to inflate such matters above all others. And so he gives us a parody of such an attitude in the "syren" passage. If we imagine ourselves in a conversation or dialogue with the narrator, we are more likely to hear his tone of mockery than if we think of the narrator as someone who is "above" us and his fiction, and who speaks in one voice alone.[5]

However attractive we might find the notion of a dialogic Thackeray, it seems necessary to recognize that his dialogue has its limits. This is hardly surprising. We are, after all, all of us historical beings, and that means that none of us can possible escape the impress of our own age completely. The depiction of Becky herself is a case in point. Shortly after the mermaid passage, Thackeray's narrator depicts a drowning, in imagery that demands to be taken more seriously than that of mermaids or pickled victims. The narrator tells us that Becky's "*abattement* and degradation did not take place all at once: it was brought about by degrees, after her calamity, and after many struggles to keep up – as a man who goes overboard hangs on to a spar whilst any hope is left, and then flings it away and goes down, when he finds that struggling is in vain" (ch. 64). To write in this vein is to take Becky's plight seriously, yet it's worth pointing out that, in his attempt to take her seriously, the narrator finds himself imagining her as a "*man* who goes overboard." For that matter, some modern readers find any suggestion that Becky is to be criticized at all repugnant, especially when they compare her with the (to them) feckless Amelia, and when they consider the oppressiveness of class and gender Becky faces in her society. Some ingenious arguments have been constructed to demonstrate that Thackeray's novel is "really" totally in favor of Becky. But this is a line of interpretation we would discourage: there are better ways of honoring our own values than by finding them everywhere we look. It would seem preferable to listen to Thackeray's narrator as a cultural "Other." One of the greatest virtues of nineteenth-century fiction is that it offers us the opportunity to enter into a dialogue with minds that try to make sense of a society much like our own, but do so in ways that are different enough from ours to lend distance and perspective to the vision of the world that comes naturally to us. (So, to compare great things to small, can entering into a dialogue with the writers of a book such as this one, who, given their own cultural and historical positions, must make assumptions about values in general, and also about the values their readers are likely to subscribe to, which may or may not strike those readers as valid.) Entering into a dialogue with Thackeray's narrator can be a training in the appreciation of cultural difference.

In any such dialogue, there are bound to arise moments of difficulty and uneasiness. One thinks, for example, of the role Miss Swartz plays in the novel. Miss Swartz, a "wooly-haired" mulatto West Indian heiress, makes relatively few appearances, all of which are entirely of a piece. From beginning to end, she is loud, impetuous, uncontrolled, and uncouth in her gushing manners and her flashy, tasteless dress. During a pivotal scene in which she appears, she is referred to as "honest Swartz in her favourite amber-coloured satin, with turquoise-bracelets, countless rings, flowers, feathers, and all sorts of tags and gimcracks, about as elegantly decorated as a she chimney-sweep on May day" (ch. 21). Thackeray drives the point home with not one but two of his drawings. One depicts her in her finery, swinging around from playing the piano, and staring the reader in the face with witless, thick-lipped surprise. The other depicts George Osborne's sisters fawning over her preposterous dress. In both drawings the racism is palpable: her smiling visage is meant to be inherently absurd and hilarious; the attention this black woman gets simply because of her money becomes a *reductio ad absurdum* of the values of Vanity Fair. There would seem to be no dialogue occurring here, only the monologic restatement of racist norms.

Or is there? Miss Swartz's appearance in the Osborne drawing room occasions a break between George and his father. The father orders the son to marry Miss Swartz for her money; the son refuses, and at the prodding of Dobbin, marries Amelia instead, only to be disinherited. This might seem to be a noble act on George's part. It isn't. Thackeray makes it abundantly clear that George is acting selfishly throughout. When he argues with his father about Miss Swartz and Amelia, he tosses off the following statement:

> "Who told me to love her [Amelia]? It was your doing. I might have chosen elsewhere, and looked higher, perhaps, than your society: but I obeyed you. And now that her heart's mine you give me orders to fling it away, and punish her, kill her perhaps – for the faults of other people. It's a shame, by Heavens," said George, working himself up into passion and enthusiasm as he proceeded, "to play at fast and loose with a young girl's affections . . ." (ch. 21)

This speech makes it abundantly clear that what motivates George is not love or even concern for Amelia, but instead a young man's wish to master his father, as well as a strong dose of personal vanity (we've seen him admiring himself in mirrors several times). He really deserves something better than Amelia, he tells his father, but now that she's in love with him, he must be gallant, since that's what superior people do. To emphasize the factitiousness of the "passion and enthusiasm" George works himself into, Thackeray has him echo a phrase Dobbin had earlier used with angry sincerity in persuading him to remain faithful to Amelia ("to play at fast and loose with a young girl's affections"). This is the only part of his speech that rings true.

George goes on to cap his inadvertent demonstration of his own shallowness, vanity, and snobbery by ending his part of the argument as follows: "'Marry that mulatto woman?' George said, pulling up his shirt-collars. 'I don't like the colour, sir. Ask the black that sweeps opposite Fleet Market, Sir. *I'm* not going to marry a Hottentot Venus'" (ch. 21). Now by this point an attentive reader is likely to view George with distaste and even anger. We are thus programmed to find in everything he says layers of inadvertent irony that tell against him. His blatant, arrogant racism here becomes part of this pattern, but when it does so, something unexpected begins to happen. If *this* racism is distasteful, an index of callow egotism, what about the racism of Thackeray's drawings of Miss Swartz a few pages earlier? Were we right in assuming that we were expected to enjoy and participate in the racism there? We have reached some tricky ground here. It seems to us facile to suggest that Thackeray has created a subtle and knowing critique of racism, by first involving us in the enjoyment of racist comedy (or trying to do so), and then, through George, showing how distasteful racism in fact is. Thackeray's irony in this case seems less programmatic than that. We suppose that, in fact, he considers Miss Swartz ridiculous, and that he does so in part simply because she is black. (Such a view would be unsurprising in a man of his time, nationality, and social class, though of course they were not universal – and of course the final evidence here must be the novel itself.) He may despise George, but that is primarily because of his unfairness to Amelia, not to Miss Swartz, whom he doesn't bother to endow with anything approaching estimable emotions or an inner life. But the novelistic texture he has created has the capacity to transcend his own attitudes and intentions: it can lead to a more far-reaching critique of racist comedy, the sort of critique our own cultural context demands. Here Bakhtin's view that, regardless of the intentions of individual speakers, language itself carries with it layers of sedimented dialogue, may provide a useful model. Perhaps we might say that the dialogic quality of mind and practice Thackeray's fiction at its best embodies, the way it keeps casting up new possibilities and perspectives on what we had thought were simple situations, inherently has a way of moving in directions that Thackeray himself may not intend. Who are we to say that Thackeray himself might not have been carried along in such a direction?

We have been stressing dialogic possibilities in Thackeray's narration that put his audience on equal terms with the narrator. Such a stance is one of the hallmarks of his art. His works gain peculiar power when the narrator enacts the position of someone who is trying to make ethical sense of a world that is dismaying, who feels compelled to express his outrage at cruelty and injustice and his admiration for the few figures he observes who escape such crimes. (The wish to find a place, somewhere, free from cruelty and injustice helps to account for his idealization of childhood.) A narrator removed from the human condition could not stage such a protest as effectively, and a narrator placed firmly above the world of the novel could not involve us as fully. But though this is an important side of Thackeray's narrative art, it is not the only side. Our dialogue with the narrator is not always on equal terms, and we wouldn't want it to be. We read Thackeray in part because of moments when the narrator expresses insights beyond us. (Here we return to his debt to the eighteenth-century moral essay, which can also have just this appeal.)

We will conclude this chapter by mentioning one such moment, as a way of putting the side of Thackeray's narrator we have been stressing in dialogue with the narrator's other qualities, and also of stressing the extraordinary variety of voices the narrator produces. (We hope our readers will listen for them as they read *Vanity Fair*!) In the narrator's commentary on Pitt Crawley's refusal to acknowledge even to himself the ethical debt he incurred when he received the inheritance his brother had expected, we can only admire the psychological penetration displayed and summarized as follows: "So, in a word, Pitt Crawley thought he would do something for his brother, and then thought that he would think about it some other time" (ch. 44). But it is a passage that occurs a few lines earlier, commenting on the limited remorse Pitt feels for stepping between his brother and the inheritance, that truly takes one's breath away:

I have no doubt that Pitt Crawley's contrition, or kindness if you will, toward his younger brother, by whom he had so much profited, was only a very small dividend upon the capital sum in which he was indebted to Rawdon. Not everybody is willing to pay even so much. *To part with money is a sacrifice beyond all men endowed with a sense of order.* (ch. 44)

Perhaps our readers feel equal to producing the final sentence, and insight, here. We do not. In the end, it may be that Thackeray's crowning achievement is the creation of a narrator who can move from tone to tone and voice to voice in a way that encompasses so broad a spectrum of relationships, from authoritative to companionable, with his readers as they enjoy the extended conversation that is *Vanity Fair*.

Chapter 6

Mary Barton

Mary Barton was a popular success on its publication and has remained more or less continuously in print ever since. The novel, published anonymously, was Elizabeth Gaskell's first, and early reviewers rightly predicted that its author would go on to a successful career as a novelist (Dickens, who was convinced that the author was female – a matter of some debate among readers and reviewers – soon commandeered Gaskell to write for his magazine *Household Words*, to which she became a regular contributor). It is also significant as representative of a small grouping of novels written mostly in the 1840s and early 1850s, including Disraeli's *Sybil*, *Coningsby*, and *Tancred*, Kingsley's *Alton Locke*, Dickens's *Hard Times*, Charlotte Brontë's *Shirley*, Gaskell's own later novel *North and South*, and (with some stretching of the temporal boundaries) Eliot's *Felix Holt*. Variously termed the "Condition-of-England" novel (a phrase derived from Carlyle's *Past and Present*), the social problem novel, or the industrial novel, these works engage directly with the conditions and prospects for the growing class of urban factory workers, whose grievances and potential for civic and economic disruption had recently been made evident by the growth of trade unionism, the rise and fall of the Chartist movement, and the widespread suffering generated by a severe depression in trade from 1837 to 1842, known as the "hungry forties." Disraeli, in *Sybil*, had coined the phrase "the Two Nations" to describe the stark gap between rich and poor in industrial areas, and nearly all these novels share a desire to raise their predominantly middle- and upper-class readers' consciousnesses – and quicken their consciences – about a class of people with whom many of them would have had little or no direct contact.

Mary Barton was one of the most successful of these novels on its publication, and it is certainly now, with *North and South*, one of the most highly regarded. It shows the human warmth and keen eye for social and psychological detail that would continue to characterize Gaskell's fiction in this and other genres. *Mary Barton* is also distinctive among industrial novels in that its story is set almost entirely within the working class. Readers are asked to sympathize and identify directly with working-class characters rather than with a more familiar middle-class mediator-figure whose gradual discovery of and response to the workers' condition could drive the plot. Instead, the plot is generated by political and private conflicts intrinsic to the lives of the workers themselves.

The idea that a novel could offer information and moral instruction as it entertained – and even that the form might prove to be uniquely well suited to that aim – was nothing new, but the industrial novel involved a qualitatively different form of quilting of fiction to reality, in that it professed to offer very particular truths about very contentious contemporary issues: what was it really like to be a factory worker in Manchester in the 1840s? What were *they* like, and how did they feel about their lot? What responsibilities did manufacturers, the government, or other individuals have for alleviating their distress? Gaskell stresses the novel's documentary aspirations with the frequent footnotes and asides that make reference to published or living authorities to validate her representations, with the gestures toward a Scott-like anthropological rigor in accounts of Lancashire dialect and customs, and in her direct claim in the Preface to personal acquaintance with the thoughts and feelings of representative Manchester workers.

Unsurprisingly, responses to industrial novels, then and now, and particularly assessments of their worth, almost invariably get caught up in questions of accuracy and political values. Charges of factual inaccuracy or misguided conclusions are often seen as invalidating the whole project of the novel to a degree that they would not in more mainstream realist novels of the period. It may be useful to know how accurate is Dickens's portrayal of Chancery in *Bleak House*, or how practical are his suggested responses to its shortcomings (in both cases, not particularly), but the novel will hardly stand or fall on our conclusions, while the discovery that navy officers were not, after all, particularly notable for their domestic affections would have no bearing on our appreciation or judgment of *Persuasion*. At the time of its publication, praise for *Mary Barton* tended to coincide with more or less detailed affirmations of its sociological accuracy, and validations of its aim of promoting greater sympathy between classes, while more conservative readers resistant to its social aims – particularly its implied critique of "the masters'" seeming indifference to the periodic sufferings of their workmen – attacked its facts, sometimes in astonishingly petty ways, as when one reviewer scornfully observed that a man walking from Manchester to Liverpool would not in fact pass through Hollings Green, and consequently the author must know little about Manchester! Among twentieth-century critics Gaskell has been more likely to be critiqued from the left: as denying the reality of class conflict and advocating instead clearly inadequate gestures of paternalistic charity, or as seeking to redirect her readers' potential political energies into the purely private melodrama of the romance plot.

But to criticize Gaskell for offering individualistic responses to systematic evils is, to some degree, to hold her to anachronistic standards. The ground of abstract, systematic analysis of industrial relations was at this time firmly held by "Political Economy," by which is meant, in brief, the principle that markets of rational self-interested actors will self-regulate to produce the greatest benefit to the greatest number. What we would now term "class conflict" can under this model only result from a misunderstanding of the nature of the economy and the best interests of its participants. (Harriet Martineau was publishing her popular narrative *Illustrations of Political Economy* with the avowed aim of forestalling just such misunderstandings.) The social conclusions dictated by this mode of thought were not uniformly accepted, but neither Gaskell nor her immediate contemporaries yet had the conceptual tools to challenge Political Economy on its own – abstract, systematic, avowedly "scientific" – terms. While she clearly shares her class's anxiety – and ignorance – about the methods and aims of Chartism, Communism, and trade unions (all of which she lumps together under the term "combination"), she portrays John Barton, an enthusiastic participant in all of the above, respectfully as well as sympathetically, stressing his intelligence, responsibility, generosity, and idealism. Meanwhile, she neatly sidesteps the question of what Political Economy would have to say about the conditions she describes: "I know nothing of Political Economy, or the theories of trade. I have tried to write truthfully; and if my accounts agree or clash with any system, the agreement or disagreement is unintentional" (Preface). By disavowing (somewhat disingenuously) any knowledge of Political Economy, Gaskell avoids the obligation to reconcile its precepts with the "truth" of her own experience of conditions among Manchester workers. The weapons Gaskell opposes to the authoritative conservative logic of Political Economy are the moral judgments that arise from direct personal exposure to the suffering of others. Faced with an actual starving child, it becomes difficult to attend to arguments about the risks of food aid dangerously distorting the economic judgments of the poor, however irrefutable they may appear on purely logical grounds. We will address some of the consequences and implications of this approach in our discussion of "sentiment" in the novel.

The Narrator

The authorial narrative voice of *Mary Barton* is highly personalized. She frequently confesses her own doubts and limitations, and addresses the reader disarmingly as someone who will of course share her own desire to be honest and decent:

> It is so impossible to describe, or even faintly to picture, the state of distress which prevailed in the town at that time, that I will not attempt it; and yet I think again that surely, in a Christian land, it was not known even so feebly as words could tell it, or the more happy and fortunate would have thronged with their sympathy and their aid. (ch. 8)

One could just about imagine Dickens writing something like this, but it would be dripping with irony – both as to his own descriptive incapacity and as to the good intentions of the "happy and fortunate." Gaskell's narrator, by contrast, wants us to take this, if not quite straight, at least a good deal straighter. She presents the reader with the gap between what she personally knows – "the state of distress which prevailed in the town at that time" – and the actions she believes that knowledge would have to produce in a humane person "in a Christian land." Since those actions were manifestly not forthcoming, there must be something wrong somewhere. She is willing to give us the benefit of the doubt that it is the information, not the humanity, that's missing, and to take on the job of informing us despite her limitations. She is able to be effective, in other words, because she is capable of identifying sympathetically not only with the suffering workers, but with moral aspirations of the happy and fortunate. The passage is disarming – she won't harangue us about our failings – but also a challenge: now that we can no longer say we don't know, how *will* we demonstrate our humanity?

At moments like this, as in her Preface, Gaskell positions herself in the familiar role of a mediator or translator: someone who can make the experience of Manchester workers, viewed from above as objects of interest and pity, available and comprehensible to her more prosperous audience. But there are other ways in which the narrator troubles this easy division, to place characters, narrator, and reader on the same plane, and facing the same interpretive and moral challenges. Consider this passage:

> It is a pretty sight to walk through a street with lighted shops; the gas is so brilliant, the display of goods so much more vividly shown than by day, and of all shops a druggist's looks the most like the tales of our childhood, from Aladdin's garden of enchanted fruits to the charming Rosamond with her purple jar. No such associations had Barton; yet he felt the contrast between the well-filled, well-lighted shops and the dim gloomy cellar, and it made him moody that such contrasts should exist. They are the mysterious problem of life to more than him. He wondered if any in all the hurrying crowd, had come from such a house of

mourning. He thought they all looked joyous, and he was angry with them. But he could not, you cannot, read the lot of those who daily pass you by in the streets. How do you know the wild romances of their lives; the trials, the temptations they are even now enduring, resisting, sinking under. You may be elbowed one instant by a girl desperate in her abandonment. . . . You may pass the criminal, meditating crimes at which you will to-morrow shudder with horror as you read them. You may push against one, humble and unnoticed, the last upon earth, who in Heaven will for ever be in the immediate light of God's countenance. Errands of mercy – errands of sin – did you ever think where all the thousands of people you daily meet are bound? Barton's was an errand of mercy; but the thoughts of his heart were touched by sin, by bitter hatred of the happy, whom he, for the time, confounded with the selfish. (ch. 6)

In one respect, this is a familiar evocation of what might be termed "the urban sublime": a reflection that takes advantage of the contrast between the fullness of our own experience of selfhood and our attenuated sense of the person-hood of others in a crowd to invite us to enter into the vertiginous imaginat-ive experience of attempting to grant to others the same fullness. The passage appears at first glance to be explaining how Barton could have been led into the perceptual and moral error of assuming and resenting the selfish indiffer-ence of the wealthy to his plight: a kind of "pity their ignorance" move that invites sympathy at the price of reducing the poor to inferior objects. The first part of the passage models for us the process of entering sympathetically into the consciousness of people different from ourselves: Barton doesn't have the same associations with druggists' shops that "we" do, but evoking our associ-ations can still help us to appreciate the contrast he experiences between this magical space and the ugliness of his own situation. But from here the subject of perception (or misperception) slides around in ways that subtly undercut the univalence of this approach: the social contrasts that torment Barton are also "the mysterious problem of life to more than him" – perhaps, by implica-tion, to the narrator as well, who has elsewhere expressed her puzzlement that "a Christian land" could permit contrasts on quite this scale. And it is not only Barton who "could not . . . read the lot" of those he passes: "you can-not" either. The "wild romances" that hide behind his perception of the pros-perous cheer of others also potentially hide behind other, and even "your," perceptions of him: for all "you" know, he may be "a criminal, meditating crimes" or a humble, unnoticed man whose Christlike virtue will place him in the "imme-diate light of God's countenance" – and in fact, Barton's later actions will have elements of both roles. The novel as a whole has the effect of unveiling the "wild romance" that might be hidden in the lives of any of the anonymous mass of Manchester workers, but the problems of knowability and moral judg-ment ultimately come to apply with equal force along all three sides of the triangle of narrator, working men, and readers. It is her direct, unassuming, "engaging" mode of address to the reader that allows Gaskell to induce the reader to enter into a reciprocal relationship with the imagined Barton, one in which we cease to look at him from above and begin to imagine that we might be as mistaken about him and his motivations as he is about the motivations of "the happy." Gaskell speaks to us directly, admitting her own perplexities and difficulties in understanding the motivations and inner lives of others, be they rich or poor, and we listen to her in a way we might not were she to preach our duty to us.[1]

Sentiment

Gaskell makes use of the "sentimental" frequently in *Mary Barton*: the novel is chock-full of emotionally intense, "tear-jerking" scenes, which occur with a frequency matched only by Dickens (who famously summed up his fictional formula as: "Make 'em laugh, make 'em cry, make 'em wait"). As we suggested in the Introduction, though, pointing this out by no means exhausts the significance of these occasions. Emotional connection with suffering others, the obstacles to it, and the personal and social consequences of its success or failure, are vexed subjects in *Mary Barton*, and they are central to the novel's aesthetic and its aims.

Actual scenes of suffering and loss in the novel are presented with the hard-edged emotional realism of a keen observer with a wealth of experience of her own and others' grief – there are none of the conventionally sweet, teary scenes of pious deathbed instruction and farewell so endemic to bad Victorian novels (and which even Dickens indulged in). Instead we get the "terrified" Mary providing "automaton-like" assistance to the midwife as her mother screams in agony before her death in childbirth; Mrs. Wilson bitterly relinquishing her dying child to another's arms in deference to the folk belief that her "wishing" him not to die will make his death-struggle harder; the normally pious Davenport snatching at a jug of tea intended for his half-starved wife "with animal instinct, with a selfishness he had never shown in health" (ch. 6); and even Alice, the novel's most sentimental figure, oblivious to her visitors and sawing the air "in a monotonous, incessant way, very trying to a watcher" (ch. 19) as she lies slowly dying of a stroke.

Significantly, too, Gaskell does not set out initially to make factory workers the objects of readerly sympathy and charitable impulse: the novel opens with a scene of relative prosperity, with a minute description of a house "crammed with furniture" and a family who, while they must count their pennies, are not too poor to treat their old neighbors to a substantial tea. The first death – of Mary's mother, in childbirth – seems unrelated to the family's socio-economic status (except indirectly, in Barton's comment that "she's never been the same body since poor Tom's death"). But such a death would have provided an immediate point of commonality for readers of all classes in a period in which maternal mortality was generally high. The first reference to specifically economic suffering comes with the brief retrospective account of Tom's death, used to explain the roots of John Barton's bitterness against "the masters" – crystallized when he spots the mill-owner's wife buying expensive delicacies for a party as his own son dies for want of decent food. But the real focus of sympathy here is not young Tom, whose illness and death is hastily summarized, but John Barton's grief and rage in the face of it. Relegating Tom's death to background material enables Gaskell to keep her focus in the first part of the novel predominantly on her characters' roles as the *subjects* of sympathetic connection and charitable aid. Barton praises Alice Wilson's generosity by saying "she's a poor woman, and can feel for the poor" (ch. 1), an observation in keeping with his resentful litany of charitable actions he cannot expect from the rich: "No, I tell you, it's the poor, and the poor only, as does such things for the poor" (ch. 1).

Gaskell largely agrees: in describing the consequences of a widespread industrial depression a few chapters later, she points out that in addition to the sins and crimes generated by the suffering that follows,

> there was Faith such as the rich can never imagine on earth; there was "Love strong as death"; and self-denial, among rude coarse men, akin to that of Sir Phillip Sidney's most glorious deed.[2] The vices of the poor sometimes astound us here; but when the secrets of all hearts shall be made known, their virtues will astound us in far greater degree. (ch. 6)

Before and during this economic crisis, her narrative maps out in some detail the contours of a network of mutual support and assistance among the poor, operating via the multiple and criss-crossing ties of neighbors, relations, and coworkers, and carried out with a practical skill and matter-of-fact self-sacrifice that suggest its habitual nature.

The poor help each other because they "can feel for the poor." Can fiction accomplish the same aim for its non-poor readers? And if so, might it lead, not only to charitable action, but to the kind of resentment and violence John Barton is driven to? Gaskell stages a number of scenes in which characters, the narrator, and sometimes the reader, are put in the position of responding to a work of art – a song, a poem, a drawing – that depicts the suffering of the laboring poor. In the process, she dramatizes and works through some of the implications of publishing fiction that relies on sentimental appeals to produce targeted social or political effects.

In the first such scene, in chapter four, a working-class young woman, Margaret, at the request of her elderly friend, Alice, sings a song called "The Oldham Weaver" for her new friend Mary Barton, a performance Alice says "can make me cry at any time." Gaskell's narrator rather self-consciously invites the reader to join the audience: "Do you know The Oldham Weaver? Not unless you are Lancashire born and bred, for it is a complete Lancashire ditty. I will copy it for you." This is a good example of "engaging direct address," a metafictional moment which seeks to blur the boundaries between the authorial narrator, the reader, and her subjects. The text of the song is transcribed in a broad Lancashire dialect that's quite difficult to make sense of (in sharp contrast to the readily comprehensible semi-dialect Gaskell uses to present characters' dialogue elsewhere in the novel).

After the song, Gaskell adds:

> The air to which this is sung is a kind of droning recitative, depending much on expression and feeling. To read it, it may perhaps, seem humorous; – but it is that humour which is near akin to pathos, and to those who have seen the distress it describes it is a powerfully pathetic song. Margaret had both witnessed the destitution, and had the heart to feel it, and withal, her voice was of that rich and rare order, which does not require any great compass of notes to make itself appreciated.

Accordingly, Alice sheds "tears of holy sympathy" at the song, and Mary is also deeply moved.

The reader's own response, though, Gaskell suggests, is unlikely to follow suit, and may indeed be diametrically opposed to that of the intratextual audience – we may perceive the text as humorous, whereas they perceive it as pathetic. This is because the reader is triply distanced from the effect this particular song produces on these particular listeners. First, the Lancashire dialect makes the text difficult for a non-Lancashire person even to understand, let alone respond to on an emotional level. Second, readers cannot hear the deeply felt "droning recitative" with which Margaret sings – though Gaskell's direct address invites us to feel personally part of the scene, her emphasis on the power of music excludes us from it. But finally, and most important, the well-heeled reader (Gaskell clearly perceives her audience as middle class) lacks the painful first-hand experience with absolute want that makes the song's apparent comedy actually pathetic: the song describes a bailiff pulling a stool – their last remaining possession – out from under the weaver and his wife, tumbling them to the floor, and the last verse has the wife resolving to "sew up her mouth and end" since, without food, neither is of any use to them.

Here we might say that Gaskell is preparing the reader to bridge the gap between his or her experience and that of Manchester factory workers by giving us an estimate of just how wide the gap is. She does not so much ask us to sympathize directly with the suffering of a Lancashire weaver as ask us to notice how hard it will be to do so – how much stands in our way.

Gaskell offers a different "audience-response" moment a little later, in chapter nine, when Margaret and her grandfather Job share with the Bartons a poem written by Thomas Bamford, a real Victorian poet who was also, as Job points out, "a weaver like oursel." The poem consists of five stanzas detailing various scenes of suffering from cold, exhaustion, and starvation, each beginning and ending "God help the poor!" John Barton, sunk in depression after the failure of his London journey to appeal to the government for help, is moved enough by it to rouse himself to an "Amen" after the reading, and he asks his daughter Mary to copy the poem out for him on a scrap of paper. As with "The Oldham Weaver," Gaskell includes the text in its entirety, but there is none of that explanatory back-and-forth scurrying across the sympathy gap we saw with the earlier song. The poem is referred to by the narrator simply as "Bamford's beautiful little poem": Gaskell clearly expects her readers to be as readily moved by the poem as its intratextual audience is. This is partly because Bamford has done some of the mediating already. Though a weaver himself, he takes a step away from the dialect-based oral culture evident in "The Oldham Weaver" to the formal English of print culture: note that though the poem is read aloud, Barton's response to hearing it is not to ask to hear it again but to have it copied over in writing.

At this point, then, the gaps between narrator, characters, and reader appear to be closed. As Gaskell, her characters, and (she presumes) her readers join in admiration of Bamford's pathetic poem, the circuit of feeling is complete. In a sense, the poem is represented as performing the same function Gaskell hopes her own novel will perform, so that the rationale Job gives for allowing Mary to copy the lines – "more they're heard and read the better, say I" (ch. 9), applies equally well to Gaskell's decision to publish her novel, and to give this poem a broader audience by taking this opportunity to reprint it in her novel.

The next scene of artistic response in the novel, in chapter eleven, is actually one of creation as well, and is considerably less positive. In this case, the art object is a drawing – a caricature, drawn by Harry Carson, a mill-owner's son, of the ragged and starved-looking delegation of workers that has come to negotiate with the mill-owners for higher wages. The drawing is adorned with a hasty quotation from "the fat knight's well-known speech in Henry IV"

– probably "no eye hath seen such scarecrows" or "There's not a shirt and a half in all my company."[3] It is quietly passed around the room among the mill-owners, earning a smile and a nod from each, before being crumbled and tossed into (or as it turns out, just short of) the fire.

Within the text, this artwork's initial function is actually to forestall sympathy: the caricature makes the working men the objects of ridicule, while the quotation also evokes a shared familiarity with Shakespeare that most likely unites the mill-owners while excluding the working men. The drawing thus helps to pave the way for the mill-owners' ultimate unresponsiveness to the workers' demands, and for Harry Carson's own leadership role in articulating their position to the workers in the harshest possible terms: the mill-owners are divided – some leaning toward sympathy, and some toward harshness – so that Carson's drawing could be seen as tilting the balance. Gaskell gives the reader neither the artwork nor the actual quotation, though her knowing reference to "the fat knight's well-known speech" certainly casts the reader with the group that can be expected to know their Shakespeare.

The drawing takes on an afterlife when one of the workers manages to retrieve it. Pored over by the workmen in the late-night meeting, the drawing unwittingly completes its work of generating intra-class solidarity at the expense of inter-class sympathy. The men acknowledge the drawing as an accurate and closely observed representation – "That's John Slater! I'd ha' known him anywhere, by his big nose. Lord! How like; that's me, by God, it's the very way I'm obligated to pin my waistcoat up, to hide that I've getten no shirt" – but understandably find the comedy to be in rather poor taste: "I could laugh at a jest as well as e'er the best on 'em, though it did tell again mysel, if I were not clemming [starving]," says one man, "and if I could keep from thinking of them at home, as is clemming; but with their cries for food ringing in my ears, and making me afeard of going home . . . – why man, I cannot laugh at aught. It seems to make me sad that there is any as can make game on what they've never knowed." For the working men, then, the starved bodies and ragged clothes depicted in the drawing signify not just – or even primarily – their own suffering but, more powerfully, that of the families dependent on them.

We might see the drawing as a kind of mirror-image of the situation of the Oldham Weaver: in both cases, removing an artwork from the class and cultural context that produced it to be read in a different context potentially reverses the emotional valence of the work: the Oldham Weaver, which is pathetic to its intended audience – Lancashire working-class folks – risks being perceived by Gaskell's middle-class audience as merely comic; while the drawing, intended to be comic to the mill-owners, comes across to the workers as powerfully pathetic.

But in another sense the episode simply extends the logic of the Oldham Weaver example: just as the reader might see comedy rather than pathos in the predicament of the Oldham Weaver, so Harry Carson and his peers do see comedy in the dilapidated condition of the workers' delegation. But whereas Gaskell's narrator forestalls the risk with the Oldham Weaver, using the occasion instead to call our attention to the obstacles to sympathetic response and thereby to attempt to overcome them, in this case the substitution of comedy for sympathy is already implicit in the style of the drawing itself.

Characteristically, it is John Barton who makes the rhetorical transition from inserting the pathos back into the parodic drawing to directing his anger at its artist: "It makes me more than sad, it makes my heart burn within me, to see that folk can make a jest of striving men." Their anger drives the decision to assassinate one of the mill-owners, and pieces of the drawing itself are used to draw lots to select the murderer. Here the tangible evidence of Harry Carson's refusal to respond sympathetically to the suffering in front of him – the drawing – is literally recycled into an agent of retaliatory violence.

From the Oldham Weaver, then, we might trace two possible trajectories: one, which "gets" the Oldham Weaver's pathos despite all the obstacles to sympathy, which points toward a closing of the gap for an unmediated sympathetic connection (as with the Bamford poem), and the other, responding to its potential comedy and rejecting sympathetic connection, which points towards the widening of the gap, and leads directly to an act of violence. So far so good.

But the Bamford poem actually makes an odd reappearance later at the scene of violence, when it turns out that the scrap of paper Barton used as wadding for the pistol was torn from his copy of the poem – it is the recognition of Bamford's words on the paper that tells Mary that her father is the murderer. As with the drawing earlier, the tangible artifact is literally used as a tool in the production of violence. This is reflected more directly in Barton's rhetoric in guiding his fellow-workmen toward their sinister resolve, in which he offers a sequence of images of suffering closely reminiscent of those presented in Bamford's poem: the "old granny, who shivers with the cold . . . the poor wife who lies in labour on the damp flags . . ." and the "childer, whose little voices are getting too faint and weak to cry aloud wi'hunger . . . the helpless ones that cling to us in the keen wind." Ultimately, then, what drives Barton to murder is not just the millowner's failure of sympathy but his own excess of it, as his vicarious suffering on behalf of all the victims of poverty demands an outlet in retributive violence.

This sinister recycling of scraps of paper bearing works of art seems to reflect anxiety about the ultimate destination of published works of fiction, like this one, that seek to evoke strong and consequential responses in their readers, but that, through the impersonality of publication, necessarily relinquish control over the scene of their own reception. In other words, while the realist novel seems to hold the promise of integrating the particular (its richly realized individual human story) to the general (the mass audience who will read it) without losing its emotional force, the same process risks generalizing the wrong feelings. The Bamford poem's afterlife as wadding for an assassin's bullet prefigures the anxiety of Gaskell's more conservative reviewers, who feared the novel's sympathetic treatment of workers' grievances would feed violent social unrest. At the end of the novel, the conclusion of John Barton's story engages with this problem in different terms: for Mr. Carson, recognition of the depth of his own retributive rage after the death of *his* son ironically becomes the very ground of his sympathetic connection with the dying Barton.

Domesticity and Gender

When Mrs. Barton dies at the beginning of the novel, we are told that "one of the good influences over John Barton's life had departed . . . one of the ties which bound him down to the gentle humanities of earth was loosened" (ch. 3). When Mary tells Jem that she will "never" marry him, he cries out that her "cruelty" will drive him to become "a drunkard, . . . a thief . . . and maybe a murderer" (ch. 9). Statements like these, along with the negative portrayal, via Mrs. Wilson's and Esther's experiences, of the effects of factory work on women, reveal the novel's links to the cultural values associated with domestic femininity. In their most conventional form, Victorian values relegate the wife and mother to a distinctly domestic "separate sphere," kept pure of the agonistic values of the marketplace, a sphere in which men can be emotionally refreshed and morally recentered after their daily encounter with the struggle and ugliness of the (implicitly male) public sphere. Gaskell is clearly invested in some of the values associated with domesticity, particularly its valorization of emotional ties and selfless devotion to the needs of others over the rational self-interest that is supposed to govern the marketplace.

But it is worth noting that the domestic "sphere" in *Mary Barton* is neither separate nor strongly feminized. Actual wives and mothers in the novel are far from idealized: Mrs. Wilson's habitual crankiness makes her home something of a trial to its inhabitants. Mrs. Barton is described as having "something of [a] deficiency of sense," so that Mary's later belief that her mother would have been a help to her in her troubles, the narrator suggests, is probably inaccurate. Alice, the most clearly idealized female figure in the novel, is unmarried and has only a minimal domestic space of her own: she operates as something of a freelance Angel in other people's houses, while in the Davenport episode we see men like George Wilson and John Barton performing similar acts of selfless charity with equal sensitivity and skill. And while the economic independence created by factory work is shown to be a bad influence on young women, Margaret's very public and lucrative career as a singer is treated in entirely positive terms.

The Trial

After the murder, the novel appears to turn its emotional energies altogether elsewhere: Jem's arrest and Mary's anguished struggle to save him from conviction without exposing her father as the real murderer, combined with John Barton's disappearance from both the narrative and Manchester itself, direct attention away from Barton's moral and emotional struggles and the social and political questions with which they are bound up. This turn of the plot is generally read as an abandonment of the novel's political interests in favor of more conventional melodrama and romance. Certainly this portion of the novel comes across as less skillful (and more dated) than what has gone before: the courtroom drama, soon to be established as a staple of popular narrative, was still in its infancy, and Gaskell's handling of it is inexpert – particularly in the suspense-killing move of signaling the "Not Guilty" verdict in advance, in the chapter title! But the trial and the events around it are not as disconnected from the political plot as they may appear. They represent Gaskell's engagement with an alternative model for mediating the relations between classes, or, more broadly, between abstract generalities and lived human particulars: that of the law. More directly than in her sidestepping of Political Economy, the treatment of the trial stresses the inadequacy of formal reasoning to produce or uncover human truth, in comparison to direct, sympathetic human contact.

Consider Mary's efforts to bring Will to court to establish Jem's alibi: Mary is wandering the harbor in helpless desperation, unable to get the information she needs about Will's ship. Her cry that "some one must die for my negligence!" engages the interest of the boy Charley "at once." As he takes on her quest as his own, his "sympathetic 'we' gave her heart and hope." Charley helps her to engage boatmen to chase the ship, but negotiations for their pay break down until in desperation she offers to throw in her shawl as part of the bargain, "in such a tone of voice, that they must indeed have had hard hearts who could refuse such agonized entreaty." In the boat, "her patience, her grief, and perhaps her silence . . . win upon the men" so that they do their utmost to catch the boat, and when (barely) within hailing range, to convey her message to Will. Only the boy's and the men's sympathetic response to Mary's contagious desperation, then, makes the necessary contact with Will possible, and even then Will's own personal commitment to Jem and Mary must overcome his captain's stated indifference.

In Job's consultation with the solicitor they have hired for Jem, Mr. Bridgenorth, we see again the superiority of direct personal response to judicial modes of interpretation: in Bridgenorth's meeting with Jem, the latter's tone and manner in refusing to offer any exculpation for himself is, ironically, exactly what convinces Bridgenorth personally of Jem's innocence, of which he was doubtful before, though he acknowledges that that belief is worth nothing in the actual trial Jem faces. But the defense barrister, who encounters the human elements of the case only at second hand, has no such conviction, and remains "still doubtful" of the prisoner's innocence even when informed of the exculpatory testimony Will has arrived to offer. And the opposing barrister responds to Will's testimony with a trumped-up tone of outrage whose artificiality Gaskell attacks scathingly. Will's testimony proves effective not only because it is "clear and distinct in every corroborative circumstance" but because he goes on to give a stirring "account of the singular way in which he had been recalled . . . and the terrible anxiety he had felt, as the pilot-boat had struggled home against the wind." As a result, the jury find their opinion "shaken and disturbed in a very uncomfortable and perplexing way." When Will's credibility is challenged by the opposing barrister, Gaskell suggests that his passionate sincerity, "his bright clear eyes, flaming with indignation," carries conviction even to the opposing barrister, "whose look fell at last before that stern unflinching gaze." That is, Will's ability to convey emotion in an immediate and personal way is at least as important as the facts he brings to bear in saving Jem by swaying the jury.

Even with this heroic intervention to prevent a miscarriage of justice, the judicial proceeding does not so much arrive at "truth" here as agree to fail to arrive at it. The jury refuse to convict because the stakes are so high, but "The verdict they had come to was unsatisfactory to themselves at last; neither being convinced of his innocence, nor yet quite willing to believe him guilty in the teeth of the *alibi*." This failure of the courtroom to establish Jem's innocence decisively is what will lose him his position back in Manchester and ultimately drive him to emigrate: too many workers and masters – *except those that know him personally* – will continue to believe him guilty based on what they read in the papers about the trial.

The trial, then, can be read in part as a further reflection on the relationship of "fact" to "feeling." It is not that feelings take the place of fact, or render the facts irrelevant. Jem's innocence is a fact, but one that would be likely to go unrecognized on the public stage were it not for thoughts and actions made possible by sympathetic connections between people. The narrator takes up the same issue again with reference to its political and economic themes in its penultimate chapter, with Mr. Carson's debate with Job over the masters' duties to their workmen. Faced with Job's claim that the masters should do more to relieve workers' sufferings during unavoidable depressions of trade, Carson evokes the familiar argument of Political Economy, that "facts have proved, and are daily proving, how much better it is for every man to be independent of help, and self-reliant." Job responds that "You never can work facts as you would fixed quantities, and say, given two facts, and the product is so-and-so. God has given men feelings and passions which cannot be worked into the problem, because they are forever changing and uncertain" (ch. 38). Because of the networks of sympathetic feeling and mutual aid among the poor, no one is truly "independent," and the suffering of one fuels the sympathetic pain and resentment of many more. Fiction like Gaskell's held the promise of working "feelings and passions" into the problems of economic suffering and industrial unrest. As one contemporary reviewer wrote, "What philosophy, so styled, has failed to do, philosophy flinging aside even the dignity of its name . . . will one day effect. In this case, as in many others, we may live to employ fiction to arrive at the truth, and of this we think [*Mary Barton*] a striking example."[4] *Mary Barton* is exemplary of some of the complex roles fiction was able to play in the cultural process of making sense of and responding to new social and economic developments. It invokes interpersonal sympathy as a vital source of *knowledge* as well as values, and, importantly, of *reciprocal* knowledge between classes, and suggests that the failure of Political Economy to allow such knowledge to be "worked into the problem" has rendered it unable to respond adequately to the social and moral challenges posed by the Industrial Revolution.

Chapter 7

Bleak House

When Charles Dickens published the opening installment of *Bleak House* in 1851, he was a novelist at the height of his powers and popularity. The novel is in many ways exemplary of his best work: in its dazzling stylistic and tonal virtuosity, its deft management of multiple, complexly intertwined plotlines over nineteen months of serial publication, in the seemingly endless proliferation of engagingly idiosyncratic characters (which had by this time become Dickens's literary signature), and in its deeply felt social conscience. At the same time, *Bleak House* represents something of a turn in his work toward a darker and more comprehensive vision of the social world. Its narrative method is unique in Dickens's work (and as far as we know, in fiction of the period) in its alternation between an authorial narrator narrating in the present tense, and a first person retrospective narrative by the novel's central female character. The success of this method, particularly in the handling of Esther's character and voice, was much debated by reviewers at the time, and it has proved an enduring source of critical contention since.

Seriality

Serial publication is more important to Dickens's work than to that of any other major nineteenth-century novelist. He began his literary career writing "sketches" for periodicals, and his first major success, *Pickwick Papers*, evolved out of this form. He always wrote for serial publication, usually in monthly installments, sometimes in periodicals (often founded and/or edited by himself), more often, as in *Bleak House*, in freestanding "shilling numbers." This relatively inexpensive method allowed him to reach a much broader audience than those that could afford whole books, or even library subscriptions.

Indeed, from *Pickwick Papers* onward Dickens was notable – and widely noted and praised – for appealing to a broader social range of readers than other authors, who had by the 1830s mostly divided themselves between the purveyors of "Newgate novels" of low-class criminal adventures and those of "silver fork novels" of upper-class manners and courtship.

Dickens tended to write as he published: though he began a new novel with a basic plotline already worked out, and mapped out plans for upcoming numbers at least a little in advance, the actual writing took place as the pace of publication demanded. Trollope, who himself viewed serial publication as just another marketing strategy for a finished manuscript, would criticize this habit, pointing out that it deprived the author of the opportunity to revise earlier portions of the narrative in light of what emerged from the writing process later. But, for Dickens, the awareness of an expectant audience was obviously crucial to his self-image and motivation as a writer – while Trollope cast himself as a plodding but conscientious craftsman, Dickens was more like a theatrical performer: feeding and fed by the energy of an enthralled audience, and prepared to improvise brilliantly if the contingencies of the moment demanded it. Though he rarely altered specific narrative plans in response to readers, their impact is sometimes evident in the novels, as in his rather defensive listing of scientific authorities for spontaneous combustion in the part following Krook's fantastic demise. More importantly, the potential for such interaction cast write-as-you-go serial publication as a sustained mutual relationship between writer and audience – a relationship Dickens would take to its natural conclusion in 1858 when he began doing public dramatic readings of his work.

Once *Bleak House* was completed and issued in volume form, the boundaries of individual parts, comprising three or four chapters apiece, disappeared, remaining only as a kind of buried rhythm in the narrative.[1] But it is worth reading the novel with an awareness of these original units, and even pacing one's reading by the installments, as it gives an appreciation of Dickens's phenomenal skill in managing his readers' experience: sustaining their interest in an array of major and minor ongoing plots and characters, and also ensuring that each month's purchase would give satisfaction in its own right.

The novel opens with a virtuoso description of London at its foggy, muddy worst:

London. Michaelmas Term lately over, and the Lord Chancellor sitting in Lincoln's Inn Hall. Implacable November weather. As much mud in the streets, as if the waters had but newly retired from the face of the earth, and it would not be wonderful to meet a Megalosaurus, forty feet long or so, waddling like an elephantine lizard up Holborn Hill. Smoke, lowering down from chimney-pots, making a soft black drizzle, with flakes of soot in it as big as full-grown snowflakes – gone into mourning, one might imagine, for the death of the sun. Dogs, undistinguishable in mire. Horses, scarcely better; splashed to their very blinkers. Foot passengers, jostling one another's umbrellas, in a general infection of ill-temper, and losing their foot-hold at street-corners, where tens of thousands of other foot-passengers have been slipping and sliding since the day broke (if this day ever broke), adding new deposits to the crust upon crust of mud, sticking at those points tenaciously to the pavement, and accumulating at compound interest.

Fog everywhere. Fog up the river, where it flows among green aits and meadows; fog down the river, where it rolls defiled among the tiers of shipping, and the waterside pollutions of a great (and dirty) city. . . . Fog in the stem and bowl of the wrathful skipper, down in his close cabin; fog cruelly pinching the toes and fingers of his shivering little prentice-boy on deck.

As is common in Dickens's literary set-pieces, the passage relies heavily on repetition and parallel constructions to build intensity. It is extremely visual, almost filmic in its movement between broadly panoramic views and particularized closeups like the horses "splashed to their very blinkers," and the "shivering little prentice boy on deck." But it also exaggerates and extends its descriptions into the fantastic – a Megalosaurus, the death of the sun – juxtaposing the apocalyptic and the familiar to comical (and slightly sinister) effect. Along the way, the way the passage briefly borrows and incorporates the language of banking – "adding new deposits . . . and accumulating at compound interest," subtly linking the city's commercial preoccupations with the foul and dehumanizing qualities of the scene. Finally, in its descriptive exuberance, the writing calls attention to its own virtuosity; it signals to an audience that they are in the hands of a familiar and distinctive master: this is Dickens being self-consciously and conspicuously "Dickensian."

The first three paragraphs of the novel, which paint the exterior scene, are made up entirely of sentence fragments: each sentence simply posits an object – mud, dogs, fog, gas, etc. – and omits any main verb, relegating all action to participial phrases. This avoidance of verbs subtly reinforces the sense of stagnation and entrapment of the description, while also giving particular weight to the novel's first full sentence: "The raw afternoon is rawest, and the dense fog is densest, and the muddy streets are muddiest, near that leaden-headed old obstruction, appropriate ornament for the threshold of a leaden-headed old corporation, Temple Bar." The first significant *action* of the novel, then, is the narrator's metaphorical linkage between the exterior scene and a public institution, a linkage that the remainder of the chapter carries out at greater length. A similar linkage makes the transition from Chancery to Lincolnshire and the Dedlock household at the opening of the second chapter:

It is but a glimpse of the world of fashion that we want on this same miry afternoon. It is not so unlike the Court of Chancery, but that we may pass from the one scene to the other, as the crow flies. Both the world of fashion and the Court of Chancery are things of precedent and usage; oversleeping Rip Van Winkles, who have played at strange games through a deal of thundery weather; sleeping beauties, whom the Knight will wake one day, when all the stopped spits in the kitchen shall begin to turn prodigiously!

Just as the obscuring and slippery fog and mud is like the Court of Chancery, so Chancery's self-enclosure and stagnation, its resistance to change, is like that of the aristocracy as represented by the Dedlocks, and both are like the fairy-tale frozen-in-timeness of Sleeping Beauty or Rip Van Winkle. Like the opening chapter, this one paints its scenes with a vivid realism heightened at times to the point of surrealism. The language directly appropriates and parodies that of "the fashionable intelligence," and just as the omission of verbs in the first chapter evoked the stagnation of the scene, here the more mannered style reinforces the sense of the Dedlocks as rigid and hidebound – making it all the more startling when Lady Dedlock "impulsively" bursts out, "Who copied that?" But it also ranges more casually through a variety of literary, classical, and pop-cultural references, from Gulliver to Alexander to Rip Van Winkle to Shakespeare. Dickens's prose in this regard is exemplary of what Bakhtin considered one of the most significant features of the realist novel in this period: its capacity to bring into relationship with each other a diverse range of linguistic styles, each of which carried its own distinctive values and modes of perception. In Dickens, these juxtapositions are often self-consciously satiric, but at times they come so thick and fast that they convey the sense of the novel's prose emerging from a kind of primordial linguistic soup, of newspapers, books past and present, street slang, sermons, and the various specialized languages of commerce, law, politics, and medicine.

After two chapters of this heightened style, Esther's intimate, personalized perspective in chapter three comes as something of a relief. While the authorial narrator flits across England "as the crow flies" on the wings of metaphorical connections, Esther keeps her narrative perspective firmly on the ground, with the variety of characters she introduces linked metonymically through their fortuitous intersection with her own humble "progress." And while the earlier narrator inundates us with sweeping critical judgments about what he perceives, Esther's narrative conspicuously avoids them, offering a naïve, trusting perspective that assumes the best about others even when, as with her aunt, the details of their actions seem to demand a more critical assessment. With her meeting with Ada and Richard before the Chancellor, and the introduction of Miss Flite at the end, the part comes full circle, returning us to the figures of the opening chapter, now granted distinct identities and personalities.

The opening part, then, not only establishes the main plot and thematic clusters that will organize the book – the court of Chancery, the Dedlocks, and the Jarndyce household – it also introduces the rhetorical division of labor between the two narrators. The novel is divided roughly equally between them. The alternation follows no fixed pattern, except that, until near the end of the novel, each monthly part contains at least one chapter from each narrator. While both voices have recognizable similarities to the narrators of Dickens's earlier novels, they take on contrasting elements of his stylistic range. The voice of the authorial narrator is impersonal, descriptively exuberant, and stylistically ambitious, frequently launching into extended virtuoso flights of rhetoric, often with a satiric edge. The use of present tense, combined with the largely externalized perspective, richness of visual detail, and a tendency toward panoramic views, gives this voice film-like quality, but it also places a heavier emphasis on analytic connections and judgments. Esther's voice is more personalized and less ambitious, limiting itself to what she herself sees, hears, feels, and thinks. Because she limits herself to a sequential account of her own experiences, her sections tend to be easier to keep track of, even as subplots and minor characters begin proliferating, and her focus on personal connections and feelings makes them easier to care about as well. While the authorial narrator's bird's-eye perspective enables him to articulate thematic and causal connections among the novel's various plots, Esther's more emotionally rich account more effectively conveys the human costs of the social evils it portrays.

The Esther Problem

The decision to use Esther as a narrator was probably influenced by the success of *Jane Eyre* four years earlier. Dickens's previous novel, *David Copperfield*, begun just a year after *Jane Eyre* was published, was his first to make use of a first person, autobiographic-style narrator, and the childhood portion of that novel draws heavily on the plot and emotional effects of Brontë's: young David bears a much closer resemblance to young Jane than he does to any of Dickens's earlier children, and he goes through a strikingly similar sequence of experiences at home and school. With Esther, Dickens offers another female version of the abused orphan in quest of "a little love" (Esther's childhood circumstances also echo Jane's, though more briefly), but one largely stripped of the conflicted self-assertion that made both Jane and David compelling children. Instead, she returns much more closely to conventional expectations of virtuous femininity. She opens her narrative with exactly the sort of apologetic and deferential gesture Brontë had so pointedly omitted, disclaiming any literary ambition and locating the impetus for the writing clearly outside herself: "I have a great deal of difficulty writing my portion of these pages, for I know that I am not clever." And Esther, unlike Jane, *is* pretty, pious, deferential to authority, almost painfully modest. Dickens may have intended to capture the kinds of immediacy and emotional intensity *Jane Eyre*'s narrator achieved, while avoiding the controversy associated with its defiantly improper heroine, but the result also makes for an uneasy fit between Esther's considerable narrative responsibilities and the qualities assigned to her as a character.

Since Esther is quickly established as the moral as well as the narrative center of her tale (and indeed of the novel as a whole), making her the sole narrator of her own portion of the story creates the problem of having her convey her own transcendent virtue and goodness without implying any vain consciousness thereof. Hence her frequent assertions of humility, and her detailed recording of the praise and devotion of others, accompanied by simultaneous disclaimers like "(The idea of my wisdom!)" (97) or "It was only their love for me" (426). She even expresses surprise at her own narrative centrality, which she suggests has emerged despite strenuous efforts to the contrary:

> I don't know how it is, I seem to be always writing about myself. I mean all the time to write about other people, and I try to think about myself as little as possible, and I am sure, when I find myself coming into the story again, I am really vexed and say, "Dear, dear, you tiresome little creature, I wish you wouldn't!" but it is all of no use. (ch. 9)

Esther's narration also works to de-emphasize both her retrospectivity (the fact that she is writing from a point after the story has finished) and the fact that she is *writing* at all. While *Jane Eyre* self-consciously reproduces the intimacy and immediacy of epistolary fiction, Dickens reproduces as well its characteristic moments of confusion, ignorance, and self-contradiction. Hence the narrator of the opening chapter tells us that her godmother was "a good, good woman" (ch. 3) and that she herself culpably "never loved [her] as I ought to have loved her," without making a distinction between what she felt or believed as a child and her current perspective. In later chapters, though, we learn from Esther that Jarndyce has described the godmother to her as "cruel" and "distorted" (ch. 17), that she deceived both Esther and her mother cruelly, and that Esther now believes she should not have "been punished for birth" (ch. 36). The narrative perspective of Esther's opening chapter, then, is aligned with that of the narrated self of Esther's childhood rather than with the self she becomes before she begins that narration. Recursiveness – the capacity to edit or revise what she writes – is similarly effaced. Such comments as "six quiet years (I find I am saying it for the second time)," or "that particular . . . which I have no intention of mentioning any more, just now, if I can help it" (ch. 37), suggest that Esther's words, once written, cannot be altered.

Nowhere is the effacement of both retrospectivity and recursiveness more apparent than in the treatment of Woodcourt, whose every appearance is marked by abrupt self-corrections: "I think – I mean, he told us" (ch. 17); denials: "Ada laughed and said – But, I don't think it matters what my darling said" (ch. 14); or other signals of hesitation or embarrassment. Since his appearances provide the outlines of the romance plot a reader conventionally expects in the narrative of a young and attractive heroine, they take on a prominence out of proportion to their frequency. These self-correcting gestures suggest that Esther cannot simply cover up her hesitations and second thoughts by editing out the slips she makes, while the embarrassment and uncertainty they signal about the possibility of Woodcourt's love are obviously more appropriate to the narrated self than to the narrator, who has been happily married to him for seven years. They again associate her writing with personal letters, but they come even closer to the effect of oral conversation. We can almost see Esther blushing, tittering, shaking her head, trying to change the subject. Such moments, in other words, seek to efface our consciousness of Esther *as narrator* altogether.

Positive accounts of the dual-narrator strategy in Dickens criticism tend to stress the ways Esther's perceptual and analytic limitations act as a counterweight to the too bleakly comprehensive social vision of the authorial narrator: she is described as a "brake" on his runaway imagination, or as a figure "quarantined" from its infectious despair, or a model for the semi-willful blindness to the sheer scope of the social mess needed to work positively within it. But the majority of contemporary reviews included some criticism of what Dickens's biographer and friend John Forster would later term Esther's "too conscious unconsciousness" as a narrator, even when they approved of what she stood for as a character, complaining in one case that "Esther Summerson fatigues us by the pains she takes to show how wonderfully good she is, and how unconscious of her goodness,"[2] and in another that "there is no affectation so disagreeable as the affectation of ingenuous simplicity."[3]

Chancery: Systematicity, Inheritance, and the Pursuit of Claims

Bleak House takes as its primary theme the social and personal evils generated by a corrupt institution: the Court of Chancery. Most of the characters in the novel are brought together, directly or indirectly, by their connection with the court or the lawyers or suitors involved in it, and the progress, or lack thereof, of the entangled case of Jarndyce and Jarndyce provides one of the main supporting arcs of the novel's multiple plotlines. Chancery was in fact in dire need of reform. Dickens was careful to base his fictional treatment of its failings (albeit somewhat loosely) on actual cases, some of which he cites in his Preface, and the novel's publication did, as he had hoped, heighten the public pressure to reform some of Chancery's worst abuses. But Dickens also makes Chancery a stand-in or metaphor for a broader range of social and conceptual problems – as is evidenced in the way he appears to lay at its doorstep social problems, like the dire living conditions of the London poor in rookeries like Tom-all-alone's, that could hardly be plausibly traced to the court of Chancery itself. One of the qualities that make Chancery more broadly emblematic is its status as a large, institutional *system*. At a historical moment when government bureaucracies, businesses, and even philanthropic organizations were becoming organized on larger and larger scales, *Bleak House* shows Dickens wrestling with the problem of how individuals can engage with the dehumanizing scale and complexity of large institutions, and with the seemingly autonomous will of institutional systems to perpetuate and expand themselves, generally at the expense of those they are meant to serve. As a representative sample of Chancery proceedings, the Jarndyce and Jarndyce case is inhuman in its scale both synchronically and diachronically: it is "so complicated, that no man alive knows what it means," and the span of the suit extends beyond the lifespan of any of the suitors engaged in it. For the Chancery lawyers employed in it, though, its proliferating complications are a source of livelihood as well as professional amusement. Jokes about it help to socialize young professionals into the ethos of Chancery practice, sharpening their legal wits while relaxing their social consciences.

For those on the outside (or receiving end) of such an institution, its complexity and scale are both maddening and debilitating. Consider Gridley. When Mr. Jarndyce condoles with him on "being unjustly treated by this monstrous system," Gridley bursts into a tirade about the whole idea of treating an institution as a system:

"There again," said Mr. Gridley, with no diminution of his rage. "The system! I am told, on all hands, it's the system. I mustn't look to individuals. It's the system. I mustn't go into Court, and say, 'My Lord, I beg to know this from you – is this right or wrong? Have you the face to tell me I have received justice, and therefore am dismissed?' My Lord knows nothing of it. He sits there to administer the system. I mustn't go to Mr. Tulkinghorn. . . . *He* is not responsible. It's the system. But if I do no violence to any of them here . . . I will accuse the individual workers of that system against me, face to face, before the great eternal bar!" (ch. 15)

Gridley's response to the Chancery "system" is to deny its systematicity, to insistently personalize it by holding "the individual workers of that system" accountable for the actions of the system as a whole. We might expect this to be Dickens's approach as well: he certainly takes pains to illuminate satirically the process by which Chancery's "individual workers," like Vholes or Kenge, evade personal responsibility for the human suffering that results from their profession. In general, as we saw in *Mary Barton*, social-issue fiction works precisely by putting a human face on social abstractions, reducing them to a human scale. But in *Bleak House*, irreducible scale, to a large extent, *is* the problem. Though Dickens presents Gridley sympathetically, his strategy for tackling Chancery's abuses proves worse than useless: not only does he wear himself to death without having any perceivable effect on his adversary, but, more disturbingly, the spectacle of his persistant resistance is itself simply incorporated into the Chancery system as "half the fun of the fair," alongside Miss Flite's madness, and later, Richard's desperate obsession with his case.

Dickens himself resists embodying Chancery's evils in any one character: *Bleak House* is actually the first of Dickens's novels to lack a clear-cut human villain. There is no shortage of villainous characters, and they frequently embody aspects of the evils associated with Chancery as a whole, but only partially: Skimpole evokes Chancery values in his evasion of personal responsibility, but not in his aversion to work; Tulkinghorn in his sinister retentiveness, but not in the grim speed and efficiency with which he brings his "case" against Lady Dedlock to a conclusion. The Smallweeds reflect its greed, Krook its chaotic accumulation of legal litter, but neither has the court's social standing and authority. And many of the characters most directly associated with Chancery are not wholly bad: Kenge is a glib apologist for the court but also acts as the legal agent for Jarndyce's benevolence; Guppy proves capable of being inspired by Esther to at least a degree of disinterested devotion, and even the Lord Chancellor makes a positive appearance in the novel's first installment, interviewing Richard "altogether with more ease and less ceremony

– as if he still knew, though he was Lord Chancellor, how to go straight to the candour of a boy" (ch. 3).[4] Vholes, the vampire-like solicitor who feeds Richard's dangerous obsession with the suit for his own profit, probably comes closest to embodying the evil of the court in a single individual, but by the time he is introduced, Richard's fatal course has already been set, and eliminating him would only create a vacuum for another Vholes-like lawyer to fill: Vholes is a classic symptom of Chancery's evils, but not their driving force.

The villainous, dehumanizing scale and reach of "the system," then, is both a central theme and a narrative problem in *Bleak House*. It cannot be vanquished, or even significantly impacted, by individual characters on the level of plot. Yet efforts to address its damages more sytematically, through large-scale philanthropy like Mrs. Jellyby's or Mrs. Pardiggle's wholesale schemes, only extend the problem of dehumanization. Its destruction will be evoked metaphorically and proleptically midway through the novel with the Spontaneous Combustion of Krook, which Dickens rather wishfully labels "the death of all Lord Chancellors in all Courts, and of all authorities in all courts under all names soever, where false pretenses are made, and where injustice is done . . . inborn, inbred, engendered in the corrupted humours of the vicious body itself" (ch. 32). But the very unlikeliness of this as a model for the fate of an abusive institution (leave it alone and it will blow up by itself!) suggests the intractibility of the problem. It therefore also highlights the need for a counterfigure like Esther, whose focus is so determinedly localized that the debilitating scale of the problem never becomes evident. Except, perhaps, in her dreams: the two recurrent nightmares of her illness symbolically recapitulate Gridley's experience, first of being worn down by the sheer scale of the task of fighting Chancery, and then of being simply absorbed into it as "half the fun of the fair"; she dreams of "labour[ing] up colossal staircases, ever striving to reach the top, and ever turned . . . by some obstruction, and labouring again" and later endures the "worse" dream of a "flaming necklace, or ring . . . of which *I* was one of the beads . . . when it was such inexplicable agony and misery to be part of the dreadful thing" (ch. 35). Esther's literal blindness, of course, also resonates with this theme.

If part of Chancery's significance lies in its status as a public institution, it is no coincidence that it is one that concerns itself centrally with adjudicating inheritances. Inheritances real and symbolic, lost, threatened, contested, stolen, or miraculously recovered were fertile plot devices for nineteenth-century novelists, since they could plausibly produce drastic changes in condition quite suddenly, and, in a period in which inherited status and wealth still tended to be more highly valued that their self-acquired versions, could represent a wide range of social struggles. In fiction of the period, recovery of a material inheritance generally goes hand in hand with the reclaiming of a social birthright, often arriving as a kind of magical reward after the hero or heroine had proved their innate gentility without it (as in *Oliver Twist* and *Jane Eyre*). Dickens had always been ambivalent about the values of inherited worth, either social or financial, but in *Bleak House* (and subsequently), inheritance of any kind become an almost wholly negative force. Esther must repudiate her aunt's assertion that she inherits her mother's shame and sin, just as Woodcourt's mother needs to let go of her preoccupation with her son's much-diluted Welsh royal blood, and Ada cheerfully sacrifices her modest fortune to her love for Richard. Chancery's evil influence on Richard's life, by contrast, as on Miss Flite's, is not so much that it denies him an inheritance as that it seems to promise him one, thus sapping his will to make his own living. His fatal inheritance is finally nothing more than an ingrained sense of entitlement.

The rather odd exception to this is John Jarndyce, who, despite his family's embroilment in Chancery and his having no visible form of paid employment himself, seems to have no end of cash for his various benevolent purposes. In some respects, Jarndyce is a holdover from Dickens's earlier days: while he has moved beyond the need for an arch-villain in *Bleak House*, he does conjure up one of the familiar archangels who act as *dei ex machina* in many of his early novels: cheerful, eccentric men whose benevolence is matched only by their access to ready money. But even here, the figure is darkened by the uncomfortable treatment of his attraction to Esther, and the rather sadistic mind game of setting up both her and Woodcourt to believe she must renounce her true love in favor of a dutiful but passionless (on her side, anyway) marriage to Jarndyce.

Jarndyce's peculiarities also point to a more buried strain in the novel. The horror of Chancery may reflect ambivalence not just about inheritance *per se*, but more broadly about pursuing "claims" on others at all. That we all have duties toward others is a truth emphasized continually throughout the novel, and one central characters ignore to their cost, but its seemingly obvious corollary – that others have duties toward us, which we are entitled to expect them to fulfill – is treated with deep discomfort. Jarndyce's most noted eccentricity is his profound resistance to being thanked – as if to allow someone to repay kindness with thanks would convert benevolence itself into little more than a sordid bargain. That he seeks to reward himself for his goodness to Esther by taking her as a wife – and that her chief motivation for taking him is gratitude for that goodness – is the surest sign that the marriage ought not to take place, while his last-minute switch at the altar constitutes even Esther's and Woodcourt's marriage as a gift to each of them from Jarndyce, rather than as an exchange between them.

Throughout the novel, Dickens's numerous highly critical portraits of characters who fail to recognize or fulfill their duties to others are matched by celebration of their victims' unwillingness to recognize or challenge that failure. When Caddy Jellyby responds to Esther's gentle reminder of her duty to her mother by bursting out, "where's Ma's duty as a parent? All made over to the public and Africa, I suppose! Then let the public and Africa show duty as a child" (ch. 5), her resentment seems like a reasonable response, given what we have already seen of Mrs. Jellyby's conspicuous dereliction of maternal duty, and the demands she makes on Caddy. But one of the first fruits of Caddy's efforts to educate herself in womanly skills on her own is that it makes her "more forgiving to Ma," and the result of her happy success is that she whole-heartedly takes on her future husband's massive and completely unreciprocated sense of "duty" to support the pompous and parasitical Mr. Turveydrop.

Lady Dedlock: Class, Motherhood, and Violence

Alongside Chancery, Lady Dedlock's buried secret, with all the various and intertwined subplots it sets in motion (i.e., of Jo, Guppy, the Bagnets, the Snagsbys, George, Tulkinghorn, etc.), forms the other major center of gravity in the novel. Here the central thematic concern is not the qualities of an insti-tutional "system" but the governing classes' isolation from and indifference to the sufferings of the poor. When the narrator asks "What connection can there be, between the place in Lincolnshire, the house in town, the Mercury in powder, and the whereabouts of Jo the outlaw with the broom, who had that distant ray of light upon him when he swept the church step?" he is ask-ing a question that resonated powerfully for his Victorian audience, to whom the unbridgeable social gap between the very rich and the destitute seemed far more evident. As we saw with *Mary Barton*, the novel as a genre had proved itself well suited to modeling answers to that question.[5] Dickens's empathy for the sufferings of the poor, and the indignation on their behalf it feeds, are deeply felt, and his vividly grotesque accounts of the living conditions endured by the brickmakers and the denizens of Tom-all-alone's are, horrifyingly enough, fairly consonant with contemporary non-fictional accounts. His passion animates some of the novel's most powerful scenes, most notably when, over Jo's dead body, the narrator reaches out to address the audience directly, to insist that children just like Jo are "dying thus around us every day." Dickens has also learned something from *Mary Barton*: that paying tribute to the depth and effect-iveness of the poor's charitable commitment to each other could prove at least as powerful as portraying unrelieved, abject sufferings directly. *Bleak House* places a much greater emphasis on "what the poor are to the poor" than his previous novels: the mutual support of the brickmakers' wives, the efforts of neighbors to relieve the orphaned Necketts, Jo's willingness to fetch medicine for the brickmakers' families, and their care for him in return, and George's sheltering of Gridley and then Jo in their final illnesses. When Jo's death is followed immediately by the murder of Tulkinghorn, who had contributed to the boy's harassment, and then by the arrest of George, who had sheltered Jo in his final illness, on suspicion of it, the indignation expressed at Jo's death seems, as in *Mary Barton*, to have found vent in a political assassination.

But while the Dedlock plot provides occasions for introducing characters and scenes that make vivid the conditions of the poor (especially by juxtaposing them with those of the rich), conceptually it seems a rather unlikely vehicle for such concerns: Lady Dedlock's connection to Jo's death has less to do with her class indifference than with her buried sexual past, which links her secretly with a man who had befriended Jo. Lady Dedlock herself is not aristocratic by birth, and though she may well have married Sir Leicester for his money and position, it is never directly indicated that class ambition played a role in the failure of the romance that led to Esther's birth – in fact, we never learn which, if either, of Esther's parents abandoned the other, though we do know that the hushing-up of Esther's survival and upbringing was carried out without her knowledge or consent. And Tulkinghorn's death, we discover, was not an act of retaliation for Jo's death, or a measure of Lady Dedlock's determination to preserve her position, but an ill-motivated attack by a moody and violent French maid.

But the surface incoherence here masks a complex pattern of symbolic substitutions or displacements within parent/child relationships which link Lady Dedlock indirectly to characters of lower social classes. Esther, raised as an unwanted orphan and left with nothing at her aunt's death, might well have wound up as neglected and destitute as Jo. Jo, meanwhile, has had an affectionate (if rather slight) relationship to Nemo, Esther's father. By these means Jo becomes a kind of equivalent or substitute for Esther. Lady Dedlock also takes the servant girl Rosa under her wing, substituting her for the daughter she lost – but also potentially locking her into her lower social position by ruining her chance to marry an industrialist's son. Rosa's position as favorite in turn displaces Hortense, who then becomes, symbolically, another rejected child, but one associated directly with violent class revolution through her French identity and her comparison to "a woman from the Reign of Terror." Finally, in her flight from Bucket, Lady Dedlock changes places and clothes with the brickmaker's wife whose baby had earlier died and been covered by Esther's handkerchief, producing yet another symbolic substitution for the original, lost, mother-daughter pairing.

This pattern of substitutions and slippages allows Dickens to engage with class issues on an emotional and symbolic level while avoiding the kinds of overtly political representations that made *Mary Barton* so controversial. When Hortense murders Tulkinghorn and tries to pin the crime on her former mistress, she is acting out the aggression she feels toward Lady Dedlock for being "so very high" (perhaps rightly perceiving that exposing Lady Dedlock to public shame and opprobrium would be a worse punishment than killing her outright). More directly, she is acting on her anger at having been used and then summarily dismissed by Tulkinghorn, an anger that could more reasonably have been felt by Jo (were he not so angelically long-suffering) and that is felt by George, on Jo's behalf as well as his own, in ways that initially make him a likely suspect for the murder himself. By using a Frenchwoman to express what is really a violent class anger, Dickens finds a way to vent the genuine resentment of the sufferings of the poor he has been building in his audience while obscuring its roots in the class structure, and thereby avoids troubling the tenuous confidence of the English public, in the face of European revolutions, that "it could never happen here."

Mapping class issues onto the mother/child pairing also allows him to substitute for large, "systemic" social problems the more manageable (to him) issue of women's proper role and place. While substituting a variety of lower-class figures for Esther in the role of Lady Dedlock's daughter, the novel also quickly instates Esther in the role of substitute mother for every neglected or motherless child who comes her way, from Caddy Jellyby to Charley Neckett to (however briefly) Jo himself.

What are we to make of a situation in which the novel, on the one hand, reflects outrage at the mistreatment of the poor and anger at the mistreatment of children, but on the other hand allows that anger to center itself fully and effactually only in the figure of Hortense, where it is immediately distanced and disavowed as something foreign, excessive, and out of control? This question echoes the questions we earlier raised about why Esther is never allowed to evince a consistent knowledge of how she has been mistreated and oppressed, and why Jarndyce, in running away from being thanked, seems to evade the expression of a reciprocal duty between humans being to acknowledge their responsibilities to care for one another? On one level, it is tempting to explain such paradoxes as the results of Dickens's own ideological self-mystification. Dickens, we might say, is genuinely outraged by the situation of the poor, but at the end of the day, given his own class allegiances, he finds terrifying the possibility that the poor might turn outrage at the treatment they receive into violent, revolutionary action. He thus finds it necessary to embody that sort of reaction in the figure of Hortense, whose nationality (given the fact that memories of mass violence during the French Revolution haunted the genteel consciousness of Europeans throughout the nineteenth century) is designed to make it unacceptable. Meanwhile, in the gentle, unassuming, unselfconscious, and uncomplaining Esther, Dickens creates a kind of anti-dote to the anger against social injustice he himself feels and expresses. The displacement and defusing of class anger via Hortense, the scapegoating of female sexuality (Lady Dedlock appears to be punished not for any upper-class neglect of the poor but instead for having had an affair with Nemo) for social ills that have more systemic roots, could be seen as part of the same pattern. So could the valorization of long-suffering characters like Esther, Jo, and Charley. In the light of all this, we could easily conclude that, in *Bleak House*, Dickens acknowledges social ills only to sweep them firmly under the rug.

Despite the attractiveness of such an explanation, we cannot in the end accept it. To begin with, it is worth pointing out that, though Hortense may indeed deflect the reader's attention abroad and away from social issues within England, in other parts of *Bleak House*, as we have already noted, Dickens uses his full rhetorical powers to remind his readers that the plight of people like Jo is intimately connected with the privileged position of people like the Dedlocks. "What connection can there be," the narrator asks, "between X and Y?" The novel's developing action transforms this question into the implicit and threatening proposition that English society will in the end be unable to suppress the real connections between the wealthy and the poor. If things don't change, these connections will take the horrifying form of transmitted diseases, of plagues that move from East to West London, plagues that will prove to us that we are all mortals after all. This is just the dynamic that is enacted when Esther loses her sight and her looks to the same disease that kills Jo, an out-come that is the more frightening in that Esther is an innocent victim who has neglected no one.

Bleak House is indeed ambivalent through and through with regard to what it would mean to frame a just response to the social problems it relentlessly uncovers, but underlying its ambivalence lie forces more complex and more interesting than the supposed class inhibitions of the successful and wealthy Charles Dickens. Ideological constraints and fears (in particular, the fear of what the lower classes might do, given how they have been treated) doubtless play an important part in producing his ambivalence, but they play only a part, and they are balanced by a clear and effective wish to lash out at injustice and inhumanity wherever it appears. What needs to be explained is why both impulses are at work in *Bleak House* – why the novel seems at once to be marching right up to a violent confrontation with social injustice, but at the same time to be slipping away from it and disguising its nature. Why can't Esther lash out at the forces that have oppressed her and that kill Jo? Why does it have to be Hortense?

One answer is that Dickens refuses to "center" the definition of the social problems in the novel into easily identifiable confrontations between single characters, because he wants to show how broadly and deeply the problem exists in society: the problem, precisely, is that though there is plenty of culpability and guilt, it *has* no simple center. There is also, however, a more immediately literary aspect at play here, which involves the particular kind of relationship Dickens, from the beginning of his career, had been creating with his audiences. We would argue that in *Bleak House*, Dickens is guided by his intense desire (evident throughout his works) to create a moment-by-moment relationship with his audience in which his narrator wins ("extorts" might be a better word), through displays of imaginative brilliance, its enthusiastic approval. On one level, the social criticism never entirely centers itself because he doesn't want to alienate his audience by presenting its members with too threatening a picture of the social reality that surrounds them. But beneath that, he wants the power of his novel to center on and radiate from his own narrative brilliance, which involves in part just the shifting and unpredictable pattern of equivalences among characters that can from one point of view seem to be simply an ideological evasion, keeping a character like Esther from the "contagion" of anger.

In the case of *Bleak House*, this desire to keep the power of his narrative in the center of the reader's experience is coupled by an uncanny ability to pick up and use for his own purposes fictional techniques developed by others. Just as *Jane Eyre* had shown him that a first person narrator could make up in vivid immediacy and emotional intensity what she sacrificed in comprehensiveness of vision, so *Mary Barton* suggested the rhetorical possibilities of a deliberate humility of narrative tone, both in its "unliterariness" of manner and in Gaskell's refusal to engage directly with the systemic implications of a richly realized portrayal of its characters' experience of social suffering (that is, her claim to "know nothing of Political Economy"). Characteristically, though, Dickens put these insights to work by incorporating them into yet another form of virtuoso literary performance: a narrative form that alternates between the humble immediacy of Esther's vision – with her emphasis on healing social wounds on a local scale rather than understanding them on a larger one – and the rhetorical ambition and outrage of the authorial narrator, whose capacity to see and convey to a vast audience the vertiginous scale and resilience of a systematically exploitative institution just might provide the tools to go after it. For as Trollope would reluctantly acknowledge in his critique of "Mr. Popular Sentiment" in *The Warden*, Dickens's tackling of real social issues in his novels did often produce results. If Dickens's slippages and displacements of uncomfortable issues sometimes seem to sacrifice his passionate sense of wrong to his drive to keep his audience coming back for more, he also found ways to make them serve each other. And they also allow his narratives to fill his novels with an imaginative variety and intensity unmatched by any of his contemporary novelists, and perhaps by any other novelist in the British tradition.

Dickens at Work: Part Ten

Any of the monthly "parts" in which *Bleak House* originally appeared could be used to exemplify the powerful variety with which his narrator performs for us. Particularly notable is the pacing of the parts: the brilliance with which Dickens juxtaposes and moves between contrasting moods and themes, in a way that always keeps the reader intensely aware of the narrator's skill, that maintains the relationship between narration and audience we have argued is so important to Dickens. The narrator constantly keeps us off balance; the climaxes, for instance, don't quite fall where we would expect. But this situation offers the intense delight of a controlled vertigo, an imaginative roller-coaster that we know will continue to provide unexpected ups and downs and new vistas.

Part ten opens with Esther, and Caddy's marriage: her preparations for her wedding, and the wedding itself. This chapter offers a familiar form of light social comedy, in Caddy's and Esther's efforts to get the house and Mrs. Jellyby in a state to host a wedding breakfast without the slightest assistance on her part, and in such humanizing details as Charley's childish sense of delighted self-importance at her mounds of sewing work. The scene provides an opportunity for Dickens to broaden his critique of organized philanthropy beyond the particular variety represented by Mrs. Jellyby and the Pardiggles. It also completes the story of Caddy's rehabilitation: having met Caddy in chapter four as an inky and embittered girl, angry at her mother for the chaos of her home and at her own inability to tackle it with anything like the gracious ease modeled for her by Esther and Ada, we now see her, an accomplished young lady, forgiving and accepted by her mother, entering with competence and joy into the womanly role of dedicated wife and helpmeet. For an audience now only at the midpoint of a very long and complex novel, such localized conclusions provide a welcome sense of closure, thus helping to keep the number of ongoing storylines to a manageable level.

The next chapter moves to Jarndyce's home, Bleak House. It continues with Esther's voice but quickly strikes a more ominous tone with the appearance of Jo (hitherto a figure confined to the authorial narrator's sections). Significantly, Jo finds his way into the household via Charley Neckett. Having been herself assisted by neighbors on her father's death, she has quickly made herself part of the network of support among the poor of St. Albans. Jo's arrival at Bleak House, delirious from fever and exhausted from having been "moved on" interminably, having found his only refuge among brickmakers almost as poor as himself, occasions a bitter commentary on the failure of philanthropy and public health policies to address the real needs of the poor, suggesting a darker side to the sleek self-absorption of the philanthropists we met at Caddy's wedding.

Skimpole's reaction is also significant: his selfish unconcern is to be expected, of course, but note that he then goes into a back room and plays a sentimental song about a "poor orphan boy, bereft of his parents, bereft of his home." It is a song he says "always makes him cry." Like the various scenes of artistic creation and response in *Mary Barton*, this one carries a certain amount of self-referential freight. Dickens knows how to make his audience cry, and he knows they like it when he does so. He is about to do it again. Like Gaskell, he hopes to transmute their tears into real-world compassion. But he knows that weeping over novels can be a substitute rather than a rehearsal for the kind of empathy that makes real demands upon us. So he dramatizes precisely the response he fears, in a character we should already know to despise, under circumstances that dramatize the egregiousness of his failure.

The remainder of the chapter gives a moving account of the course of the disease in Charley and then Esther. In moments like this, the intimacy and immediacy of Esther's narration are at their most effective: she gives full play to what is affecting in Charley's decline (we get the full sentimental Victorian deathbed treatment, minus the death) but is more reticent and indirect about her own fears and sufferings, preferring instead – as she often does in response to personal distress – to focus on protecting Ada from whatever is disturbing her. Her self-effacing narrative gives us the indulgence of sympathetic weeping, and also reminds us why we should admire and care about Esther. The final line, though, is a bombshell. Since Esther is narrating her portion of the novel retrospectively, any concern the reader might have felt about her contracting a dangerous illness is bound to be moderated by the awareness that she has to survive to tell the story. That she might go blind is unexpected, and more shocking for that reason, and its shock value moves us as much backward as forward in the narrative: we wonder whether she will recover from her blindness, of course, but we wonder too how our understanding of her narrative to date might have to be reinflected by the knowledge that it was narrated by someone now blind. At the midpoint of the novel, Dickens gives a powerful jolt that not only gets his audience wondering what will come next, but gets them thinking back over the whole of what they've read to date.

Blindness is also a symbolically loaded affliction, particularly for a narrator who has been important in part for what she can't perceive. In myth, blindness is often figured as a punishment for forbidden knowledge, for seeing what should remain hidden. When Esther confronts, in Jo's abjectness, the heart of "the system's" capacity for human damage, we might say, on the metaphoric level, that she has to go blind to survive at all. But as in the familiar image of the blind prophet or poet, physical blindness is also associated with spiritual insight.

In a lesser novelist, we might expect the installment to end at this power-fully climactic moment. Dickens, however, does nothing of the kind. The following chapter shifts dramatically, to the authorial narrator and to a seem-ingly ordinary evening scene in Cook's Court, Cursitor St. In his structuralist analysis of the multiple functions of literary language, Roland Barthes observed that "unmotivated detail creates the effect of the real." Details that don't in themselves appear to carry any particular narrative or thematic "point," in other words, convey something of the "just-thereness" of many aspects of real life. The first three paragraphs of this chapter exemplify this observa-tion perfectly. The proximity of Chancery is of only geographic relevance here: the phatic chit-chat of the women, the rampaging boys, the sounds of pop-ular entertainment drifting from the pub, could belong to any lower-middle-class neighborhood anywhere; they point to nothing beyond themselves. Dickens does this sort of thing beautifully, if rarely, and nearly always at just this social level: the inhabitants prosperous enough to be secure, but not too genteel for the men to go to the pub, or for the women to hang around out-side with a pint to gossip and watch their children play in the street. It is the level at which he seems most at ease as a writer, and the one from which the majority of his most beloved characters are drawn.

But of course there is a point to doing this kind of writing precisely *here*: after the complexly intertwined narrative and rhetorical motivations of the pre-vious chapters, and the emotional roller-coaster of their affect, this passage conveys a stillness far more profound than that of the evening air. It allows the reader to step back after the emotional blow of the previous chapter's stun-ning final line, to catch their breath (perhaps literally, if, as was commonplace at the time, they have been reading that sob-inducing material aloud), before the very different literary effects that are to come.

The description segues unobtrusively into the gradual buildup of tension in the main portion of the chapter. Notice how skillfully Dickens uses the gradual accumulation of small but telling details to build a growing sense of disgust and mystery (never read this chapter on a full stomach). By the time he has actually given a name to Krook's death, the sense of mounting horror has reached such a pitch that the absurd unlikelihood of his mode of dying is less likely to strike us: like the best horror writers, Dickens uses a vivid realism of effects to induce his audience to suspend their disbelief about causes, and the background of calm, unsuspecting ordinariness plays a key role in this. Notice, too, that while Dickens builds suspense quite effectively here, he also relieves it before the chapter ends, solving the mystery and naming the horror. Throughout the novel, and in sharp contrast to many lesser serialists, Dickens rarely relies on the crude cliffhanger mode of suspense to build interest in the next part. He is far more concerned to leave readers satisfied with the experience of reading. In this part, that means doing something with the distress that the previous chapter should have left us in. We have just seen social neglect achieve its most hideous effects, in the spread of a crippling and often fatal disease to two of the few characters in the novel who actually care about, and for, the poor. As in *Mary Barton*, the sympathy we feel for the victims is likely to (*ought* to, if the novel is working) carry with it a charge of anger on their behalf. Krook's explosive death releases this charge on the emotional level, much as Tulkinghorn's murder will do immediately after Jo's death. That there is little causal or logical relation between the two events is beside the point; Dickens connects them symbolically by making Krook's death a metaphor for the fate in store for the institution Krook personifies. Again, the fact that the connection here is *only* a metaphor might be seen as an evasion, but there's no doubt that part of Dickens's motivation in creating the scene of the spontaneous combustion is to "wow" his audience – what other novelist could get away with such a thing, could make us believe (if only within the intense circle of the imaginative experience he has created) that such a thing could happen, instead of rejecting it out of hand? We can only mentally applaud – which is just what Dickens wants. But such intense effects, metaphorical or not, can have a larger power and significance; we recall again Trollope's somewhat rueful acknowledgment that a fiction like Dickens's might have an effect on the real world his own could not. Whatever we decide about such matters (and whether or not, in the end, we care about the social and ideological effects of novels), there is perhaps one thing on which readers of Dickens can agree, namely that his narration does have a kind of power we simply don't find anywhere else in the nineteenth-century novel.

Chapter 8

The Warden and *Barchester Towers*

Trollope would seem to be the most unspiritual of authors. In describing his work as a novelist, he is openly scornful of creative inspiration. What novelists need, he insists, is not access to a divine spark, but time spent glued to their chairs, putting words on paper. They should be at least as workmanlike as shoemakers or tallow chandlers. He himself kept a strict account book in which he recorded how many words he had written each day: his goal was generally 40 pages of 250 words per week, and if he fell short one week, he would make it up the next – a practice that allowed him to produce more than fifty novels.[1]

The world of Trollope's novels seems just as down-to-earth. Nathaniel Hawthorne wrote that Trollope's fiction is "just as real as if some giant had hewn a great lump out of the earth, and put it under a glass case, with all its inhabitants going about their daily business, and not suspecting that they were being made a show of . . . these books are just as English as beef-steak."[2] Despite this earthiness, Trollope often turns his focus on the church. The society that both *The Warden* and *Barchester Towers* depict is clerical society. Both novels are concerned almost exclusively with the doings of Church of England clergymen associated with Barchester, a fictitious cathedral town in the south of England. Such a focus may seem alien to American readers and quaint to British ones. What does the study of this segment of a self-contained and provincial locale offer us as modern readers? Why should we care who becomes the Warden of Hiram's Hospital or the Dean of an English cathedral?

There are excellent reasons for us to care. It is not merely that Trollope's focus on this small segment of society, like Austen's focus on the gentry, allows him to capture subtleties of human behavior less easily explored in a more amorphous society. Nor is it that, in the nineteenth century, the Church of England remained a potent force in British society and thus deserves the attention of those with historical interests. Beyond these considerations, the clerical society Trollope depicts provides an ideal basis for contemplating a crucial modern problem, the conflict of reform with tradition. The coming of modernity occurs, Hegel tells us, when the fact that something has been done in a certain way since beyond human memory no longer suffices. We can no longer rely on custom and tradition for our values, but must seek justifications from within ourselves. The nineteenth-century novel's characteristic concerns – about human conduct; about individual thought, emotion, and freedom; about how the complex course of a society moving through history impinges on individuals – arise from the predicament modernity presents to societies and individuals. Without the guidance of tradition, how can they find their way? This is the problem that *The Warden* addresses and *Barchester Towers* replays with a slight but significant change of terms – the extent to which traditional values can be of use in a modern world. On the level of the individual, this becomes the question of how men and women are to find a decent path forward in an increasingly complex world, where change seems necessary and inevitable, but the direction change should take remains unclear and its consequences elusive. For an author who wished to look at all sides of this problem, clerical society was an inspired choice of subject. The nineteenth-century Church of England was a powerful institution with a complex history and every reason to respect tradition; it was also an institution dedicated to fostering ethical and spiritual values in the modern society surrounding it. But it was ripe for change.

Trollope's underlying subject in *The Warden* and *Barchester Towers*, then, is the same as Scott's in *Waverley* – how does change over time occur, how do societies cope with the changes that history brings, and what of value can be saved from the past as we leave the past behind? In *Waverley*, Scott deals with these subjects in a direct and dramatic form, depicting politics, rebellions, war, and a change of dynasties. Trollope's clerical canvas is tame by comparison: the spotlight falls on individual characters and their ethical choices. This is not to say that Trollope's characters possess the dramatic inwardness and sharp sense of self that we find in the novels of the Brontës. Emily Brontë's characters are vividly aware of worlds transcending ours. Where in *The Warden* do we find a scene like the one Lockwood half-dreams in the opening chapters of *Wuthering Heights*? There is something more spiritual, in at least one sense of that word, about the perceptions of Cathy and Heathcliff than those of the clergymen Trollope depicts. Spiritual elevation is as rare in Trollope as in Scott. Trollope instead emphasizes, as Scott does, his characters' implication in a web of social relations – an emphasis that, among other things, makes possible the genial comedy characteristic of both authors. Yet Trollope breaks ground the other novelists we have studied do not. The relatively sheltered field on which issues involving the coming of modernity are played out in Trollope allows for an exploration of personal feelings and ethical responsibility that is much more fine-grained than in Scott, but at the same time supports an exploration of the nature of institutions in the modern world hardly to be found in the Brontës.

The Warden: Reform and Modernity

The Warden is organized around two mutually involved lines of action, involving the reformer John Bold on the one hand, and Septimus Harding, the Warden of the almshouse Bold wishes to reform, on the other. Bold is the protagonist of a traditional love plot: he wishes to marry the Warden's daughter, Eleanor, who is in love with him. Bold believes that the Warden's income from the Hospital is too high and the benefits the old men who live there receive are too low. His attempt to reform Hiram's Hospital provides the obstacle to marriage that traditional love plots require. The climax of this side of the novel occurs when Eleanor decides to sacrifice herself to save her father's position by begging Bold to end his lawsuit to reform the administration of the almshouse. This will be a sacrifice, because she decides that, if she is to ask Bold for this favor, she can never consent to marry him. Otherwise, she might seem to be offering to sell herself to Bold in return for her father's continued prosperity. In the end, she does ask Bold to stop the lawsuit and he agrees, but despite her heroic intention not to marry Bold, when he proposes, her love triumphs and she consents. All of this is what any reader might expect: we share the narrator's amusement at Eleanor's attempt at heroics without thinking less of her, either for indulging in them or for ultimately abandoning them. She is punished for her heroic airs by having to retreat from the somewhat histrionic position she has taken, and that's that, so far as she is concerned.

More surprising is the severe punishment meted out to Bold. Some sort of rebuke does seem in order, because Bold's grasp of his own motivations is slim. He hardly realizes how much his wish to improve the lot of the old men of Hiram's Hospital stems from his own vanity and his wish to make a noise in the world. One might have thought, though, that having to stop the suit just when it promises to bring him fame would be rebuke enough for his egotism. But when he goes to Archdeacon Grantly (who is the Warden's son-in-law and leads the opposition of the church to his suit) to announce that he is going to end the suit, instead of receiving the gratitude he expects, he finds himself enduring a humiliating half-hour during which Grantly rakes him over the coals, belittling his attempt to ruin Eleanor's father and impugning his motives for abandoning the suit. (Grantly at this point knows nothing of Bold's engagement to Eleanor; he also knows, as Bold does not, that the suit is bound to fail in any case.) Bold, as he slinks back to his house after this excruciating session with the Archdeacon, exclaims to himself that having to endure Grantly's abuse was "the bitterest moment" in his life (166). We will turn shortly to the question of why Bold should be made to endure it.

The novel's other line of action involves the Warden himself, and it has nothing to do with love. Septimus Harding has unreflectively relied on tradition to justify holding the comfortable position of Warden of Hiram's Hospital, which provides him with a considerable income and a handsome house to live in. The novel's engagement with the problem of modernity begins when "modern" reforming pressures (starting with John Bold's lawsuit, but soon extending to editorials in England's premier newspaper, the *Jupiter*) force Harding to shake loose from this traditional grounding and to ask himself whether the role he is playing is truly justified, and if so, how. With Archdeacon Grantly, who defends the traditional privileges of the Warden, and with Bold and the *Jupiter* (a thinly veiled version of the London *Times*), the controversy becomes a matter of tactics, prejudice, and the will to triumph over an adversary. For Harding, once he is forced to look at the situation, the issue is one of principle and self-respect, felt as a matter of whether other individual men and women, whether he knows them or not, would be justified in condemning his actions. One of the comic elements in Eleanor's attempted sacrifice for him is that he does not want it and cannot use it. What matters to the Warden, and all that matters to the Warden, is that he has come to feel that he has no right to the perquisites attached to the almshouse, and he cannot bear that others should accuse him of taking what is not rightfully his. And so he resigns.

The consequences of this admirable, self-denying action are depressing. The men in the almshouse, who had hoped to profit financially from a change, do not profit at all; indeed, they lose a small sum that Harding had been giving them out of his own pocket. They also lose the presence of a resident Warden, for when Harding resigns, the Bishop refuses to appoint a successor, fearing that anyone he would appoint would find the position as untenable as Harding did. Thus the men's condition worsens in every way. Even the physical condition of the hospital deteriorates. In the closing pages of the novel, the narrator informs us that

> the whole place has become disordered and ugly. The warden's garden is a wretched wilderness, the drive and paths are covered with weeds, the flower-beds are bare, and the unshorn lawn is now a mass of long damp grass and unwholesome moss. The beauty of the place is gone; its attractions have withered. Alas! a very few years since it was the prettiest spot in Barchester, and now it is a disgrace to the city. (ch. 21)

Such, it seems, are the fruits of reform. Bold is punished for beginning the process of reform; the hospital and its inhabitants are punished because it was begun. Why should this be?

The answer is certainly not that Trollope wishes to demonstrate that reform is simply unnecessary because the old ways are always the best ways. Harding himself, who provides the closest thing we are given to a moral center of gravity in the novel, decides that maintaining the status quo is untenable, and he is surely right. Several answers present themselves. On one level, the grim fate of Hiram's Hospital at the end of the novel underlines the fact that, however inadequate inherited values may be, forging new ones and applying them to the complex situations in which history leaves us is not the simple, easy task such superficial actors as John Bold and the *Jupiter* imagine. On such a reading, what is punished is the glib, presumptuous self-seeking that too often accompanies attempts at reform, however well-meaning. Like Scott, Trollope believes that the virtues of the past are worth saving. John Bold's approach to reform is unlikely to accomplish such an end.

Such a lesson, however, hardly accounts for the mordant sense of waste epitomized by the "wretched wilderness" the Warden's garden becomes. To explain *that*, it seems necessary to seek a less rational level. (Readers of novels should always resist the impulse to explain too quickly and easily the powerful emotional effects they generate.) There, two investments on Trollope's part present themselves, an emotional and even sensuous love for certain legacies of the past on the one hand, and a fear and hatred of modern mass society on the other. Trollope loves the aura of past ages. In *Barchester Towers*, for instance, he describes a country house that possesses "that delicious tawny hue which no stone can give, unless it has on it the vegetable richness of centuries. . . . No colourist that ever yet worked from a palette has been able to come up to this rich colouring of years crowding themselves on years" (I, ch. 22). In *The Warden*, this sensuous/aesthetic appreciation of the fruits of time is nicely combined with an implicit admission of the shortcomings of the past, in a description of the church adjoining Archdeacon Grantly's rectory (the expensive, heavy ugliness of whose more modern furnishings the narrator goes out of his way to criticize):

Few parish churches in England are in better repair, or better worth keeping so, than that at Plumstead Episcopi; and yet it is built in a faulty style. The body of the church is low – so low that the nearly flat leaden roof would be visible from the churchyard, were it not for the carved parapet with which it is surrounded. It is cruciform, though the transepts are irregular, one being larger than the other; and the tower is much too high in proportion to the church. But the colour of the building is perfect; it is that rich yellow grey which one finds nowhere but in the south and west of England, and which is so strong a characteristic of most of our old houses of Tudor architecture. The stone work is also beautiful; the mullions of the windows and the thick tracery of the Gothic workmanship is as rich as fancy can desire; and though in gazing on such a structure one knows by rule that the old priests who built it, built it wrong, one cannot bring one-self to wish that they should have made it other than it is. (ch. 12)

It seems clear enough where at least part of Trollope's emotional investment lies when we read a passage like this one. The church at Plumstead Episcopi is, by strict and abstract architectural standards, imperfect, but it is also human and loveable, possessing qualities that arise from time and tradition. Trollope has great tolerance for human imperfection, particularly when it finds a place in an orderly tradition. For Trollope, there remains a strong tempta-tion to resist changes that will destroy lovely things that take centuries to come into being. Were such feelings allowed full rein, he would simply reject out of hand any attempt to reform the fruits of history. He does not go so far, but the strength of his attachments does help explain a deep distrust toward anyone who could imagine that the work of reforming old institutions is straightforward and easy.

The Threat of Mass Culture

The sense of desolation at the end of *The Warden* also arises from a less mellow emotional source – a fear and hatred of modern mass society. When John Bold decides to discontinue his suit against the Barchester almshouse, his punishment includes not only the painful interview with Archdeacon Grantly, but also a visit to his friend Tom Towers, a writer for the *Jupiter*. As we have noted, it was the appearance of these articles (published anonymously though written by Towers), which suggest that the Warden is stealing money from the inmates of the Hospital, that more than anything else moves the Warden to resign. Bold realizes how devastating the articles have been to the Warden, and he quite reasonably feels that, as part of his promise to Eleanor to aban-don his attack on the Hospital, he must not only drop his lawsuit but must stop them as well. In fact, however, he can do nothing whatever about them. Towers not only refuses to stop writing the articles, he refuses to admit that he wrote them in the first place or that he has any power over their continua-tion. He does so, he tells Bold, in defense of the freedom of the press.

Tom Towers is a troubling figure. It is not merely that he is arrogant; it is that his arrogance takes the form of a delight in wielding power that is entirely without checks or boundaries because it is anonymous. (Newspaper articles and editorials, in Trollope's day, were unsigned.) Towers, the narrator tells us,

> loved to sit silent in a corner of his club and listen to the loud chattering of politicians, and to think how they all were in his power – how he could smite the loudest of them, were it worth his while to raise his pen for such a purpose. . . . to whom was he, Tom Towers, responsible? No one could insult him; no one could inquire into him. He could speak out withering words, and no one could answer him; ministers courted him, though perhaps they knew not his name . . . Tom Towers never boasted of the *Jupiter*; he scarcely ever named the paper even to the most intimate of his friends; he did not even wish to be spoken of as connected with it; but he did not less value his privileges, or think the less of his own importance. It was probable that Tom Towers considered himself the most powerful man in Europe; and so he walked on from day to day, studiously striving to look a man, but knowing within his breast that he was a god. (ch. 14)

The studied neutrality of the narrator's language in this description only intensifies our sense of his fear and loathing of situations in which mass audiences are addressed and manipulated by anonymous media – a situation with which we have become entirely familiar, but which was still relatively new when Trollope wrote *The Warden*. For Trollope, the heart of the problem appears to be that this impersonal manipulation has replaced face-to-face contact between individual human beings – a particularly ominous situation when newspapers promote themselves as powerful agents of reform. Perhaps mercifully, Trollope was spared the rise of the cult of media personalities. He never had to endure, as we do today, a situation in which manipulative news reports are delivered by pleasant, synthetically earnest television anchorpersons who, with a simulation of personhood, accompany the "spins" their controllers place on the news they report with, as appropriate, either a smile or a look of concern on their faces. That such persons may come to believe that they actually are expressing their own ideas merely adds to the depressing comedy of our present era.

Trollope's dismay at the media of his own day explains an odd aspect of *The Warden*, its inclusion (in the chapter depicting Bold's encounter with Towers) of two pieces of extended literary parody, one of Thomas Carlyle (referred to as "Dr. Pessimist Anticant") and the other of Trollope's fellow novelist Dickens (referred to as "Mr. Popular Sentiment"). Both Anticant and Sentiment had written attacks on Hiram's Hospital, and Trollope produces a selection from each attack. In both cases, what emerges is a gross oversimplification of the actual situation, which drains the humanity from everyone depicted, including the inmates of the Hospital. The strong implication is that in the process, a human relationship between author and reader disappears, too: the author becomes a maker of caricatures, not an artist capable of nuance, and the reader is reduced to one of the "masses," instead of being treated as an individual human being capable of looking at all sides of a question. What Trollope seems to find most distressing is that he can see no way out of this situation. He ends his parody of Dickens with the following, rather surprising, attempt to do justice to the method he imputes to Dickens: "The artist who paints for the million must use glaring colours, as no one knew better than Mr. Sentiment when he described the inhabitants of his alms-house; and the radical reform which has now swept over such establishments has owed more to the twenty numbers [installments] of Mr. Sentiment's novel, than to all the true complaints which have escaped from the public for the last half century." This is, to be sure, something of a backhanded compliment, in that it's not entirely clear that a *radical* reform is really what would be best for Hiram's Hospital. It is also telling that Mr. Sentiment's complaints are contrasted with complaints that are "true." We nonetheless recognize that Trollope's narrator is here attempting to be fair to Mr. Sentiment in a way Mr. Sentiment's own method does not allow him to be fair to others, by imagining the specific, socially produced situation Mr. Sentiment inhabits. Or to put it another way, Trollope's narrator is here insisting on confronting Mr. Sentiment in a face-to-face manner, in a way that takes into account Mr. Sentiment's situation as an individual author writing in a concrete social and historical situation – and that treats the members of Trollope's own audience not as objects to be manipulated but as intelligent beings capable of grasping the full complexity of that situation.

The Warden himself finds the attacks of the *Jupiter* intolerable, precisely because he insists on giving them the undeserved dignity of face-to-face criticisms made by one person to another. He cannot bear the idea that any of their readers might be justified in believing the attacks to be true, because he imagines the readers as if they were his next-door neighbors. Archdeacon Grantly knows better: he cannot imagine worrying about the *Jupiter*, stating that its attacks "can break no bones." For him, the Warden's sensitivity is mere "cowardice" (ch. 9). But the weakness here has its own wisdom and strength. It may be viewed, on one level, as the Warden's heroic insistence that human beings continue to hold themselves accountable to ethical standards based on face-to-face encounters, not on a world of statistical norms and faceless averages of acceptable behavior. On another level, we may view the Warden's stance as enacting Trollope's own protest against mass society and the quality of communication it brings with it. It is no coincidence that the *Jupiter* is published in London, the center of mass society in England, nor that Bold's encounter with Tom Towers and the literary parodies that accompany it have a London setting.

The Warden has his own London encounter with another avatar of faceless modernity, the Attorney General Sir Abraham Haphazard. Sir Abraham is the lawyer who represents the Diocese of Barchester against Bold's suit. He is a man without close ties of any kind. Cold and heartless, like Tom Towers, he has an almost supernatural power that comes from his ability to manipulate an arcane system (in this case, the legal system) from behind the scenes. In a nice piece of irony, he reveals that Bold's suit is certain to fail because, as it turns out, it will be impossible for Bold to discover just who he should sue. Bold himself doesn't realize it, but he will always find himself suing the wrong person! Bold, the champion of progress and reform, will be defeated by the shifty facelessness that characterizes urban modernity. His legal situation is a nice parody of how modern mass anonymity cancels the face-to-face relationships that the Warden himself relies on to conceptualize his place in the world.

When the Warden refuses to continue the lawsuit, he is rejecting anything less than direct, authentic human contact. The Warden, as it happens, unconsciously acts out his protest against all that Sir Abraham represents when he visits him in his London chambers. As the Warden pours out his woes to Sir Abraham (in a way that the latter, unsurprisingly, finds incomprehensible and embarrassing) and states that he is going to give up the suit whether or not he would win it, he absentmindedly begins to accompany his verbal recital with the gestures he uses when he plays his cello – a favorite way he has of sharing his feelings with his friends in small, private, face-to-face concerts. Waving one's arms about for no apparent reason is, to be sure, disconcerting behavior, and Sir Abraham concludes that the gesticulating Warden must be deranged. Elements of his same inherent incompatibility with all that London represents appear repeatedly in the rest of the Warden's trip to London. His consistent failure to connect with the London realities around him (at one point he innocently falls asleep in a quite disreputable house of entertainment) reflects an inability to comprehend, much less mix with, modern urban life.

Such scenes provide a comic version of the protest against mass society that, we are arguing, gives energy to the dark side of the novel, which is epitomized by the "wilderness" Hiram's Hospital becomes. Their profusion also underlines the seriousness of the issues involved. Trollope, with his face-to-face recognition of human and social complexity, realizes that the problems created by the coming of modernity admit of no easy solution. If London and reform were simply and obviously wrong, rejecting them would be simple. The energy Trollope expends in his various symbolic rejections of modern mass society suggests that things are in fact anything but simple. (We again urge our readers to pay particular attention to what looks like excess, especially emotional excess, in the conduct of a novel.) The life of the hospital before it is attacked by Bold was in many ways beautiful and humane; yet it was also corrupt. The energy behind the novel's attack on London reflects, in part, a defensive reaction to the justified claims of modernity. The comedy in the London scenes allows Trollope at once to express and at the same time disown ("it's just a joke") a depth of antipathy toward modernity he knows is not entirely justifiable. If it were possible simply to reject the claims of progressive reform, having Archdeacon Grantly humiliate Bold would suffice.

Trollope's Narrator

Most readers warm to Trollope's favored characters, such as the Hardings, and are amused by the likes of Archdeacon Grantly. But it may be that the most striking presence is the narrator. If we move from the level of content to that of form, much that is characteristic of Trollope's narrative technique can be explained as an alternative to the norms of mass society and the impersonal, sometimes manipulative relationships it brings with it. We have suggested in passing that, in his final judgment on the novelistic practice of Mr. Sentiment, Trollope's narrator attempts to maintain the respectful, personal relationship to his own audience he finds lacking in Mr. Sentiment's novels. The wish to create a companionable, face-to-face relationship with his readers informs the stance Trollope's narrator assumes throughout his novels.

Trollope's narrator has a remarkable stability in his relationship to the reader. Trollope admired the work of Thackeray, whom he considered the greatest of contemporary novelists, and to some degree he sought to emulate him. Both create garrulous, personal, "intrusive" narrators, who resemble one another more than they resemble the narrators of Dickens or the Brontës. But Trollope's narrator never produces the panoply of shifting tones and inflections Thackeray is so skillful at creating, sometimes in the space of a single paragraph. It is telling that when Trollope's narrator engages, uncharacteristically, in literary parodies in *The Warden*, he cordons them off from the rest of his narration. The parody of Carlyle is enclosed in quotation marks and clearly identified as a written text John Bold is reading. The parody of Dickens is, in similar fashion, marked as a summary of an independent text, not a performance or reenactment of that text by the narrator. We never get the sense that Trollope's narrator is himself acting out a series of parodic roles in rapid succession, as Thackeray often does; we also never feel that Trollope's narrator is acting out an outraged or anguished reaction to the world he has created. Instead, the narrator converses with us. Trollope, like Thackeray, may announce that he has met his characters; he may inform us from personal experience how it feels to dine with them or visit their homes or shake hands with them, but the effect is different. When Trollope's narrator tells us how unpleasant it was for him to shake hands with Mr. Slope, the effect is to intensify our picture of Slope, to focus our contemplation on *him*. We focus on Slope, not on the narrator's attempt to frame an adequate response to him – among other things because framing an adequate response to Slope isn't particularly difficult. Slope is easily and completely knowable.

Trollope's narrator also evinces a respectful concern for the moral well-being of his readers – a concern that may seem antiquated or even unwelcome to modern readers. This concern is unobtrusive: few characters in the novels play the part of moral teachers even by example. *Barchester Towers* in fact contains an attack on the presumption of young clergymen who feel competent to give sermons, an attack that is doubtless meant to be playful but that nonetheless betrays enough irritation to make one wonder whether anyone of any age is justified in sermonizing. "There is, perhaps no greater hardship at present inflected on mankind in civilised and free countries," the narrator announces, "than the necessity of listening to sermons" (I, ch. 6). Trollope's art is often an art of the unspoken that leaves readers to form their own conclusions. In a conversation among equals, one doesn't keep making ethical judgments about this or that acquaintance, or one is likely to seem overbearing and lacking in respect for alternative viewpoints. There are nonetheless moments when his narrator feels obliged to speak out, delivering judgments on his characters that are pellucid and unanswerable. This impulse is at work in the narrator's valedictory comment at the end of *The Warden* about Archdeacon Grantly:

And here we must take leave of Archdeacon Grantly. We fear that he is represented in these pages as being worse than he is; but we have had to do with his foibles, and not with his virtues. We have seen only the weak side of the man, and have lacked the opportunity of bringing him forward on his strong ground. That he is a man somewhat too fond of his own way, and not sufficiently scrupulous in his manner of achieving it, his best friends cannot deny. That he is bigoted in favour, not so much of his doctrines as of his cloth, is also true: and it is true that the possession of a large income is a desire that sits near his heart. Nevertheless, the archdeacon is a gentleman and a man of conscience; he spends his money liberally, and does the work he has to do with the best of his ability; he improves the tone of society of those among whom he lives. His aspirations are of a healthy, if not of the highest, kind. Though never an austere man, he upholds propriety of conduct both by example and precept. He is generous to the poor, and hospitable to the rich; in matters of religion he is sincere, and yet no Pharisee; he is in earnest, and yet not fanatic. On the whole, the Archdeacon of Barchester is a man doing more good than harm – a man to be furthered and supported, though perhaps also to be controlled; and it is a matter of regret to us that the course of our narrative has required that we should see more of his weakness than his strength. (ch. 20)

We believe in the "regret" that the narrator expresses here; we also recognize the narrator's need to put Grantly in his place (in several senses), as a man whose wish for power indeed "ought to be controlled."

One reason why Trollope's narrator is sparing in producing definitive judgments on his characters may be that he takes a huge delight simply in contemplating their antics. Trollope remarks in his autobiography that he "sometimes regretted" having killed off Mrs. Proudie after she had appeared in a number of his novels, "so great was my delight in writing about [her], so thorough was my knowledge of all the little shades of her character" (177). His investment in face-to-face relationships in a knowable society not only has ethical and historical roots and resonances but an aesthetic dimension. In the case of Mrs. Proudie, it involves an admiration for her energy and self-consistency, even though it also involves a vivid sense of her narrowness and the potentially evil consequences of such narrowness on the sense of community that is so important to Trollope.

The wish to maintain a face-to-face, respectful relationship with his readers, and a delight in observing in detail just how it is that knowable characters will behave in shifting circumstances, combine to explain probably the most notorious aspect of the behavior of Trollope's narrator, his "intrusive" deflation of plot-suspense and the reader's suspension of disbelief. In both *The Warden* and *Barchester Towers*, Trollope's narrator is at pains to short-circuit the plot suspense that the author of another kind of fiction would attempt to heighten. In *Barchester Towers*, for instance, the narrator informs us early on that we needn't worry that Eleanor Bold will marry either of the two suitors we immediately recognize to be unsuitable. He adds the following comment: "the novelist . . . ventures to reprobate that system which goes so far to violate all proper confidence between the author and his readers, by maintaining nearly to the end of the third volume a mystery as to the fate of their favourite personage." He invites us instead to read the last chapter of *Barchester Towers* first, if we please, and to "learn from its pages all the results of our troubled story, and the story shall have lost none of its interest, if indeed there be any interest in it to lose. Our doctrine is, that the author and the reader should move together in full confidence with each other." Otherwise, readers become "dupes" (I, ch. 15).

There is much to remark on in this brief, "intrusive" commentary, with its eschewal of dealing with the reader or "spectator" (I, ch. 15) through a veil of mystery and suspense. On one level, we may suspect that a certain virtuosity is being flaunted here. Trollope is letting us know that he can keep our interest even without calling on one of the novelist's most reliable interest-sustaining devices. The paradoxical assertion that knowing how the plot will work out should not in any way detract from a novel's "interest" also seems to follow from the notion that the reader should become a certain kind of "spectator," one who focuses on what the characters are like and how their personalities and values mesh with the society around them. We need to concentrate on what really matters, not on what will happen next. To be sure, these are issues that we must attend to in reading any serious novel; what is unusual in the claim Trollope's narrator makes is the extreme weight given to them. If we attend to our experience while reading the novel, we may in fact feel that the claim is a bit too extreme. Even though we have been assured that Eleanor Bold will not marry Slope or Bertie Stanhope, we still feel a certain interest, perhaps even anxiety, to discover just how this will prove true. Yet even this anxiety in fact corroborates the larger point the narrator is making, since our anxiety finally involves our inability to grasp, until we reach the novel's end, the exact process by which the action will work out along a certain path, not a question of what the path will be.

A more fundamental issue, however, is suggested by the narrator's emphasis on the importance of maintaining a relationship of "confidence" with the reader. The level of companionability here seems to exceed that even of Scott's narrator, much less Thackeray's, who is not at all above "duping" us from time to time. Trollope seems concerned that absolutely nothing disrupt the trusting, face-to-face relationship his narrator hopes to create with us, as an alternative to the dishonest, histrionic manipulation he finds in literature that appeals to the masses, not to individuals.

Trollope's assurance that Eleanor Bold will not marry either Slope or Stanhope is the sort of disruption of illusionism that many post-Victorian novelists found particularly trying, interpreting it as reflecting a failure to take the claims of fiction seriously. The condescension such authors directed toward the supposedly "garrulous" and "intrusive" narrative stance typical of many of the authors we are considering in the present book thus derives from a change of aesthetic priorities. It may also, however, be seen as their own reaction to the coming of modernity. They despair of achieving a face-to-face relationship with their audience and turn, by way of compensation, to the production instead of a dramatic vividness that would indeed be spoiled by the sort of narrative intrusiveness Trollope engages in. One can respect this alternative way of going about writing novels without accepting the idea that Trollope and authors like him are simply unserious and artistically inept when they allow their narrators to "intrude" into their fictions. Instead of promoting one kind of fiction at the expense of the other, it would seem better to attempt to approach them on their own terms. It is at any rate difficult to imagine that anyone could enjoy Trollope's novels without enjoying the presence of his narrator. It has been our purpose in this section of the discussion to try to bring into focus just what that narrator is like, why, and to what effect.

Barchester Towers

If we turn to *Barchester Towers*, we can observe the same general subject matter and the same underlying issues repeated, but with significant differences. To put it briefly, we may say that the issue of modernity versus tradition recedes in favor of a focus on individual characters. The Proudies and Slope would seem to represent modernity, in that they come from London and lack any respect for tradition, but they lack the frightening abstractness one finds in Tom Towers or Sir Abraham Haphazard in *The Warden*. When Archdeacon Grantly opposes them, he is in some sense battling against modernity, but we are more aware that an argument is taking place between members of two different segments of the Church of England than that the values of past and present are colliding. The issues here seem, in several senses, more parochial than they were in *The Warden*. In similar fashion, the quandary facing the Warden in the book that bears his name is displaced, in *Barchester Towers*, into a problem about the happiness of quite a different sort of character, Arabin. The "history" of this problem is the history of Arabin's own development: through his early life, he is uninterested in marriage and worldly advancement; what matters to him is a spiritual struggle about whether to join the Catholic Church. In middle age, however, he discovers that he is no longer indifferent to gaining a loving wife and a good income, but he fears he has waited too long. The resolution of this problem involves the larger issue of how to come to grips with the worldliness in general, not the modern world in particular.

We earlier remarked that in *The Warden* Trollope refuses to allow the love story to "solve" the novel's problems. He takes a more conventional path in *Barchester Towers*. By the novel's end, Arabin gains a high position in the church and an ideal wife in Eleanor Bold. With this shift in focus comes a resolution of the painful impasse the reader is left with at the end of *The Warden*. Hiram's Hospital does not regain a Warden of the moral stature of Harding, but it is physically restored and does a certain amount of good, and for a larger number of people – including the new Warden, who is a man with a large family to support. (We note again how the mundane problems facing individuals predominate in *Barchester Towers*.) It is not that we cannot make connections between the characters and incidents in *Barchester Towers* and issues of tradition versus reform. We can, for instance, associate the good luck of the new

Warden with the more democratic distribution of wealth that modernity brings (or is supposed to bring). Such connections can be drawn; it's simply that they seem, to us at least, less rich and compelling than they are in *The Warden*.

Yet the more conventional turn Trollope takes in *Barchester Towers* brings with it significant compensations, which many (perhaps most) readers may feel more than overbalance anything that has been lost. This emphasis allows Trollope to concentrate on what he does best – creating a set of concretely knowable characters and chronicling their activities with an amused delight. The comedy of the novel can be delicious. It is telling that Trollope, as we have seen, wrote of his "delight" in writing about Mrs. Proudie and "all the little shades of her character." His ability to immerse himself in the contemplation of his characters is so pronounced that it leads him to write two major series of novels in which characters make repeated appearances from one work to the next – and some of the characters appear in his other novels as well. Harding, for instance, appears in all six of the "Barsetshire" novels which begin with *The Warden* and *Barchester Towers*. Some of Trollope's most intriguing and successful characters (Lady Glencora in the Palliser series, for instance) come most fully into their own when they cease to be protagonists in a novel but then reappear in subsequent works, where we see them in different lights and expanded perspectives, and at different stages of their lives. It is fascinating to observe how a woman we meet as a rebellious teenage bride behaves once she is the mother of teenage daughters herself. One feels that Trollope's interest in his characters requires more than one novel and plot to express itself fully.

Trollope and Social Control

One of the novel's most interesting readers, however, senses more serious issues behind that delight. Working in a line of thought initiated by the French thinker Michel Foucault, D. A. Miller questions the contemplative attitude of Trollope's narrator, which seems to him to involve a kind of covert surveillance.[3] He is particularly suspicious of the narrator's announcement that "moderate schism" in the church (that is, a certain amount of infighting about matters of doctrine, ritual) is actually a good thing: "We are much too apt to look at schism in our church as an unmitigated evil. Moderate schism, if there may be such a thing, at any rate calls attention to the subject, draws in supporters who would otherwise have been inattentive to the matter, and teaches men to think upon religion" (I, ch. 20). Foucault has demonstrated with considerable persuasiveness the naïveté of supposing that the power that keeps societies in order primarily involves naked, top-down coercion. The most effective agents in policing society aren't tyrants ruling from above, he argues, but instead the habitual, everyday practices we all engage in, for those are what keep us behaving in our usual, set ways, creating the sense of what is "normal." For Miller, the doctrine of limited schism provides a perfect instance of this sort of policing; engaging in limited schism keeps the Barchester community playing a certain game in a certain way. In Miller's skilled hands, nearly everything about *Barchester Towers* is interpreted as participating in this larger process of making members of a society attend to the same things in the same ways, and hence perpetuating the existing relations of power. If you busy yourself about differences of church doctrine, you are not likely to ask whether there should be a church in the first place.

We urge readers of *Barchester Towers* to read Miller's essay on it as well, if only because it provides a compact and brilliant example of what Foucauldian criticism (with a generous admixture of gender criticism) can accomplish. We believe that the critique of modern society Foucault offers is of compelling interest and importance. We will add that suspicion of the ideological allegiances and effects of literary works has been a vigorous, perhaps dominant, part of the practice of literary criticism for many years now, and this is something of which readers should be aware. (Our readers may notice that this chapter itself reflects a level of suspicion of mass society and the media, though not of novels.) We also relish the texture of Miller's prose. We do not, however, subscribe to his conclusions.

We remarked in discussing *The Warden* that the novel contains a sadness that its attempt at a happy ending cannot contain. A Foucauldian reading could recuperate that element as just one more element of the "game" that novel gets us to play. We take it more seriously, and we find echoes of that side of *The Warden* in *Barchester Towers* as well, though they are transformed into quite a different mode. Miller suggests that what Trollope holds against the Stanhopes is that they are not serious enough about religion, but this simply is not true: what he in fact holds against them is that they have "no real feelings, could feel no true passion" (I, ch. 19). On one level, the Stanhopes are indeed an expression of the forces in a society that are concentrating on "the game." They play the social and institutional network provided by the church for all that it is worth, and if this were all there was to them, they could indeed be viewed simply as relays of power, without significant beliefs or affections. They might therefore by seen as the perfect embodiments of the Foucauldian mechanisms Miller finds dominant in the novel, and to a significant extent, in all nineteenth-century novels. (On another level, they might also be seen as individual expressions of the faceless anonymity of mass society that so disturbs the vision of *The Warden*. To be sure, in this case we do know their names and faces, but one could argue that there is nothing genuine behind either.)

Yet at least two of the Stanhopes should not be so easily dismissed. In *Barchester Towers*, much of the pleasure Trollope offers us comes, as we have been arguing, from a narrative stance we are invited to participate in, in which we observe and enjoy the actions of knowable characters. One thing that makes them knowable is that they are members of a knowable and predictable society, with a predictable set of values and way of dealing with their fellows. It is doubtless true that Trollope finds much to commend in an orderly society that is respectful of tradition. When someone like Slope comes along, someone who doesn't fit into that society, we can be sure that he will in the end be expelled – as Slope is in *Barchester Towers*, to our considerable satisfaction. But the Stanhopes are different. Bertie Stanhope's refusal to take up any steady line of work, conjoined with his genuine good humor, are amusing and attractive objects of contemplation. There are few things more pleasurable in the novel than when he patiently explains to Eleanor Bold (with genuine sorrow at the insult he is inflicting on her) that for the sake of family peace he needs her to pretend that he has proposed to her, but that in fact he doesn't want to tie himself down to her. One cannot help liking Bertie for that. Bertie's insistence on going his own non-way (reinforced in parodic form by his series of religious conversions) delights us in part because it is a negation of the conditions of normality in Trollope's world, and they surely delighted Trollope for the same reason. A knowable community, with its predictable rules and personalities, can be charming, but also stifling.[4] Eleanor Bold herself senses this at an early point in the novel: we are told that

> she began to think that she was getting tired of clergymen and their respectable humdrum wearisome mode of living, and that, after all, people in the outer world, who had lived in Italy, London, or elsewhere, need not necessarily be regarded as atrocious and abominable. The Stanhopes, she had thought, were a giddy, thoughtless, extravagant set of people; but she had seen nothing wrong about them, and had, on the other hand, found that they thoroughly knew how to make their house agreeable. (I, ch. 21)

She changes her views as she discovers more about the Stanhopes, but her initial impulse remains significant. Bertie Stanhope's actions are quite unpredictable by Barchester standards; he may indeed have no fixed personality at all. That is why we enjoy him.

His sister, Madame Neroni, has a similar charm. Her theatrical appearance in the Bishop's Palace during a party, and her routing of Mrs. Proudie when the latter tries to bring her to order, are high points in the novel. She has the added virtue of deepening the sense of what can be known about others beyond the confines of what Barchester standards could imagine, much less voice. She sees through Arabin's conflicts and quandaries with ease. She penetrates and plays with the sexual desires of Slope and even old Thorne. A Foucauldian reading would suggest that she transgresses such norms of perception and action simply to reinforce them. She stirs things up a bit, helps to provide grounds for Slope to be ejected from Barchester, helps Arabin find a suitable wife in Eleanor Bold, and then returns to Italy, leaving Barchester intact. The reader must decide whether such a diagnosis fully captures her part in our experience of the novel. For us, it does not.

Conclusion

It is common to point out that Trollope's novels about clergymen have little to do with religion and spirituality. We ourselves have operated under this assumption throughout this chapter, which began by suggesting that the Church of England is an excellent subject for *The Warden* and *Barchester Towers*, not because it allows Trollope to depict, say, spiritual struggle, but because its social and historical dimensions are useful for exploring such issues as the coming of modernity. In fact, however, even though Trollope does not parade issues of spirituality, they make their presence felt. It is perfectly true that Trollope's treatment of the Church of England stresses the church as a social institution. But there are moments when we hear a different music, one that breaks through the this-worldly norms of Barchester society as surely as do the antics of the Stanhope family. Perhaps the finest example is the following passage describing the feelings of Harding as he awaits an interview with Slope at the Bishop's Palace, an interview that will determine whether he will reassume the Wardenship. This is, for a number of reasons, a natural moment for him to think about the meaning of his life as a whole. As he stands looking out the window at the Bishop's garden, he feels how different a place the Bishop's Palace was for him when his dearest friend, the previous bishop, lived there:

> The ex-warden stood up at the window looking into the garden, and could not help thinking how very short a time had passed since the whole of that house had been open to him, as though he had been a child of the family, born and bred in it. He remembered how the old servants used to smile as they opened the door to him; how the familiar butler would say, when he had been absent a few hours longer than usual, "A sight of you, Mr. Harding, is good for sore

eyes;" how the fussy housekeeper would swear that he couldn't have dined, or couldn't have breakfasted, or couldn't have lunched. And then, above all, he remembered the pleasant gleam of inward satisfaction which always spread itself over the old bishop's face, whenever his friend entered his room.

A tear came into each eye as he reflected that all this was now gone. What use would the hospital be to him now? He was alone in the world, and getting old; he would soon, very soon have to go, and leave it all, as his dear old friend had gone; go, and leave the hospital, and his accustomed place in the cathedral, and his haunts and pleasures, to younger and perhaps wiser men. That chanting of his! – perhaps, in truth, the time for it had gone by. He felt as though the world were sinking from his feet; as though this, this was the time for him to turn with confidence to those hopes which he had preached with confidence to others. "What," said he to himself, "can a man's religion be worth, if it does not support him against the natural melancholy of declining years?" And, as he looked out through his dimmed eyes into the bright parterres of the bishop's garden, he felt that he had the support which he wanted.

Nevertheless, he did not like to be thus kept waiting. If Mr. Slope did not really wish to see him at half-past nine o'clock, why force him to come away from his lodgings with his breakfast in his throat? (I, ch. 12).

It is typical of Trollope to return us, at the end of this passage and with something of a thump, to the real world in which even saintly men do not enjoy being kept waiting after having bolted down their breakfasts. It remains important to keep in mind, however, that the genial contemplative stance Trollope invites us as readers to share with him can, at times, take on a very broad scope indeed.

Chapter 9

Lady Audley's Secret

Mary Elizabeth Braddon's *Lady Audley's Secret* (1862) is one of the best examples of the "sensation novel," a genre that arose in the 1860s. In addition to several novels by Braddon, the genre includes fiction by Wilkie Collins, Mrs. Henry Wood, and other more minor imitators. The term was initially coined by a contemporary reviewer to describe what appeared to be a new phenomenon in popular fiction: novels written for serial publication that were characterized by page-turningly suspenseful plots, outlandish characters, hidden or stolen identities, lurid secrets, and unspeakable crimes, whose primary function seemed to be to thrill their readers. Reviewers generally identified the trend to decry what seemed a degeneration in both readers and in the novel as an art form, as audiences seemingly followed the new authors in abandoning the more serious work of realist fiction. We will be focusing on *Lady Audley's Secret* in part as a representative sample of features common to sensation fiction more generally – especially that of Collins – rather than solely in relation to Braddon's own fiction.

The dark subject matter and heavy use of suspense in sensation fiction were not in themselves new: Gothic novels at the end of the previous century had traded heavily in both, and, as we saw in *Bleak House*, Dickens also employed them readily. Indeed, the novels we have already discussed here contain among them most of the sensationalistic plot elements featured in *Lady Audley's Secret* and other sensation novels: privately incarcerated madwomen, bigamy, false identities, dastardly manipulations of marital property and inheritance laws, the awkward return of long-lost relatives presumed dead, and murder, to name a few. What made sensation fiction distinctive was partly the sheer concentration and centrality of such "sensational" elements, but it was also their location in seemingly ordinary middle-class settings: unlike the Gothic novel, sensation fiction did not exile its horrors to looming castles or the primitive and alien reaches of the Italian Alps or German forests (or, for that matter, the remote Yorkshire moors). Its characters are mostly minor English landed gentry and their tutors, governesses, lawyers, doctors, and other professionals, all in the mainstream of British polite society: roughly the same settings and cast of characters, in short, from which Austen and Trollope crafted their relatively sedate novels of manners. But sensation fiction took the roles and relations of prosperous domesticity and made them the locus of dastardly intrigues and shocking crimes: monstrous husbands, murderous wives, sinister governesses, and the everpresent threat of the insane asylum. Sensation fiction, in other words, gained its particular thrills by imagining terrifying truths seething beneath the peaceful surface of British middle-class domesticity.

Dickens had done similar things, but as we have seen, his sensationalistic tendencies are also linked to a profound interest in contemporary social issues and in understanding how individuals relate to vertiginously vast and powerful social structures and institutions: the terrifying truth unveiled behind the comforts of domesticity is the very real social horror of Tom-all-Alone's or Chancery corruption as much as it is any private secret. Sensation fiction, while it occasionally engages in flights of generalized social commentary – LAS's narrator periodically launches into reflections on such matters as women's rights and class prejudices – for the most part sinks these issues from view. Sensation novelists, in other words, took from Dickens the focus on managing the reader's emotional experience, and his penchant for strange and distinctive, almost cartoon-like characters, while largely dropping out the overt focus on broader social concerns – though as we shall see, this does not mean the novels have nothing to do with them.

Sensation fiction features a wide range of narrative methods. Collins, in *The Woman in White* and some of his later fiction, pioneered a narrative form loosely modeled on the epistolary novel, in which the novel is presented as a collection of first-person narratives assembled by the hero (a form Bram Stoker would pick up and elaborate, with great effectiveness, for *Dracula*). *Lady Audley's Secret*, by contrast, has a familiarly garrulous authorial narrative voice of the sort we might find in Trollope or Thackeray, though with vital differences from both, as we shall see. But for all the formal differences among them, sensation novels share important features in the forms of emotional and interpretive engagement they invite. *Lady Audley's Secret*, like many sensation novels, features an initially marginalized protagonist (usually though not invariably male, as here) with aesthetic predilections, who is gradually transformed and empowered by the process of unraveling a dark secret that threatens or victimizes someone he loves. In this respect, sensation fiction is one of the most significant precursors to contemporary detective fiction, and especially to those branches of it that feature "amateur" detectives forced into action by personal circumstances, so that the plot of detection becomes also a plot of self-discovery and personal development.

Sensation novels also tend to feature strange, unlikely, and often uncannily hyper-competent villains and villainesses who undertake – and but for the protagonist, carry off – plots of audacious scope. In this sense, sensational villains can be a form of stand-in for the author, in that their plots work by constructing a convincingly "normal" surface reality of conventionally acceptable motivations and unremarkable coincidences (such as those that repeatedly prevent Lady Audley from being introduced to George Talboys, for example), that in fact conceal a deeply structured and coherent pattern of action and meaning.

For the protagonist, the process of uncovering and tracing this unlikely pattern in the most seemingly innocuous, unrelated, or random elements of his experience – including hints of violent intentions toward himself if he continues his investigations – is alarmingly similar to paranoia, or as the Victorians would term it, monomania. By the end of the novel, the protagonist must perform a virtuoso act of interpretive reconstruction, heroically challenging a given order of reality and substituting for it one authorized solely by his own investigative efforts. This interpretation is so radically different from the socially accepted one, so shocking, and on the face of it so unlikely (in that it assigns the most sinister motivations and actions to highly respectable figures) that there is some danger of the hero being seen – and at times, seeing himself – as simply insane for believing in it. Sensation fiction then characteristically invites us to share in the protagonist's paranoia, as well as his fears for his own sanity. This particular form of psychological thriller had actually been pioneered by William Godwin (with a sharper political edge), in his singular masterpiece, *Caleb Williams*, but in sensation fiction it becomes a familiar feature of the form. Godwin's novel ends, in one version, with its protagonist actually driven mad by his inability to convince others of any wrongdoing by the man who has destroyed his life, but sensation novels that rely on this plot device generally end more cheerfully, with the hero's sanity safely affirmed by the social validation of his interpretation of events, while the specter of madness, if not eliminated altogether, is at least transferred elsewhere.

This empowerment of an aesthetically oriented figure by means of a project of sensational interpretation also potentially makes the protagonist something of a stand-in for the reader, who, as in most mystery novels, is paralleling him in the effort to make sense of the range of sinister hints and clues with which both we and he are presented. The problem-solving effort of the reader and protagonist becomes a source of narrative pleasure, reinforced by the ways the protagonist is ultimately socially and romantically rewarded for his successful efforts.

If the protagonist is a model for the heroically empowered reader, Fate or Providence often stands in for the author. At the same time that the hero perceives his interpretive project as carried out in defiant social isolation, he also perceives himself as being led on by an external force variously termed Fate, Providence, or, as in *Lady Audley's Secret*, "a hand stronger than my own," which operates by such means as prophetic dreams and (most frequently) uncanny coincidences to give him the impetus, tools, and allies to solve the mystery. In a kind of bizarre reversal of realism, sensationalist interpreters bring to everyday life interpretive practices we normally reserve for reading fiction: the sensitivity to foreshadowing and omens, the presumption that all details brought to their attention, even those that seem trivial, random, or unrelated, are relevant to their central preoccupations, and the faith that everything they learn and experience can ultimately be integrated into a coherent narrative trajectory leading to an ethically and emotionally satisfying resolution. The critic Frank Kermode once pointed out that anyone responding to the real data of their lives as if they inhabited a coherent, teleologically plotted novel would be diagnosed with paranoid schizophrenia; the insanity these protagonists fear in themselves, and are accused of by others, could be seen as an earlier version of this insight.

In one sense, then, sensation fiction is notable for its refusal of the forms of intellectual, artistic, and social seriousness we have been stressing in the other novelists we discuss here. Its thrill derives in part from its destabilization of "the real": its constitution of the reader as a heroically empowered interpreter, challenged by radical if localized gaps between social appearance and reality, but reassured by an authorial Fate that is as thoroughly proper in its ultimate aims as it is weirdly idiosyncratic in its methods.

But cutting loose from the restraints of social realism also allowed sensation fiction to channel and exploit more inchoate social anxieties. For readers today, these novels offer, in addition to their enduring readerly pleasures as thrillers, a window onto the landscape of those anxieties. These novels feature demonic figures hiding behind the most approved social facades and exploiting the credibility that comes with an accepted social position or fixed social roles. Their worst-case scenarios of sinister social posing suggest an uncomfortable awareness of the degree to which social status and credibility are fictionally constructed and self-reinforcing, particularly as the society becomes more mobile and urbanized, and therefore less "knowable."

Many sensation novels gain part of their power to disturb by a destabilization of conventional gender roles, evident here not only in *LAS*'s angelic-looking villainess, but in the powerful, determined female allies who in many sensation novels serve to prop up and drive on an initially aimless protagonist. More particularly, sensation novels often call attention to the legal and social vulnerability of women, especially within marriage. *The Woman in White* offers a wife victimized, incarcerated, and all but murdered by the forms of economic and social control granted to husbands. *Lady Audley's Secret* appears to offer just the opposite: a woman who uses her attractiveness to catch and exploit a rich second husband, and later to shield her murder of the first, but even here it is hinted that women's economic and social vulnerability relative to men, and the preoccupation of men with women's physical beauty, are contributing factors to her villainy.

The Narrator

Lady Audley's Secret opens in a fairly conventional manner by setting a scene, with an extended, detailed description of Audley Court:

> It was a house that could never have been planned by any mortal architect, but must have been the handiwork of that good old builder, Time, who, adding a room one year, and knocking down a room another year, toppling down a chimney coeval with the Plantagenets, and setting up one in the style of the Tudors; shaking down a bit of Saxon wall, allowing a Norman arch to stand here; throwing in a row of high narrow windows in the reign of Queen Anne, and joining on a dining-room after the fashion of the time of Hanoverian George I, to a refectory that had been standing since the Conquest, had contrived, in some eleven centuries, to run up such a mansion as was not elsewhere to be met with throughout the county of Essex. (ch. 1)

There are clear echoes of Dickens's style here: in the quirky and varied language, the animation of inanimate objects – such as the front door tucked in a corner "as if it was in hiding from dangerous visitors, and wished to keep itself a secret" – and the extensive use of parallel constructions to pile up descriptive details. In its content, though, the passage seems more reminiscent of Trollope's affection for ancient buildings (and by extension, the institutions they embody), with their charming, if "incorrect," designs and their inimitable patina of age. Trollopian, too, is the narrator's familiar, chatty address to the reader – "a smooth lawn lay before you"; "a house in which you incontinently lost yourself," etc. – which seems to invite the reader to join the narrator in a leisurely, reflective tour of the house and grounds.

But the description is laced through with more sinister undertones: the door is "in hiding from dangerous visitors," the "secret chamber" carries its reminder of the "cruel days" of Catholic persecution, the lime-tree walk "seemed a place in which a conspiracy might have been planned," and there is a strangely repeated emphasis on the hidden and disused old well. Readers aware of the conventional Victorian association of women with ivy, adorning and supported by the oak of manhood (as in the conclusion to *Vanity Fair*), might also be struck by the description of the house's chimneys, "so broken down by age and long service, that they might have fallen but for the straggling ivy which . . . wound itself around them and supported them." More generally, the sense of "Peace" the whole setting evokes is said to produce in a visitor "a yearning wish to have done with life, and stay there forever," suggesting a death-like quality to the ancient stillness of the place. This is the kind of symbolic loading of descriptions of landscape and buildings we expect in Dickens or the Brontës, but here it is much more covert: we cannot fail to notice the metaphoric linkage between Chancery and the fog and mud of London, or between stormy weather and emotional chaos at Wuthering Heights, but we might well pass over the dark hints dropped in Braddon's otherwise genial Trollopian tour, unless we've been made suspicious by the title's indication that the Lady of Audley Court has a "secret." This effect is actually as far as possible from Trollope's narrator, who goes overboard to give away his narrative secrets early so that we can stay focused on the (to him) more interesting matters of character and social portraiture.

The opening's warm evocation of "Peace" at Audley Court retroactively acquires a further sinister subtext six chapters later, when the narrator, having left Robert Audley and his friend George Talboys smoking by an inn window and looking out "at the peaceful prospect" of the countryside, launches into the following digression:

> We hear every day of murders committed in the country. Brutal and treacherous murders; slow, protracted agonies from poisons administered by some kindred hand; sudden and violent deaths by cruel blows, inflicted with a stake cut from some spreading oak, whose every shadow promised – peace. In the county of which I write, I have been shown a meadow in which, on a quiet summer Sunday evening, a young farmer murdered the girl who had loved and trusted him; and yet, even now, with the stain of that foul deed upon it, the aspect of the spot is – peace. No species of crime has ever been committed in the worst rookeries about Seven Dials that has not been also done in the face of that rustic calm which still, in spite of all, we look on with a tender, half-mournful yearning, and associate with – peace. (ch. 7)

While the opening of the novel created a subtle dissonance between surface and depth, description and meaning, this passage seems to assert their sheer incommensurability: there is simply *no* necessary linkage between the emotions a given landscape evokes and the human actions for which it might serve as a setting. But placing the passage, seemingly apropos of nothing, at this precise point in the narrative – just after George Talboys has experienced in this very landscape "a kind of sensuous rapture" that is "the nearest approach to enjoyment that he had ever known since his wife's death" – also acts as a clear hint that some "foul deed," perhaps by a "kindred hand," is indeed on the way. It is as if the narrator is saying, "don't pay attention to scenery, pay attention to *me*."

Introductions of major characters operate similarly, especially in relation to the two main antagonists, Lady Audley and Robert. Again, we know already that the former has a "secret," so when she is initially described at the second hand, through the perceptions of the people around her who are so enraptured with her innocent-looking blond beauty that they credit her with the best possible character and motives, we are well primed to assign more significance to hints offered by the narrator in minor details and parenthetical asides about her mysterious past and lack of any concrete demonstrations of benevolence or generosity. By the end of the first chapter, with the account of her strange distress at Sir Michael's proposal and the hidden ring she wears round her throat, most readers probably already feel pretty sure of what the secret is (though of course there will be more to it than that . . .).

The gap between public presentation and reality is more comically displayed in the introduction of Robert, who is "supposed to be a barrister," having acquired the credentials and chambers of one, but who "had never either had a brief, or tried to get a brief, or even wished to have a brief" in his life (ch. 4). But if Robert is initially presented as a "lazy, care-for-nothing fellow" with a "listless, dawdling, indifferent, irresolute manner," we will soon find that this too is a facade which conceals depths of will and intelligence unguessed at by his friends and relations, or perhaps even Robert himself. Robert in turn initially judges Clara Talboys to be "as heartless as her father" (ch. 22) based on her outward manner, only to find that her still surface conceals passionate resolution beyond his own.

We have discussed in other chapters the way, in our view, the best authorial realist narrators embody modes of perceiving and responding adequately to a complex social world, modes that, far from claiming any unique privilege of "omniscience," present themselves as implicitly available to a thinking reader willing to tune and sensitize their own vision by practicing or performing them with the narrator. The contrast should make clear how Braddon resists, upends, or perhaps even parodies realist narration. To read *Lady Audley's Secret* is to engage in a game between author and reader, in which we try to sift genuine hints and clues from various forms of deliberate misdirection, and she tries to give us just enough to keep us reading to test our guesses, while still holding enough secrets in reserve to continue to surprise us. These techniques are now quite familiar to readers of mystery stories or thrillers, but it is worth remembering that Braddon and her fellow sensationalists predate – and to some degree are themselves inventing – the genre's conventions.

Lady Audley

Lady Audley's Secret tells the story of a young woman who has assumed a false identity to escape the impoverished circumstances of an early marriage, and then illegally marries a rich baronet. When exposure is threatened by the return of her first husband, she carries out a complicated plot to fake her own death, and then resorts to increasingly violent means to keep her secret safe. As the full scope of Lucy's actions become evident, the novel appears to condemn her wholeheartedly, frequently calling attention to her selfishness, vanity, and love of luxury, while inviting us to identify emotionally with George Talboys's depth of love and grief for his young wife, Robert's concern for his missing friend and reluctant horror at his dawning suspicions of his young aunt, Clara Talboys's determination to unmask her brother's destroyer, and Sir Michael's grief at the betrayal of his devoted love. At the same time, though, the novel offers a range of different, and sometimes incompatible, accounts of the circumstances and motives that drive Lucy to act as she does, some of which also suggest alternative judgments of other characters' responses to her, and especially those of her nemesis, Robert. The remainder of our discussion of the novel will be organized around these accounts and their implications, as among them they touch on most of the important social and aesthetic issues the novel raises, including the societal emphasis on feminine beauty, women's economic and physical vulnerability and the lack of legitimate outlets for their enterprise and ambition, and the ambiguous character and social meaning of "madness."

Beauty and Vanity

A major portion of what makes *Lady Audley's Secret* "sensational" is the device of attributing extensive cold-blooded calculation and a capacity for murderous violence to a figure whose appearance and manner seem to convey only innocence, fragility, and good nature. We might read this as no more than a sensationalist strategy of seeking shock value by creating the least likely villain imaginable, but this is too simple: we will see George Eliot, hardly a sensationalist, making essentially the same move in casting Rosamond, with her "perfect blond loveliness" and delicately proper manners, as one of the most negative and destructive characters in *Middlemarch*. In both cases, the lovely villainess occasions reflection on society's – especially, but not exclusively, men's – overemphasis on female beauty, and as a consequence, the negative influence such beauty can have on the characters of the women themselves. From the first chapter, we see Lucy's beauty, without any more active benevolence than a willingness to listen for "a quarter of an hour" to the compliments of a "toothless crone," earning from an old woman "senile raptures with her grace, her beauty, and her kindliness, such as she never bestowed upon the vicar's wife, who half fed and clothed her" (ch. 1). Is it any wonder, then, that Lucy sees herself as entitled to more than other women, purely on the strength of her own beauty? This is in fact the first extended explanation the narrator offers for the negative qualities of Lucy's character:

> Perhaps in that retrospective revery she recalled that early time in which she had first looked in the glass and discovered that she was beautiful; that fatal early time in which she had first begun to look upon her loveliness as a right divine, a boundless possession which was to be a set-off against all girlish shortcomings, a counterbalance of every youthful sin. Did she remember the day in which that fairy dower of beauty had first taught her to be selfish and cruel, indifferent to the joys and sorrows of others, cold-hearted and capricious, greedy of admiration, exacting and tyrannical with that petty woman's tyranny which is the worst of despotism? Did she trace every sin of her life back to its true source? and did she discover that poisoned fountain in her own exaggerated estimate of the value of a pretty face? Surely, if her thoughts wandered so far along the backward current of her life, she must have repented in bitterness and despair of that first day in which the master-passions of her life had become her rulers, and the three demons of Vanity, Selfishness, and Ambition, had joined hands and said, "This woman is our slave, let us see what she will become under our guidance." (ch. 31)

But while this passage claims to identify the "true source" of Lucy's "sin," it is actually only one of several competing explanations for why Lucy behaves the way she does, and not necessarily the most compelling of them. Usually, defending fictional villainesses as having received a "bad rap" from their fellow characters, readers or author represent the most naïve and unproductive form of feminist criticism. In the case of *Lady Audley's Secret*, though, the strains of a counternarrative surface persistently, if often unobtrusively, to suggest an alternative contextualization of Lucy's misdeeds that complicates, if it does not wholly invalidate, the easy outrage the novel apparently invites.

Feminine Enterprise

Lucy's own final confession locates the roots of her actions squarely in her experience of "poverty" and the anxieties associated with her mother's madness. The circumstances of her early childhood impress upon her "the bitterness of poverty," which separates her from her father (who must remain on active duty in the military to support her), condemning her to the care of an unloving woman "who vented her rage upon me when my father was behind-hand in remitting her money," at one point threatening to cut short her schooling altogether. Her accidental discovery, at the age of ten, that her absent mother is actually "mad" and incarcerated in an asylum reinforces her perception of the effects of poverty: her father "had loved his wife very dearly; and . . . would have willingly sacrificed his life to her, and constituted himself her guardian, had he not been compelled to earn the daily bread of the madwoman and her child by the exercise of his profession," depriving his wife of the superior care of a "devoted husband." At the same time, she suggests, the specter of hereditary madness, and the knowledge that she must keep her mother's condition secret because it "might affect me injuriously in after-life," constitutes an additional burden for her childhood self: "and it was, perhaps, this that made me selfish and heartless." In Lucy's account, significantly, these earlier childhood influences *precede* the discovery that she is "pretty – beautiful – lovely – bewitching" (ch. 34), a recognition that arrives only with adolescence.

That recognition, she suggests, comes along with "that which in some indefinite manner or other every schoolgirl learns sooner or later – I learned that my ultimate fate in life depended upon my marriage." Without connections or money, and saddled with an unreliable father and an ominous family history, Lucy is pushed into the same realization Charlotte Lucas confronted with more equanimity in *Pride and Prejudice*, that whatever one's private opinion of men or matrimony, a good marriage is a woman's "pleasantest preservative from want" – and may be her only one. With beauty as her only dowry, Lucy cannot afford to be "romantic" any more than Charlotte can.

When Lucy finally acknowledges to Sir Michael her prior marriage, she also makes a confession that proves a fatal blow to his love for her, telling him "I think I loved [George Talboys] as much as it was in my power to love anybody; not more than I loved you, Sir Michael; not so much; for when you married me you elevated me to a position that he could never have given me" (ch. 34). But realistically, given how completely dependent a woman's fate could be on the man she married, how could she *not* take financial practicalities into account in thinking about love and marriage – as, in *Pride and Prejudice*, Elizabeth's favorite aunt Mrs. Gardiner very sensibly encourages her to remember? Lucy does love Sir Michael, she says – better than she loved George Talboys – but she loves him primarily for his generosity to her and the security and luxury he can give her. How far is this from the love Cathy feels for Edgar in *Wuthering Heights*? Or even from the "gratitude and esteem" Elizabeth feels as she realizes that "to be mistress of Pemberley would be something" (which are not, to be sure, the feelings that lead her finally to accept him)? If we return to the proposal scene in the first chapter, we see that Lucy, with what is surely admirable honesty, has told Sir Michael from the start that while he is thoroughly loveable – "How good . . . how noble . . . how generous" – it is simply "too much to ask" a poor unconnected governess to be "blind to the advantages of such an alliance" in responding to his proposal. In *Middlemarch*, Eliot astutely observes that our romantic attractions are inevitably shaped by our other desires: the fact that Lydgate is a stranger to Middlemarch and has aristocratic connections, for example, is as much a factor in making Rosamond quite sincerely fall in love with him as the fact that he is tall, handsome, well dressed, witty, and fond of flirting with her, while for Dorothea, the promise of sharing in Mr. Casaubon's (presumed) intellectual wealth endows him in her eyes with attractions incomprehensible to women motivated by more conventional longings. The same might be said of Lucy's "love" for Sir Michael. To expect a woman in Lucy's position to somehow excise these vital concerns from her consciousness in considering a marriage, and to condemn her for failing to do so, might well strike us as unreasonable.

Consider, too, the circumstances that have led Lucy to the point of responding to Sir Michael's proposal: having married, at the ripe age of seventeen, the handsome, well-born, and devoted George Talboys, in the belief that he offered her an escape from the painful circumstances of her life with her father, Lucy quickly finds herself in even more difficult circumstances, for which George surely bears at least as much blame as his younger wife. Having been disowned by his father, George runs through his only remaining money with extravagant haste, and then makes only minimal efforts to get employment to support his young wife and infant son, while responding with resentment to her complaints about their increasingly desperate circumstances. Finally, rather than deal with the emotional discomfort of his family circumstances, and in an act of retaliation against his wife's reproaches, he walks out on her with no more than a farewell note and a half share of his cash on hand (despite the fact that she has a child and presumably considerably less earning capacity than him). She is left with an infant son to support, and an alcoholic, impecunious, and unreliable father who proves more a burden than a help, as his failings repeatedly thwart her otherwise successful efforts to support them all by her own efforts.

Discovering that a young woman encumbered with an infant and a disreputable father simply cannot get decent work, Lucy adopts the desperate expedient of posing as a single woman, enabling her to take a position as a teacher, but – in significant contrast to George Talboys – as soon as her financial circumstances improve she resumes contact with her father and infant son, and sends them money when she can. She also, at some risk of exposure, wears her wedding ring around her neck and keeps her son's tiny shoe as a precious memento, suggesting that her departure is not entirely an emotional abandonment of those commitments. One of the temptations Sir Michael's offer of marriage presents is the chance of access to resources to send to her secret family – as indeed she does. And after three years of complete silence from her absent husband, it is perhaps not unreasonable of her to assume that, if he is still alive, he has no intention of returning. At any rate, given the bleak alternatives she faces, it is not necessarily a stupid gamble, nor, given the circumstances of her father and young son, even an entirely selfish or immoral one, to accept the offer of becoming Lady Audley. And while she deceives Sir Michael about the facts of her identity and prior marriage, she does not deceive him about her feeling for him: he reiterates his offer of marriage in the full knowledge that her acceptance will be motivated primarily by the privileged position he can offer her.

Even Lucy's "murder" of George Talboys contains crucial ambiguities. We know that George is prone to impulsive and unreasonable anger – as is shown in his abandonment of his wife in a fit of pique at her reproaches. It is surely significant that one of Lucy's anxieties on hearing of his return is terror at his "implacable" determination: it is perhaps not fear just of "exposure," but of the direct consequences of his anger, that drives the plot to fake her own death. And indeed, when George actually does confront her, his grasp is hard enough to leave bruises on her arm, and he expresses an enraged determination to expose and punish her. The threat of male violence against a rejecting sweetheart is brought to the foreground of the novel with the relationship between the brutal Luke and Phoebe, Lucy's maid and physical double, who marries the former solely out of the conviction that he will murder her if she doesn't. Even the paragraph about peaceful country scenes quoted above, while it overtly hints at the attack on George by Lucy's "kindred hand," significantly does so by way of analogy with an incident of a young rustic killing his sweetheart – just what Phoebe fears. In the confrontation scene between George and Lucy, after he grabs her arm and berates her, she pushes him away with a strength heightened by pain and terror, and, apparently by accident, he tumbles into the decayed well. Believing him dead, she lacks the courage to destroy her own and both her families' lives by exposing herself as a bigamist and, as she now believes, a murderess as well.

The point in presenting this extended counternarrative is not that the novel has a clear-cut and airtight "secret meaning," vindicating Lady Audley, which lies coded within a surface text that appears to condemn her wholeheartedly. Certainly by the time Lucy is resorting to premeditated murder and arson, it is impossible to construe her simply as an unfairly maligned innocent. But neither does such partial vindication constitute a wholly imaginary fabrication, or an unwarranted rewriting of the information the novel gives us. Had Braddon wished to keep readerly sympathy squarely on George's side, and to constitute Lady Audley as indefensible by contrast, she could easily have made the circumstances of his departure and continuing silence less conspicuously blameworthy on his part. Instead, she calls attention to them when she first introduces George on the English-bound ship in the second chapter, both in the story he reveals and in the surprise expressed by his female interlocutor at his unwarranted confidence that he will receive a warm welcome from his wife after abandonment and three years of silence. His rather casual approach to his responsibilities is reinforced later when, after one brief visit to his son, he decides to leave him in the care of his drunken and immoral grandfather, and return to Australia! Similarly, Braddon could easily have made the economic and familial circumstances that drive Lucy to assume a false identity less compelling than they are, or omitted the evidence of her later financial support of her family. Instead, as in the sinister subtext of her opening description of Audley Court, Braddon makes available a counterreading that considerably disrupts, if it doesn't completely invalidate, the moralizing tone of both Robert Audley and, often, the narrative voice itself. In freeing herself of domestic encumbrances the better to try to earn a living, Lucy behaves with a resourceful and enterprising spirit not unlike George's. Because of her gender, though, the only gold mine available to her is in the pockets of a wealthy husband – and acting on that fact, even without the question of bigamy, opens her to moral condemnation as mercenary in a way that grabbing a share of Australia's gold never does for George.

If an implicit comparison to George troubles the novel's judgment of Lucy in one direction, parallels with Clara Talboys do so in another. Robert, after his visit to the Talboys family, finds himself sandwiched between two powerful and determined women, both of whom exercise their power largely through men: Lucy counts on her influence over Sir Michael to convince him that Robert's suspicions are the product of madness, while Clara invokes her moral claims as George's sister – and her determination, if necessary, to track down her brother's murderer herself – to compel Robert, ostensibly against his own wishes, to follow through on his investigations to the bitter end. Reflecting on this situation, Robert embarks on a series of reflections on women that are worth quoting and discussing at length:

Man might lie in the sunshine, and eat lotuses, and fancy it "always afternoon," if his wife would let him! But she won't, bless her impulsive heart and active mind! She knows better than that. Who ever heard of a woman taking life as it ought to be taken? Instead of supporting it as an unavoidable nuisance, only redeemable by its brevity, she goes through it as if it were a pageant or a procession. She dresses for it, and simpers and grins, and gesticulates for it. She pushes her neighbors, and struggles for a good place in the dismal march; she elbows, and writhes, and tramples, and prances to the one end of making the most of the misery. She gets up early and sits up late, and is loud, and restless, and noisy, and unpitying. She drags her husband on to the woolsack, or pushes him into Parliament. She drives him full butt at the dear, lazy machinery of government, and knocks and buffets him about the wheels, and cranks, and screws, and pulleys; until somebody, for quiet's sake, makes him something that she wanted him to be made. That's why incompetent men sometimes sit in high places, and interpose their poor, muddled intellects between the things to be done and the people that can do them, making universal confusion in the helpless innocence of well-placed incapacity. The square men in the round holes are pushed into them by their wives. The Eastern potentate who declared that women were at the bottom of all mischief, should have gone a little further and seen why it is so. It is because women are never lazy. They don't know what it is to be quiet. They are Semiramides, and Cleopatras, and Joans of Arc, Queen Elizabeths, and Catharines the Second, and they riot in battle, and murder, and clamor and desperation. If they can't agitate the universe and play at ball with hemispheres, they'll make mountains of warfare and vexation out of domestic molehills, and social storms in household teacups. Forbid them to hold forth upon the freedom of nations and the wrongs of mankind, and they'll quarrel with Mrs. Jones about the shape of a mantle or the character of a small maid-servant. To call them the weaker sex is to utter a hideous mockery. They are the stronger sex, the noisier, the more persevering, the most self-assertive sex. They want freedom of opinion, variety of occupation, do they? Let them have it. Let them be lawyers, doctors, preachers, teachers, soldiers, legislators – anything they like – but let them be quiet – if they can. (ch. 24)

This passage deploys rhetorical strategies often associated with gender conservatives of the period – a disparaging account of women's alleged tendency to concern themselves with "shallow" matters like social climbing, and to exercise inappropriate power by manipulating their husbands, as well as a joking reference to their inability to keep "quiet" – but it does so to mount a backhanded argument for allowing women "freedom of opinion" and "variety of occupation." It is hard not to hear the voice of Braddon – herself an astonishingly energetic woman who wrote seventy-five novels while raising eleven children – engaging in a little "stealth feminism" here behind the double mask of a masculine voice and jokey misogynistic rhetoric. But it is also not clear how seriously even Robert himself takes any aspect of this rant: he begins it by announcing "I hate women," but it has already been hinted that he is in love with Clara Talboys, making this expression of resentment of her impact on his life hollow at best. Furthermore, Robert has been presented to us as an exceptionally indolent man – surely anybody, male or female, would look energetic by comparison. Elsewhere, Robert attributes his compulsion to bestir himself in the case to Fate or Providence, and even speculates that the entire case is "God's judgment upon the purposeless, vacillating life I led up to the seventh day of last September":

> Surely this awful responsibility has been forced upon me in order that I may humble myself to an offended Providence, and confess that a man cannot choose his own life. He cannot say, "I will take existence lightly, and keep out of the way of the wretched, mistaken, energetic creatures, who fight so heartily in the great battle." . . . He can only do, humbly and fearfully, that which the Maker who created him has appointed for him to do. If he has a battle to fight, let him fight it faithfully; but woe betide him if he skulks when his name is called in the mighty muster-roll. (ch. 35)

The male pronouns and war metaphors here suggest that "tak[ing] existence lightly," far from being the normal condition of men unprodded by their wives, is a shamefully unmasculine condition. So is Clara's driving of Robert in his investigation a symptom of women's deplorable excess of energy (one that furthermore subtly links her to Lady Audley), a marker of the deplorable lack of more direct outlets for women's admirable energies, or a sign that Clara is acting as the agent of God's very particularized intention to rouse Robert from his unmanly lassitude? Or are all of these conflicting and rather ad hoc reflections symptoms of Robert's emotional turmoil, his sloppy intellectual habits, his taste for irony alternating with melodrama? Or perhaps merely of his author's careless haste in composition? We would suggest that this very uncertainty is central to the aesthetic of the novel. As with the opening invocation of "peace," no sooner is a seemingly stabilizing characterization or explanation offered than it is elsewhere undermined or cast into doubt. The result is not quite like the complex balance of emotional and symbolic forces in *Wuthering Heights*, though, or even the subtle dance of symbolic displacements by which Dickens negotiates the competing claims of social passion and narrative pleasure: it is more like a playful riot, in which disturbing possibilities are conspicuously raised and explored, only to be contradicted later or laid to rest by means of equally conspicuous narrative contrivances. Nowhere is this clearer than in the novel's treatment of "madness."

Madness: Everybody's Alibi

As we discussed earlier, the threat of madness, or of being wrongly perceived as mad, is commonplace in sensation fiction, particularly for the protagonist, who characteristically confronts indications of an order of motivations and events radically at odds with that construed as "normal" reality. It also, as here, frequently emerges as a weapon. By the time *Lady Audley's Secret* was written, mental illness had been squarely established as properly the object of professionalized medical expertise and "scientific" investigation. But its origins and diagnosis were still poorly understood, and there was considerable public anxiety about the proper criteria for declaring someone insane and the potential abuse of involuntary commitment. As Robert's investigations close in, Lady Audley defends herself by laying the groundwork to convince her husband that Robert is insane, drawing in part on the then-ambiguous distinction between actual insanity and what might be termed "harmless eccentricity." The narrator, meanwhile, periodically invokes "the narrow boundary between reason and unreason" as part of her general pattern of calling attention to potential gaps between outward appearance and hidden meaning. Just as she has earlier suggested that settings of rustic "peace" may hide violent histories, so she suggests that the "orderly outward world," especially at moments of personal crisis, is often painfully at odds with "the storm and tempest, the riot and confusion within" – so much so that although "madhouses are large and only too numerous; yet surely it is strange they are not larger . . . when we remember how many minds must tremble upon the narrow boundary . . . mad to-day and sane to-morrow, mad yesterday and sane to-day."

But in the final confrontation between Robert and Lady Audley, after her thwarted attempt at murder, it is Lady Audley's own claim to "madness" that takes center stage: "God knows I have struggled hard enough against you, and fought the battle patiently enough; but you have conquered, Mr. Robert Audley. It is a great triumph, is it not – a wonderful victory? You have used your cool, calculating, frigid, luminous intellect to a noble purpose. You have conquered – a MAD WOMAN!" (ch. 34). Lady Audley's insanity defense comes in handy for her, allowing her to disclaim moral responsibility for her presumed crimes:

When you say that I killed George Talboys, you say the truth. When you say that I murdered him treacherously and foully, you lie. I killed him because I AM MAD! because my intellect is a little way upon the wrong side of that narrow boundary-line between sanity and insanity; because, when George Talboys

goaded me, as you have goaded me, and reproached me, and threatened me, my mind, never properly balanced, utterly lost its balance, and *I was mad!*
···

As Lady Audley's confession proceeds, madness is invoked to explain not only actual criminal acts, but any occasion when her feelings or actions violate feminine expectations: when George's desertion and the hardships that result make her "subject to fits of violence and despair," she says, "my mind first lost its balance." More notably, every point at which she engages in deliberate planning and intentional action is described as one in which "the balance trembled," and "the invisible boundary was passed." When Mrs. Plowson's complaints suggest to her the plot for faking her own death, she says, "an idea flashed upon me with such painful suddenness that it sent the blood surging up to my brain, and set my heart beating, as it only beats when I am mad." Strongly negative feelings, the excitement of coming up with a workable plan to deal with a desperate situation, the determination to act: these are the mental conditions consistently equated with "madness" in Lady Audley's account.

It is tempting then, to read the claim to madness as just another convenient strategic move on Lady Audley's part – especially as it does, after all, allow her to escape prosecution for her crimes. But the narrative gives it greater weight than this. Robert has earlier puzzled over a note from Lady Audley to her father that makes reference to a momentous "Secret" over and above the secret of her prior marriage, a secret she now reveals as that of her insanity. Not only does this suggest that her own claim of madness is sincere, it constitutes the "revelation" of it as the final solution of the "secret" posed by the novel's title – the more so as the confession comes in a chapter titled "My Lady Tells the Truth" (ch. 34). If "madness" is Lady Audley's alibi for an unfeminine capacity for violent anger and ruthless calculation, then, it is an alibi at a deeper level than the conscious – and one reinforced to some degree by the narrative framework of the novel.

Robert, too, has found the contradiction between Lady Audley's actions and her femininity so disturbing that the hypothesis of "madness" seems necessary to resolve it – his own, if not hers: "I have wondered sometimes, as it was only natural I should, whether I was not the victim of some horrible hallucination, whether such an alternative was not more probable than that a young and lovely woman should be capable of so foul and treacherous a murder." Failing that, he says, he can only consider her "no longer a woman" at all, but "the demoniac incarnation of some evil principle" (ch. 34). For Robert too, then, Lady Audley's "madness" provides a handy way to reconcile his conventional ideas about what "a young and lovely woman" ought to be capable of with the disturbing facts of what one such woman has actually done. In the same way, it acts as an alibi for Braddon herself for any perceived implausibilities in Lady Audley's character: finding it hard to believe anyone who makes the relentlessly positive impression on others Lady Audley does could do the awful things she does? She's psycho!

But in her usual way, Braddon will not let the narrative rest there. Having trotted out madness as a stabilizing "truth" that explains away seeming anomalies of motive or action, she then carefully undermines our confidence in the hypothesis, and therefore in the justice of the actions carried out on the strength of it. Her mother's insanity notwithstanding, the medical expert Robert calls in to diagnose Lady Audley sees "no evidence of madness" in the truncated account of her actions Robert gives him:

> She ran away from her home, because her home was not a pleasant one, and she left in the hope of finding a better. There is no madness in that. She committed the crime of bigamy, because by that crime she obtained fortune and position. There is no madness there. When she found herself in a desperate position, she did not grow desperate. She employed intelligent means, and she carried out a conspiracy which required coolness and deliberation in its execution. There is no madness in that. (ch. 37)

It is only when Robert provides the further details of her husband's disappearance and the fire at the inn that Dr. Mosgrave is willing to examine her for insanity. When he does so, his diagnosis is disturbingly ambiguous:

> "I have talked to the lady," he said, quietly, "and we understand each other very well. There is latent insanity! Insanity which might never appear; or which might appear only once or twice in a lifetime. It would be a *dementia* in its worst phase, perhaps; acute mania; but its duration would be very brief, and it would only arise under extreme mental pressure. The lady is not mad; but she has the hereditary taint in her blood. She has the cunning of madness, with the prudence of intelligence. I will tell you what she is, Mr. Audley. She is dangerous!" (ch. 37)

If "latent insanity . . . which might never appear" is grounds for committing someone for life to a private mental hospital, then it is indeed strange, as the narrator earlier says, that madhouses are not larger or more numerous, for by her own account the world is chock full of minds that "tremble upon the narrow boundary." In fact, two chapters after Dr. Mosgrave's diagnosis, the narrator will suggest, apropos of Robert's "hypochondriacal" imagining of being haunted by George's ghost, that the condition is well-nigh universal: "There is nothing so delicate, so fragile, as that invisible balance upon which the mind is always trembling. 'Mad to-day and sane to-morrow.' Who has not been, or is not to be mad in some lonely hour of life? Who is quite safe from the trembling of the balance?" (ch. 39). The doctor's rather odd opening comment that he and Lady Audley "understand each other very well" suggests that his so-called diagnosis is arrived at by a rather cynical process of mutual agreement: Robert wants to get Lady Audley out of the way and avoid family scandal; Lady Audley wants to have a comfortable, financially secure life and avoid prosecution for murder, and Dr. Mosgrave wants to make his paying client happy and keep a "cunning" and therefore "dangerous" woman off the streets. It is a little strange, after this, that on arrival at the "maison de sante" Lady Audley should be shocked to discover that it is "A MADHOUSE!" – what on earth did she expect? – but presumably a less horrified response would undercut the narrative requirement that she suffer punishment for her misdeeds.

Madness, then, is first invoked as part of a larger narrative pattern of destabilization, and then, in relation to Lady Audley, offered as a stabilizing explanation that claims to resolve disturbing dissonances among her character, her actions, and particular social norms of femininity. But finally, that gesture of explanation is itself called attention to as a convenient fiction used quite deliberately by male characters within the story to reimpose those norms on a woman who is probably no crazier than they are.

In one sense, this is just more of the narrative fun and games Braddon obviously delights in. But its very playfulness may also act to shield a more serious interest in exploring the ways her society demands and enforces the performance of particular gender roles. We think it would be a misreading of the novel's aesthetic to see it as interested in mounting a coherent and consistent critique of the social status of women. But other sensation fiction that relies equally on disrupting gender expectations to produce sensational effects – especially the novels of Wilkie Collins – are far more thorough in reestablishing a conventionally gendered status quo in their conclusions. When a sensation novel by Wilkie Collins ends, the reader is sure that all is well, in the realm of gender relations as in all other respects. *Lady Audley's Secret* never quite stops undercutting its own stabilities. What are we to make of the narrator's closing assertion that "my story . . . leaves the good people all happy and at peace" (peace *again*!)? After following (and delighting in) the twists and turns of Braddon's unstable narrative, can we really accept at face value the idea that its manifestly conventional ending actually reflects the nature of reality, in which we will never see "the righteous forsaken, or their children begging their bread" (really? *never*?). *Lady Audley's Secret* may not offer anything approaching an analysis, explicit or implicit, of social injustice and the injustices of society to women, but it might make its best readers sufficiently uneasy that they will begin to seek such things.

Chapter 10

Middlemarch

George Eliot was among the most popular and was certainly the most respected British novelist writing in the second half of the nineteenth century. *Adam Bede* (1859) had brought her immediate and enormous success. When *Middlemarch* (1871–2) appeared, it consolidated the growing feeling that she was not only a novelist who excelled at depictions of rural life and the minds and emotions of individual characters, but an author of deep learning who was something of a philosopher and moral guide – a development that some regretted, wishing her to return to the pastoral world of her earlier fiction. In our view, she is all of these things and more, and *Middlemarch* remains the greatest single nineteenth-century British novel.

Middlemarch draws on and develops many of the concerns that have dominated the present book. Chapter 57 of *Middlemarch* begins with a scene of the Garth children reading Scott's *Ivanhoe*; its epigraph is a sonnet recounting a first encounter with *Waverley*.[1] The habit of beginning chapters with epigraphs is one Eliot drew from Scott, but his influence runs deeper than that. Eliot, like Scott, offers a meditation on what it means for individuals to live in history and for societies to progress through history. *Middlemarch* is, among other things, a careful depiction of Midlands England at the moment before the passing of the Reform Act of 1832. This provides a link not only with Scott but with Trollope's exploration of the tensions between tradition and reform. Eliot explores such matters with the fine discrimination of value we have observed in Austen, and she is alive, as Austen is, to the need to define communities of value, local and particular social institutions that support ideal human relationships, as Pemberley does in *Pride and Prejudice* and the community of naval officers does in *Persuasion*. And Eliot is just as alive as Austen to the situation of women in the actual societies in which they live.

Middlemarch explores issues of individual value and social and historical process in a setting that is largely rural, centering on a town and the surrounding countryside. The railroad is coming to Middlemarch, but it has not yet arrived. This too aligns Eliot with Scott and Austen, and it underlines an important difference between her and Dickens. *Bleak House* may depict the country estate Chesney Wold, but the heart of its matter is in the city of London, where social relations have a modern urban complexity and opacity that, as we have seen, threaten to defeat any attempt at analysis or even fictional representation. Eliot depicts a society that still seems, at least in principle, "knowable"; whether Dickens's world is knowable seems much less clear.[2] The richness with which the world of *Middlemarch* is known and depicted remains remarkable. Few novels are able to delve so deeply into individual psychology on the one hand, and social and historical process on the other. A key to this success lies in Eliot's narrator.

In discussing *Wuthering Heights*, we suggested that two of its multiple narrators define paradigmatic stances toward the experience of telling and listening to stories. Lockwood models the role of the "judicious" reader: he wants to control the telling of the story to increase his enjoyment without losing control of just how far he will allow himself to be drawn into it. Nelly, by contrast, models the role of an "involved" reader: she reacts strongly and directly as events unfold, entering the story so fully that her reactions influence its progress and outcome. Eliot's narrator seeks to make us both kinds of readers at once. She is a master of analysis, whether it be of situations or of individuals. She offers numerous frameworks for understanding the story, adducing contexts and parallels drawn from history and art and even science. All of this learning and analysis might seem likely to distance us from direct, emotional involvement. Yet she also wants to make us care about her characters and feel their plights. "Sympathy" is a cardinal virtue for Eliot: one of her purposes is to stretch our minds, hearts, and imaginations so that we will feel with the situations of others. (Here she reminds us of Gaskell, intent on creating a feeling of understanding of the Manchester poor.) To accomplish this end, Eliot's narrator employs a variety of styles and voices, sometimes summing up characters and situations with epigrammatic brevity, sometimes using language that echoes a character's own voice to reveal that character's mentality, sometimes exhorting us to pay attention, not to forget crucial aspects of a situation or judge an erring character too swiftly or too harshly or in too stereotyped a manner.

Middlemarch is a long and complex novel, which knits together (at least) four main plotlines. Yet it is a work of remarkable unity of vision, and its concerns focus most clearly on a single character, Dorothea Brooke. We will begin with Dorothea, and then consider how other characters and the plotlines they inhabit supplement the vision she creates.

"Here – now – in England": St. Theresa and Dorothea Brooke

In the early pages of *Middlemarch*, Dorothea Brooke imagines what marriage to the aging clergyman Edward Casaubon would bring:

> There would be nothing trivial about our lives. Everyday-things with us would mean the greatest things. It would be like marrying Pascal. I should learn to see the truth by the same light as great men have seen it by. And then I should know what to do, when I got older: I should see how it was possible to lead a grand life here – now – in England. (ch. 3)

A bit later, after Casaubon has proposed, Dorothea tells her uncle, with an equal measure of ardent conviction and entire naïveté, that she realizes that marriage will bring trials, and the narrator refers to her as "poor Dorothea" (ch. 4). (This language is typical of one way in which the narrator works to brings us into a gentle but firm understanding of the flaws of her characters.) Poor Dorothea indeed! She insists on marrying a man without youth, vigor, or genuine intellectual achievement – a shriveled pedant, narrow in his views and easily given to paranoid fears about his own intellectual importance, someone who will shrink from Dorothea's spiritual ardor, not to mention her strong physicality – she looks "bewitching . . . on horseback" (ch. 1) and has "powerful, feminine, maternal hands" (ch. 4) – as exhausting, unseemly, and likely to reveal his own spiritual impotence. (That his impotence is more than spiritual is suggested at a number of points, as in the reference to "this exceedingly shallow rill" that is all he can find in himself of "masculine passion" (ch. 7) or Mrs. Cadwallader's remark to Sir James that "marriage to Casaubon is as good as going to a nunnery" (ch. 6). Appreciating nineteenth-century British novels requires a sensitivity to the subtler forms of sexual reference.) Casaubon isn't a bit like Pascal, and he has nothing to do with a "grand life" in any sense. Why should we care about the problems of a character who is so deluded, and in such an odd way? How can such an extraordinary degree of blindness to obvious realities have any significance for us as readers, and especially as modern readers?

And what, in particular, are we to make of Dorothea's wish to live the "grand life here – now – in England"? If this aspiration appeared in *Vanity Fair*, we would recognize it as one more example of the vanity of human wishes and view it with a mixture of amusement and irony. Eliot's narrator registers both amusement and irony at Dorothea, whose wish to live a "grand life" in part reflects a predictable adolescent idealism arising from inexperience, but the novel ultimately makes it clear that the stakes of Dorothea's wish run deep – that, however ill-imagined, it has vital importance not just for herself but for her society and ultimately for ours.

Dorothea's wish to live a grand life raises an issue we have seen before, one we have claimed is central to the rise and significance of nineteenth-century fiction as a whole: the question of what it means to live in the "modern" (that is, post-traditional) world. *Middlemarch* opens with a "Prelude" that invokes a female figure. Though that figure is St. Theresa, not Dorothea Brooke, both women are faced with the same problem. St. Theresa did not wish to live the life of a normal aristocratic girl who read long prose romances and had her own romance, leading to conventional marriage. Instead, as a very small child, she set off to seek martyrdom for her faith. The picture Eliot's narrator paints of her and "her still smaller brother" toddling off to fight the Moors is charming; it is only right that "domestic reality . . . in the shape of uncles" should gently turn them back. But instead of growing out of her heroic visions, she found a way of realizing them. Her ability to do so depended upon the existence, in her time, of a "coherent social faith and order which could perform the function of knowledge for the ardently willing soul." This is something that "later-born Theresas" (that is to say, women like Dorothea who wish to live a heroic life that will make a difference in the world at large) cannot draw upon.

But what, exactly, is a "coherent social faith and order which could perform the function of knowledge for the ardently willing soul"? One way to approach this question is to recall the notion of "organic" society raised in our discussion of Scott. When Waverley visits the Highlands and enters Fergus MacIvor's feasting hall, he sees before him a social organism in which every individual has a natural place. All are ranked on a smoothly descending and ascending scale that knits them together. They think of themselves as the descendents of a single individual; they share the same legendary history (which for them is no legend), with its heroes, loyalties, and goals. They are one with their clan and with the landscape in which they have lived for immemorial ages.

When the narrator points to St. Theresa's convent, she is summoning up a similar organic community from a later period of human development, one that is organized not around the blood of the clan but around religious faith and doctrine. Both the clan and the convent offer a way of being in the world that is unified from top to bottom, that makes coherent sense of the thoughts, experiences, and actions of those who partake in it, a way of life in which all the parts are mutually supportive. In a convent, time is organized in a way that articulates the day into a succession of religious observances, space is organized in a way that is conducive to a focus on the worship of God, and so on. Such environments must remain imperfect because they are human, but they would help St. Theresas, ancient and modern, to focus their energies on what the Prelude describes as "some object which would never justify weariness, which would reconcile self-despair with the rapturous consciousness of life beyond self." ("Self-despair" would arise, presumably, from one's recognition that one cannot escape being unworthy of the object one is focusing on, just because it is important enough to be *worth* focusing on.) What was truly remarkable about St. Theresa (and this must be why she is the heroine of the Prelude) is that she was a woman who was famous both for her ecstatic mystical visions and also for her practical, this-worldly success in reforming the day-to-day life of an order of nuns. To achieve both of these things would suggest that St. Theresa must indeed have lived a life that was for her unified in all its aspects, from the minutely mundane ("a grand life *here – now – in England*") to the transcendently spiritual ("*a grand life* here – now – in England").

St. Theresa was doubly exemplary, then, in that she not only lived a "grand life" but created a conventual environment that would allow others to do so (to be sure, in a way less grand than hers). Modern-day St. Theresas such as Dorothea Brooke, sadly, are faced with a much greater challenge in identifying "an object that would never justify weariness" in the first place to achieve. For people in the modern world, life is in pieces. We cannot join our spiritual lives with our daily lives in a seamless way, as St. Theresa did, partly because we no longer have a unified spiritual and intellectual vision capable of bringing all parts of life into a single focus. Unlike St. Theresa, we lack a "coherent social faith and order which could perform the function of knowledge [not faith or emotion, but *knowledge*] for the ardently willing soul." This is why the narrator states, in the "Finale" with which *Middlemarch* ends, that "A new Theresa will hardly have the opportunity of reforming a conventual life, any more than a new Antigone will spend her heroic piety in daring all for the sake of a brother's burial: the medium in which their ardent deeds took shape is for ever gone." Instead of reforming a religious order (with its convents or religious "houses"), Dorothea is reduced to drawing amateurish diagrams of houses for the laborers on her uncle's estate, and then trying to persuade the men around her to build them. In the final scenes of the novel, Dorothea is still trying to solve this same basic problem: we find her trying (and failing) to decide how she can use her inherited wealth to help society at large.

The novel's Prelude, then, evokes the plight of human beings after the coming of modernity. To be sure, as we read the Prelude to *Middlemarch*, we experience a remarkable attempt at unified vision in Eliot's own mixture of storytelling (the picture of the toddling children) and philosophy (how many novels in their opening paragraphs tackle such issues as the lack of a "coherent social faith and order which would perform the function of know-ledge"?). It may be that the only rival to St. Theresa is the novel's narrator.

For all its universal philosophical scope, the Prelude to *Middlemarch* also points to something quite particular, the plight of women. This plight seems to have existed before the coming of modernity, but it had at least one escape-hatch. The religious order St. Theresa joined and reformed allowed her to elude the "social conquests of a brilliant girl" and escape marriage. The Protestant society that surrounds Dorothea Brooke offers no such refuge. *Middlemarch* takes a penetrating look at the difficulties society creates for women who have "ardently willing souls" – and at how society prevents its members (and espe-cially its female members) from having ardent wishes in the first place.

Despite the obstacles modernity and gender create, and despite the excess-ive and even absurd results that sometimes follow (Dorothea's delusions about Casaubon, for instance), it remains crucial in Eliot's eyes that we, or at least some of us, continue to strive to live what Dorothea describes, without really understanding what she is describing, as "the grand life."[3] In the final para-graph of the novel, the narrator tells us that "the growing good of the world is partly dependent on unhistoric acts; and that things are not so ill with you and me as they might have been, is half owing to the number who lived faithfully a hidden life, and rest in unvisited tombs." One suggestion here is that the world can grow better and that things can be less ill for us than they otherwise would, even if the "historic" acts that used to be performed by heroic figures such as St. Theresa have become more difficult. Part of the faith-fulness of those who "lived faithfully a hidden life" comes from wishes that, in their ardent intensity, point beyond current social norms. Despite Dorothea's delusions about what marriage to Casaubon will mean, then, there is much to respect in her wish to "lead the grand life." In deciding to marry Casaubon, Dorothea is looking for too simple a solution to the problem of heroic action in the modern world. We may smile at her (as we smile at St. Theresa and her brothers toddling out to fight the Moors), but her impulse nonetheless deserves our respect.

Dorothea, Jewels, and the Squirrel's Heartbeat

Dorothea's ardent nature is admirable, but in the opening pages of the novel it becomes clear that she lacks a deep knowledge of others and of herself. Part of the problem, again, is the "medium" in which she exists, the kinds of knowledge available to her as a provincial gentlewoman living when she does. Our first glimpse of her comes in a scene in which her considerably less ardent sister Celia coaxes her into dividing their dead mother's jewelry. Through much of the scene, Dorothea acts the part of one who is ostentatiously uninterested in such things. She hands the pieces of jewelry over, one by one, to Celia with an aura of superiority: she is above such material things, even if Celia is not. But suddenly one set of jewels captures her: " 'How very beautiful these gems are!' said Dorothea, under a new current of feeling, as sudden as a gleam. 'It is strange how deeply colours seem to penetrate one, like scent. I suppose that is the reason why gems are used as spiritual emblems in the Revelation of St. John. They look like fragments of heaven' " (ch. 1). We discover that Dorothea can be intensely alive to sensuous things (the color of the jewels "penetrates" her as if it were perfume). But Dorothea has no way of understanding and accepting this aspect of her self: she must immediately turn to spiritual abstractions. The lack of what we might call a "vocabulary" for understanding her own feelings and desires helps lead her to marry Casaubon. (This might seem a grave punishment for a slight deficiency.) More serious, in Eliot's eyes, is Dorothea's inability to feel her way into the minds and souls of others. With Casaubon, she simply projects her wishes onto him. As a result, she utterly misreads his true nature. This is a particularly dangerous error for someone with an ardent nature.

Dorothea is hardly alone, for egoism is a problem Eliot takes to be a basic part of the human condition. But Dorothea is unusual in the extent to which she comes to rise above it, as a result of the "trials" her marriage with Casaubon brings. We will not pause to trace the stages of this process here, though its depiction remains one of the great achievements of British fiction. We will instead content ourselves with quoting a narratorial comment directed (as many such comments are) as much to us as to Dorothea, at a crucial stage in the process, the moment when Dorothea first grasps that "she had been under a wild illusion in expecting a response to her feeling from Mr. Casaubon":

> We are all of us born in moral stupidity, taking the world as an udder to feed our supreme selves: Dorothea had early begun to emerge from that stupidity, but yet it had been easier to her to imagine how she would devote herself to Mr. Casaubon, and become wise and strong in his strength and wisdom, than to conceive with that distinctness which is no longer reflection but feeling – an idea wrought back to the directness of sense, like the solidity of objects – that he had an equivalent centre of self, whence the lights and shadows must always fall with a certain difference. (ch. 21)

Given the breadth and depth of her knowledge and the quality and variety of her interests, one sometimes wonders why Eliot chose to be a novelist, and not, say, a philosopher. Perhaps one reason is her belief in how important it is that ethical perceptions acquire in all of us "the directness of sense, like the solidity of objects" – a directness that fiction at its best can make live in the imagination of its readers.

What Dorothea ultimately gains with regard to Casaubon is a full imaginative sympathy. This is a remarkable achievement. But as much as Eliot values it, she recognizes that even this virtue can have its dangers – particularly for a woman. When Dorothea ceases to project her own wishes and needs onto Casaubon and sees him for the narrow, frightened man he is, her ardent nature prevents her from turning away from him and his needs. Casaubon has centered his whole existence on writing a vast theological treatise that in fact will never and can never be completed, because it is based upon ideas without substance. He has huge files of notes, but the notes will never add up to a book, and Dorothea (despite the flimsiness of her gentlewoman's education and her deep wish that Casaubon succeed) comes to realize this. On some level far beneath consciousness, even Casaubon must know this, for he keeps putting off any attempt to produce the book, until his realization that he is near death pushes him to a final desperate effort. In a last, pitiful attempt to delude himself, he tries to prepare Dorothea to complete his book after his death, and then asks her to promise to follow his wishes. Casaubon's plan is a criminal example of the egoism Dorothea has largely transcended, for had Dorothea once agreed to finish his work, being Dorothea she would have carried out this promise, even though few things could be more depressing than spending the waking hours of a long life working on a project that you don't believe in and that can't possibly succeed. In weighing her husband's request for an unconditional promise to carry out his wishes, then, Dorothea thus finds herself in an impossible dilemma, and so does the reader. We want her to remain the faithful, generous person she has become (which would mean making the promise to Casaubon), but we do not want her to ruin the rest of her life (which would mean refusing). There is simply no answer to such a dilemma. And so George Eliot allows Dorothea and the reader to have it both ways. Dorothea maintains her faithfulness by *deciding* to promise to fulfill Casaubon's wishes, but before she can actually *make* the promise to him, he suddenly dies.

What are we to make of this turn of events? In another novel, we might simply identify it as clumsy melodrama, but here, more is at stake. On one level, it comes as a response to a problem Eliot earlier identifies in another one of her brief, brilliant authorial commentaries on egoism. There she reminds us that even predictable, "normal" moments of human suffering matter, even though

---

we do not expect people to be deeply moved by what is not unusual. That element of tragedy which lies in the very fact of frequency, has not yet wrought itself into the coarse emotions of mankind; and perhaps our frames could hardly bear much of it. If we had a keen vision and feeling of all ordinary human life, it would be like hearing the grass grow and the squirrel's heart beat, and we should die of that roar which lies on the other side of silence. As it is, the quickest of us walk about well wadded with stupidity. (ch. 20)

This is a complex passage. Clearly enough, being "well wadded with stupidity" is not a state we are meant to admire: the main impetus of the passage is to goad us into being more sensitive to all kinds of human tragedy, even those that are "usual." Eliot is exhorting us to discard the wadding that blunts our perceptions. Yet the reminder that "we should die of that roar which lies on the other side of silence" is arresting, too: we would be of no use to anyone if we succumbed to the roar. Dorothea's ardent nature tends to lead her to excess, including the "death" of sacrificing oneself entirely to the needs of others. In this regard, it seems particularly important to recall that Dorothea is a woman. There is surely an implicit critique here of the "sacrificial" role assigned to women in marriage. What man would feel bound in the way Dorothea feels bound? Which is not to say that her capacity for ardent devotion is simply mistaken. In more general terms, the impasse that Dorothea faces with regard to promising away her future to Casaubon raises the quite profound issue of just how sensitive we ought to be to the suffering of others – and for that matter to the existence of others. It is immoral to be "stupid"; it is pointless to be dead. It seems likely that Eliot leads Dorothea to this impossible situation and then allows her an implausible escape precisely to underline the intractability of the issues it raises.

"How should I act now, this very day . . . ?" Sympathy and Action

Dorothea's achievement of a sympathetic understanding of Casaubon is quietly heroic, but Eliot demands even more than that of admirable characters – and of us as readers. The moment when Dorothea comes closest to living a "grand life" and achieving a state of being in which knowledge, faith, and action coalesce for her as they did for St. Theresa involves her ultimate reaction to something that at first presents itself to her as a sordid bit of sexual misbehavior, the sort of thing that would fit nicely into a sensation novel.

When Dorothea accidentally discovers Will in what appears to be a compromising situation with Lydgate's wife, she faces a crisis greater even than that posed by the earlier discovery that her own marriage was a disastrous mistake. The discovery is harrowing for Dorothea; it bites into her consciousness. It fills her with revulsion because it seems to cheapen Will and sully her own affection for him, yet the jealous rage she feels also reveals to her what she has previously avoided knowing: that she is (or was) deeply in love with Will. Dorothea spends a terrible night wrestling with her feelings. In time, her angry outrage subsides, and another current of thought and feeling takes its place:

[S]he was no longer wrestling with her grief, but could sit down with it as a lasting companion and make it a sharer in her thoughts. For now the thoughts came thickly. It was not in Dorothea's nature, for longer than the duration of a paroxysm, to sit in the narrow cell of her calamity, in the besotted misery of a consciousness that sees another's lot as an accident of its own.

She began now to live through that yesterday morning deliberately again, forcing herself to dwell on every detail and its possible meaning. Was she alone in that scene? Was it her event only? She forced herself to think of it as bound up with another woman's life – a woman towards whom she had set out with a longing to carry some clearness and comfort into her beclouded youth. . . . All the active thought with which she had before been representing to herself the trials of Lydgate's lot, and this young marriage union which, like her own [marriage to Casaubon before his death], seemed to have its hidden as well as evident troubles – all this vivid sympathetic experience returned to her now as a power: it asserted itself as acquired knowledge asserts itself and will not let us see as we saw in the day of our ignorance. She said to her own irremediable grief, that it should make her more helpful, instead of driving her back from effort.

And what sort of crisis might not this be in the three lives whose contact with hers laid an obligation on her as if they had been suppliants bearing the sacred branch? The objects of her rescue were not to be sought out by her fancy: they were chosen for her. She yearned towards the perfect Right, that it should make a throne within her, and rule her errant will. "What should I do – how should I act now, this very day if I could clutch my own pain, and compel it to silence, and think of these three!"

It had taken long for her to come to that question, and there was light piercing into the room. She opened her curtains, and looked out towards the bit of road that lay in view, with fields beyond, outside the entrance-gates. On the road there was a man with a bundle on his back and a woman carrying her baby; in the field she could see figures moving – perhaps the shepherd with his dog. Far off in the bending sky was the pearly light; and she felt the largeness of the world and the manifold wakings of men to labour and endurance. She was a part of that involuntary, palpitating life, and could neither look out on it from her luxurious shelter as a mere spectator, nor hide her eyes in selfish complaining.

What she would resolve to do that day did not yet seem quite clear, but something that she could achieve stirred her as with an approaching murmur which would soon gather distinctness. . . . [A]t eleven o'clock she was walking towards Middlemarch, having made up her mind that she would make as quietly and unnoticeably as possible her second attempt to see and save Rosamond. (ch. 80)

When the narrator tells us that it was not in Dorothea's nature "to see another's lot as an accident of [her] own," she is drawing on a quite precise philosophical terminology, in which an "accident" is "that which has no independent or self-sufficient existence, but only inheres in a substance."[4] What Dorothea is doing, then, is once again to overcome her egotism by granting to Will and Rosamond their own independent validity, their "equivalent centre[s] of self, whence the lights and shadows must always fall with a certain difference." She then goes about imagining Rosamond and Will and their centers of self quite deliberately, forcing herself to dwell on the scene as a whole and on what it might mean and how it might be saved, instead of simply recoiling from the pain it brings her. In doing this, she is building her perceptions into knowledge, and is thus operating in the realm of what the philosophers call epistemology, but it is an epistemology shot through with emotion, one that evokes Will's definition in Rome of a "poet" as one for whom "knowledge passes instantaneously into feeling, and feeling flashes back as a new organ of knowledge" (ch. 22). In Dorothea's case, the feeling is "all [the] vivid sympathetic experience" which "returned to her now as a power," and "asserted itself as acquired knowledge returns to us, and will not let us see as we saw in the days of our ignorance." She has indeed learned to conceive of the other consciousnesses in this scene "with that distinctness which is no longer reflection but feeling – an idea wrought back to the directness of sense, like the solidity of objects."

This is a good moment to pause and reflect on the relationship between Eliot's authorial narrator and her most admirable characters. Eliot's narrator, like any authorial narrator, has the privilege of seeing into the thoughts and feelings of multiple characters, a privilege none of us can actually enjoy in real life. But the intellectual and emotional work – and it is hard, exhausting, painful *work* – we see Dorothea engaging in here is actually remarkably like the work Eliot must perform to write *Middlemarch*: Dorothea is using her imagination to project the thoughts and feelings of a variety of characters different from herself, to construct and imaginatively experience the same scene from different perspectives. Like the narrator at the opening of chapter 29, Dorothea stops herself in the midst of focusing on her own feelings to ask "but why always Dorothea?" In doing so, she draws on all her experience and understanding of real life, but she does so to produce what is ultimately a work of her imagination. That her imaginative creation is wrong in at least one key respect (Will is not actually romantically interested in Rosamond) is beside the point:

it is the quality of thought and feeling in her effort that matters. Similarly, what Eliot asks of her readers is not acquiescence in any God-like comprehensiveness of vision, but an effort to engage in acts of sympathetic imagination comparable to Dorothea's.

Dorothea's imaginative leap toward a sympathetic understanding of characters who have just wounded her deeply is impressive, but in and of itself it is insufficient. In Rome, she had responded to Will's attempt to define poets simply by the quality of their thought and feeling by suggesting that poets must actually produce poems (ch. 22). Similarly, the knowledge Dorothea creates here functions, not as an end in itself, but as the necessary prelude to the crucial moment when she decides to move from the realm of knowledge to that of action and the will. It is significant that, at the moment of transition between knowing and acting, Dorothea looks out of the window of her bedroom and sees indistinct human figures beginning another day of "labour and endurance." Dorothea, as a modern, can no longer draw on a "coherent social faith and order which could perform the function of knowledge for [her] ardently willing soul," but in this case, something less substantial suffices – a necessarily vague but nonetheless powerful recognition that she is "part of [the] involuntary, palpitating life" in the world that stretches beyond the walls of her estate, joined with a sympathetic understanding of the plight of Will and Rosamond, as individual human beings with whose fates she finds herself entangled and for whom she feels responsible.

The result is not the epic reform of a conventual order, but instead a walk to Middlemarch and a conversation with Rosamond, but it remains a result that matters, a step toward redefining the "grand life" which Dorothea had naïvely imagined would be hers simply by marrying Casaubon. In the event, Dorothea is richly rewarded for her selfless generosity in trying to "save" the woman she believes has forever destroyed her happiness with Will. Even the utterly egoistical Rosamond is moved by Dorothea's selflessness. Dorothea's goodness invades Rosamond's center of self, transforming her for the moment so that she is moved to explain to Dorothea that Will had not betrayed her but instead remains deeply in love with her. The result is that the marriage Dorothea had always supposed would be impossible takes place, to her great joy.

Dorothea's marriage is a joy to her and to Will, but it has not been a joy to some readers of *Middlemarch*. As usual, Eliot is there before us, if we feel disappointed that Dorothea dwindled into a wife instead of entering into something more dramatically recognizable as a "grand life." In the novel's Finale, the narrator tells us that "Many who knew her, thought it a pity that so substantive and rare a creature should have been absorbed into the life of another, and be only known in a certain circle as a wife and mother. But no one stated exactly what else that was in her power she ought rather to have done." (The key words here, as we'll see more fully in a moment, are "what else *that was in her power* she ought rather to have done.") It is natural enough to feel a sense of regret with regard to Dorothea's fate, but it is important to recognize that the full meaning and effect of the novel depend upon the creation of such feelings of regret at lost opportunity, which extends to characters other than Dorothea. To understand why, it will be useful to turn to the other major characters in the novel, beginning with Lydgate, the man Dorothea was trying to help when she entered Rosamond's drawing room and found her with Will.

"Spots of commonness": Lydgate and Rosamond

Middlemarch, like *Vanity Fair* and *Bleak House*, is what has come to be called a multiplot novel; in less neutral terms, Henry James called such works, which lack a single plot and point of view to give them unity, "large loose baggy monsters."[5] The plotline we have been following, the one involving Dorothea, is one of four in the novel. These intersect, but never coalesce. What gives the novel its artistic unity? On the deepest level, that unity no doubt arises from the unified vision of the author. A more proximate source of unity is thematic. Central to three of the main storylines is a figure who, like Dorothea, is attempting to live a grand life, and though the fourth (the one involving the Garths) lacks such a figure, it presents a studied and symmetrical alternative to that enterprise.

At one point in the novel, Dorothea Brooke, in response to a well-meaning figure who wishes to persuade her to lead a more "normal" life, states calmly, "I never called everything by the same name that all the people about me did" (ch. 54). Tertius Lydgate has sparks of the same sort of originality and defiance of the normal; he too aspires to lead what Dorothea would call the "grand life." His vision of a grand life involves his profession, medicine. He adopts that profession in defiance of social convention (which at this period considered it insufficiently respectable for a man of his social antecedents), because he has sufficient curiosity and intellectual power to be fascinated by the idea of making scientific discoveries, and because he wishes to make people healthier. He settles in the relatively small community of Middlemarch in preference to London, believing that in London he would be drawn into the politics of his profession and a competition for patients that would hamper his pursuit of scientific discoveries and practical medical reforms. For a while, he succeeds with both projects in Middlemarch. He pursues his medical experiments, he refuses to dispense drugs (this was for his period an important step forward; it eliminated a conflict of interest), and he sets in motion a forward-looking plan for a fever hospital to cope with an impending invasion of cholera. By the end of the novel, however, Lydgate is forced to leave Middlemarch in disgrace. He subsequently abandons medical research and settles into a lucrative medical practice at a spa. There he publishes a treatise, not on the fundamentally important "primitive tissue" he had hoped to discover, but instead on a rich person's disease, gout.

Why does Lydgate fail? In the case of Dorothea, we are told that the "medium" that might have allowed her to become another St. Theresa no longer exists. With Lydgate, the problem seems to be the other side of the same coin: he is overwhelmed by the *wrong* social medium, succumbing to "the hampering threadlike pressure of small social conditions, and their frustrating complexity" (ch. 18), "the small solicitations of circumstance" (ch. 79). Lydgate discovers that the accumulated force of traditional medical practice, the small-town prejudices of the inhabitants of Middlemarch, and the demands of his wife create a current that he lacks the strength to swim against. Yet the core problem does not involve the social forces that oppose him, formidable as they turn out to be. What matters most are what the narrator refers to as his own "spots of commonness."

Though Lydgate is seeking in his medical research to discover a "primitive tissue" that underlies and unifies all life-forms, his own mental life is sharply partitioned. "Lydgate's spots of commonness," the narrator tells us,

lay in the complexion of his prejudices, which, in spite of noble intentions and sympathy, were half of them such as are found in ordinary men of the world: that distinction of mind which belonged to his intellectual ardour, did not penetrate his feeling and judgment about furniture, or women, or the desirability of its being known (without his telling) that he was better born than other country surgeons. (ch. 15)

Lydgate runs himself into debt, not because he is extravagant, but because he simply assumes that everyone who is anyone maintains a certain material standard of living (including excellent furniture in the dining room and lovely jewelry for his wife) – even though that standard of living is something he cannot afford, in part because he is unwilling to adopt some of the dubious medical practices (such as dispensing drugs) that other doctors employ to increase their incomes.

The demands and machinations of the wife Lydgate marries in Middlemarch are particularly deadly to his aspirations. When he comes to Middlemarch, he decides that achieving his goals will mean setting aside any thought of marriage for years, until he has established himself. But the attractions of Rosamond Vincy prove irresistible. Rosamond is everything a woman is, by conventional standards, supposed to be. She has an "infantine" blonde beauty, blue eyes, and exquisite manners. (As a fine example of how the narrator conveys judgments in what might seem to be neutral language, consider her description of Rosamond's "infantine blondness and wondrous crown of hair-plaits, with her pale-blue dress of a fit and fashion so perfect that no dressmaker could look at it without emotion, a large embroidered collar which it was to be hoped all beholders would know the price of, her small hands duly set off with rings, and that controlled self-consciousness of manner which is the expensive substitute for simplicity," ch. 43). What Lydgate comes to discover, to his cost, is that she also has an iron will and feels herself perfectly justified in ignoring his wishes whenever it suits her to do so, secure in the belief that her perfectly formed sentences and plans are always correct. The centers of self of others do not concern her; thus the narrator tells us that when Lydgate is beginning his romance with her, "Rosamond, in fact, was entirely occupied not exactly with Tertius Lydgate as he was in himself, but with his relation to her" (ch. 16). She wishes to lead a life that is in every respect conventional and "proper" – a life far removed from the one a medical reformer at the opening of his career could afford.

By the end of the novel, Lydgate finds himself faced with the same sort of insoluble dilemma that Dorothea faced with regard to finishing Casaubon's book. He realizes that his duty to Rosamond demands that he abandon his work in Middlemarch, which he fears will mean giving up his hopes of championing medical reform. (His fears, as we've seen, are fulfilled: in later years, when his temper frays, he bitterly remarks that Rosamond has been to him like the basil plant in a poem by Keats – something that thrives wonderfully on a dead man's brains.) Eliot does not step in to save him from this fate by arranging a providential death for Rosamond: Casaubon dies, but Rosamond lives. Why is Lydgate less favored? One reason is that Lydgate simply doesn't deserve intervention in the way that Dorothea does. Her dilemma arises entirely from her best qualities, her sympathy and generosity and imagination. His does not. There is an important way in which Lydgate deserves what he gets. Eliot finds the gender stereotypes embodied in Lydgate's view of women reprehensible. His initial view of Dorothea is particularly damaging: "She did not look at things from the proper feminine angle. The society of such women was about as relaxing as going from your work to teach the second form [that is, young schoolboys], instead of reclining in a paradise with sweet laughs for bird-notes, and blue eyes for a heaven." Eliot's animosity also appears to extend to Rosamond and women like her: there is something breathtaking in the way in which the narrator refuses to allow Rosamond to possess even a grain of her own generosity, even in the scene in which she "saves" Dorothea from her mistake about Will Ladislaw. Rosamond's apparent generosity turns out to be drawn from her as a kind of reflex by Dorothea's higher and nobler nature. Apparently a woman who embraces the female stereotypes as readily as Rosamond needs to be, so to speak, pumped up by the nobility of a better sort of woman, which invades her like an alien presence, forces her to do the right thing, and then leaves her in her former blindness.

But it won't do to accuse Eliot of simple prejudice against conventional women. Dorothea's sister, Celia, is depicted with great indulgence and affection. Though Celia's views of men and women are entirely conventional, they are made to seem charmingly so, as in her memorable statement that "men know best about everything, except what women know better . . . Well, I mean about babies and those things" (ch. 72). Celia is given a number of memorable lines, among them her response to her husband's angry outburst that he should have called Ladislaw out and shot him: "Really, James, that would have been very disagreeable" (ch. 84).

It is worth adding that Lydgate comes to appreciate Dorothea more adequately. By the end of the novel, he remarks to himself, in wonder at Dorothea's sympathetic trust in him, that "she seems to have what I never saw in any woman before – a fountain of friendship towards men – a man can make a friend of her. . . . Well, her love might help a man more than her money" (ch. 76). Many readers have wondered just why it is that his enlightenment cannot come sooner, for his good and Dorothea's. Why not arrange things so that the two of them can marry? They are ideally suited for one another, since they both wish to change the world for the better. This question is a variant on another frequent complaint. Why couldn't Dorothea grow up to be George Eliot, or someone like her? Why must Dorothea become simply someone's wife, and (as the Prelude puts it) "foundress of nothing"? To answer these questions, we need to turn to the topic of reform.

"The growing good of the world": Progress and Reform

Middlemarch is set during the period leading to the Reform Act of 1832. This Act was a significant step in the coming of modernity to British government. It was the beginning of a process that led the English Parliament to become more democratic in its membership. (Members of Parliament had hitherto been selected according to districts created in the middle ages, with no adjustment being made to reflect shifting population patterns, so that large cities in the North of England that had come into being as a result of the Industrial

Revolution had no representation at all, whereas Old Sarum, which had lost its population entirely, sent two members to Parliament.) One of Eliot's purposes in *Middlemarch* is to explore how it is that reform and progress can occur, now that the "medium" that allowed figures like St. Theresa to act in heroic and far-reaching ways no longer exists.

Given the lives portrayed in the novel, the idea that progress is possible at all can seem surprising. For the novel abounds in failed projects of one kind or another. Dorothea wants to live "the grand life," but she fails. Lydgate wants to make great scientific discoveries, but he fails. Casaubon is pursuing a grand scheme, his search for the key to all religious mythologies. His is the most obviously doomed project – its methods were hopelessly out of date long before he began it – but it bears an uncomfortable resemblance to Lydgate's search for the primitive tissue that underlies all life-forms, a forward-looking project which we must respect as a failed part of a larger enterprise that will indeed bear fruit in the long run, the spectacular advance of medical and scientific knowledge that began in the nineteenth century and shows no sign of abating today. Why does *Middlemarch* insist on the failure of grand projects and aspirations? Why couldn't Lydgate be another Florence Nightingale, to cite a real person who, several decades after the period in which *Middlemarch* is set, made a huge difference in combating disease by improving hospital practice? Why does Eliot seem bent on creating a mood of what Raymond Williams has called, echoing a phrase in the novel that describes Lydgate's attitude at its end, "sad resignation"?[6]

Let's return to politics. As it happened, though the Reform Act of 1832 was a step forward, like most political reforms it failed to produce the dramatic results its proponents had hoped for. Eliot's narrator reminds us of this in describing Will's future career: "Will became an ardent public man, working well in those times when reforms were begun with a young hopefulness of immediate good which has been much checked in our days" (Finale). For anyone who has observed political affairs, recent and not so recent, a muted sense of possibility is hard to escape. But a certain kind of realism about politics and life is not all that is in play in the novel's sober tone. It's not that Eliot believes that change cannot come and is not necessary; it's rather that she believes that heroic individuals cannot make progress occur by themselves, and particularly that she wishes to discourage the non-heroic from feeling we can leave the job of making the world better to others.

One of Eliot's central concerns in *Middlemarch* is to allow the reader to experience the nature and the power of the social fabric surrounding us all. She wants us to become aware of that power, so that we will be motivated to do what we can to create a social "medium" that will allow developments such as the Reform Act of 1832 to have an actual and positive effect in social practice.

Few of us can become Florence Nightingales, but all of us, in one way or another, produce and reproduce the general fabric of society, for good or ill. It is with this in mind that the narrator suggests, in the Finale, that the medium that allowed heroic individuals such as St. Theresa to perform their heroic deeds may be "for ever gone," but then adds that "we insignificant people with our daily words and acts are preparing the lives of many Dorotheas, some of which may present a far sadder sacrifice than that of the Dorothea whose story we know" (Finale).

Middlemarch, then, has good reasons for refusing to depict heroic success. The purpose of Eliot's art is to open our eyes to the complexities of life in history, and especially to urge us to pass beyond our own inherent egoism, so that we can make a non-heroic but nonetheless real contribution to what we must all hope will turn out to be "the growing good of the world." At the very least (to turn to the formulation Eliot balances against "the growing good of the world"), we will help create a situation in which "things are not so ill with you and me as they might have been" (Finale). She has set herself a complex task. She must create a sense of difficulty that will be sobering but ultimately energizing, that will make us want to avoid the narrowness of Casaubon and the spots of commonness of Lydgate (not to mention the deadly combination of conventionality and egoism we find in Rosamond), without taking a despairing view of the importance of striving for the good.

Dorothea's marriage to Will Ladislaw, though it is from one point of view a "sacrifice," helps to provide an answer to this problem. Some readers complain that Will is a shadowy figure. We never see him *accomplish* anything substantial, before or after he becomes an "ardent public man." But his very vagueness helps to allow him to serve as a symbol of possibility. He lacks the concentration and seriousness, not to mention the genius, of a true artist such as Naumann, but his love of beauty and pleasure adds a cheerful sensuousness to Dorothea's future that is hopeful and welcome. At one point in the novel, the narrator mentions Will's delight in acting as a kind of benevolent pied piper, leading "a troop of droll children" on "gypsy excursions" (ch. 46). This note of boyish exuberance is welcome in a novel that can tend toward sober, philosophical didacticism beneath the extraordinary richness of its depiction of character and situation.

Will Ladislaw's smile was delightful, unless you were angry with him beforehand: it was a gush of inward light illuminating the transparent skin as well as the eyes, and playing about every curve and line as if some Ariel were touching them with a new charm. . . . When he turned his head quickly his hair seemed to shake out light, and some persons thought they saw decided genius in this coruscation. (ch. 21)

We may not quite believe in the "genius" (and the narrator leaves room for us to suppose that she might not, either), but there is something attractive about the light Will brings with him.

On a more substantial and serious level, we find ourselves heartened about the possibility of a "growing good of the world" when we discover the capacity of some characters to rise to levels of personal generosity we would hardly have believed possible. Setting aside the Florence Nightingales of this world allows Eliot to remind us of how much ordinary people can accomplish. An example is the wife of Nicholas Bulstrode.

"Who can represent himself just as he is, even in his own reflections?" Bulstrode

Nicholas Bulstrode is one of Eliot's rarest achievements. One can imagine the merciless glee Dickens would take in depicting a successful banker and strict, pontificating Evangelical Christian who turns out to be linked with the receiving of stolen goods. The picture the novel paints of Bulstrode grows darker than this: it comes to include murder, when Bulstrode disobeys Lydgate's orders and allows folk medicine to be applied to Raffles, a dangerously ill man whose death he greatly wishes, and Raffles dies. The novel's judgment of Bulstrode is stern and unsparing, yet it is also compassionate and deeply wise, as it unfolds the gradual steps by which the contradictory aspects of his character evolve. We will not retrace this process, but instead will comment briefly on how Bulstrode fits into the larger patterns of the novel.

Bulstrode is, to begin with, yet another figure who tries to lead a grand life. The narrator tells us that Bulstrode had "aimed at being an eminent Christian" (ch. 53). We have seen that Dorothea's failure to lead a grand life results from the lack of a social medium that would support her efforts, the unavailability of a "coherent social faith and order which could perform the function of knowledge for the ardently willing soul." Lydgate, who also fails to lead a grand life, falls victim to the social prejudices he unthinkingly accepts, his "spots of commonness." In the case of Bulstrode, similar elements appear, but in different guises. Where Lydgate is largely unaware of the patterns of belief that help to undo him, Bulstrode is obsessively concerned with a narrow religious doctrine that blinds him to his need for power and pre-eminence. He twists a brand of evangelical piety so that it allows him to imagine that whatever he does is done because God wills it. This is not a simple, self-serving hypocrisy that he can simply discard at will: when things begin to go wrong, he concludes that God has found him wanting and is casting him out. We might say that

Bulstrode fails to become an "eminent Christian" because he attempts to find in his narrow religious ideology the sort of "coherent faith and doctrine" that no longer arises from the social fabric that surrounds him. We see here the danger inherent in allowing any faith to "perform the function of knowledge." With Bulstrode, the faith he relies on comes to *substitute* for the valid knowledge that would arise from an interplay with external reality. In discussing Bulstrode, the narrator reminds us that the weakness of this kind of thinking can infect any kind of faith, religious or secular. "There is no general doctrine which is not capable of eating out our morality if unchecked by the deep-seated habit of direct fellow-feeling with individual fellow-men" (ch. 61). (This, by the way, is why the narrator speaks of Dorothea's lack of a "coherent *social* faith and order": the "faiths" devised by individuals without a larger social dimension are perilous.) The reader will notice here yet another demonstration of the crucial importance of sympathetic imagination of the sort Dorothea achieves when she realizes that Casaubon has his own "centre of self." Bulstrode demonstrates that the stakes of a lack of sympathetic intelligence can be high, extending to complicity in murder – something that should come as no surprise to those who have seen the effects rigid political ideologies can have in our own world.

The fate of Bulstrode is chilling, but it is relieved by a moment of rare and beautiful nobility from an unlikely source. Throughout the novel, his wife, Harriet, has been portrayed as a woman with an "honest ostentatious nature" (ch. 74), much given to public piety and much satisfied with the size and decoration of her hats. There seems no reason to expect anything heroic from *her*. Yet when she learns of her husband's disgrace after a confused account leaks out of his role in the death of Raffles, she surprises us. In one of the most moving scenes in the nineteenth-century novel, instead of rebuking him or forsaking him, she simply comes down from her room (after having changed her "ostentatious" clothes to the plain clothes of an "early Methodist") and standing beside her husband (who sits with averted gaze, sick with fear that she will never again look at him with affection), lets him know that she will not forsake him. She simply says, "solemnly but kindly – 'Look up, Nicholas'" (ch. 74). This is the kind of action, the novel seems to be telling us, from which "the growing good of the world" must proceed. It means that, for Bulstrode at least, "things are not so ill . . . as they might have been."

"Things hang together": The Garths

Middlemarch is, on one level, about history. In attempting to imagine how the world might grow better without depending on heroic figures, the novel is dealing, in a forward-looking way, with the issue central to Scott's fiction: how cultures turn historical corners as the past gives way to the present and leads to the future. The character in *Middlemarch* with the strongest connection to the novel's future (and Eliot's own present) is Caleb Garth, for we see Caleb surveying land for the building of a railroad, and nothing did more to bring on the modern age in Victorian England than railroads. Yet Caleb also belongs to an earlier world. Eliot goes out of her way to cut Garth off from any connection with the capitalist economic system that underwrote the growth of the railways. To use terms Marx made famous, Caleb understands only "use value" (what you can actually do with goods and services). He cannot grasp "exchange value" (the system of commodity and labor prices on which capitalism depends). The narrator tells us that Caleb "knew values well, but he had no keenness of imagination for monetary results in the shape of profit and loss" (ch. 24). Use value is appropriate for the smaller, face-to-face social units characteristic of the world before the coming of modernity. Eliot, it's worth adding, is not sentimental about Caleb's lack of "keenness of imagination" about profit and loss; it leads him to involve himself in Fred Vincy's financial difficulties in a way that is deeply damaging to his own family. But (to adopt a locution Caleb himself likes to use) "things hang together": in the long run, Caleb's interest in "real" value is appreciated by others, increased employment results, and his financial problem is solved. His sense of value also leads him to redeem Fred Vincy. Caleb, in short, somehow more than survives being split between a simpler past and the technological forces that are ushering in a new age.

Why do things work out for Caleb? One reason is that he embodies a dedication to productive labor. When he is given a job that will allow him to build better houses for the tenants on the estates of Dorothea's uncle and Celia's husband, he takes enormous satisfaction in the chance this will afford him to do real and substantial work, viewing this opportunity as "a great gift of God" and adding (again in the "use value" mode) that "a man without a family would be glad to do it for nothing" (ch. 40). Dorothea, Lydgate, and Bulstrode all attempt to live a "grand life." Caleb does not: he is tied to the present and the local. There is, indeed, a significant exception to his immersion in the here and now. He loves the spirituality of oratorio singing, having a "profound reverence for this mighty structure of tones"; at one point, he tells his wife that Dorothea Brooke's voice reminds him of part of Handel's *Messiah* (ch. 56). His comments on attempts at political reform are more characteristic of his general outlook on life: "What people do who go into politics I can't think: it drives me almost mad to see mismanagement over only a few hundred acres" (ch. 40).

It has been said that the work of ideology is to provide imaginary solutions to real problems. The ease with which Caleb eludes key problems involved with the coming of modernity might make one suspect that his presence in the novel is highly ideological in this sense. He is connected with capitalistic, progressive technology, but he himself cares only about the local and the useful. His wife similarly "solves" some of the larger gender issues in the novel by, on the one hand, demonstrating greater practical sense than Caleb (and wielding a certain amount of power at home), but on the other hand subscribing, overtly and sincerely, to a doctrine of complete female submission. But these, we might argue, are no solutions at all to the problems the novel addresses; they pretend to confront them while turning their back on them. Such a judgment would have more validity if Caleb and his wife were the only figures in the novel. Among other things, they remind us that there are areas of freedom even in the most compelling historical processes. Older ways and values persist even in times of explosive change. Indeed, the difficulties the other characters meet in their attempts to live a "grand life" help us to gauge just how much of Caleb's character reflects wishful (perhaps "hopeful") thinking. One might add that in one sense it is precisely the function of novels to provide imaginary solutions to real problems. What matters is the quality of the total imaginative product and the way in which, as a whole, it addresses reality, not the possible wishfulness of some of its parts.

When we see the Garths, we see them as part of the countryside. Thus Mary Garth and her little sister are described as follows: "They made a pretty picture in the western light which brought out the brightness of the apples on the old scant-leaved boughs – Mary in her lavender gingham and black ribbons holding a basket, while Letty in her well-work nankin picked up the fallen apples" (ch. 40). Such a pastoral description is appropriate, for the Garths themselves are pastoral figures in a deep sense. Pastoral is a very old literary convention. In its purest form, it takes the problems of sophisticated, urban life and projects them onto a simplified version of country life, in the hopes of clarification. Shepherds and shepherdesses play out the concerns of more sophisticated, worldly-wise people. Shakespeare drew heavily on pastoral convention in his comedies, sending his characters to the forest so that they could pass, in the memorable formula of a great Shakespearean critic, "from release to clarification."[7] The Garths' place in the pastoral tradition underlines for us Eliot's knowledge that the values they embody matter, even if the solutions they seem to offer might not be directly applicable to the world of the novel in its entirety, much less to our own. In this respect, it's interesting that one of Caleb's defining characteristics is his inarticulateness. He doesn't talk in quite the way that other people do; he comes up with pithy sayings that act as a code for feelings and meanings he cannot quite express – "things hang together," for instance. But those around him know what he means, for what he means is what he is. It seems surprising that the intensely cerebral and verbal George Eliot, who always can find the right words to describe the most complex human situations, should have lovingly created such a character. Perhaps, though, it isn't really so surprising after all. Perhaps for Eliot herself, Caleb Garth's inarticulate communicativeness represents a moment of pastoral release from the demands for accurate, responsible articulateness her philosophic mind normally demands from her.

"Who that cares much to know the history of man . . .": The Mind and Voice of the Narrator

Throughout this book, we have stressed the importance of the narrator to nineteenth-century fiction. There can hardly be a narrator more central to the experience and meaning of a work than the one in *Middlemarch*. Our analysis thus far has focused on the novel's larger strategies, without a great deal of attention to how the voice of the narrator implements and mediates them. We hope that those who have read the rest of our book will by now have become accustomed (if they were not already accustomed) to attending to the narrator's presence and voice. We now bring this chapter and the book as a whole to a close by listening to Eliot's narrator speak to us, in the novel's opening sentence:

> Who that cares much to know the history of man, and how the mysterious mixture behaves under the varying experiments of Time, has not dwelt, at least briefly, on the life of St. Theresa, has not smiled with some gentleness at the thought of the little girl walking forth one morning hand-in-hand with her still smaller brother, to go and seek martyrdom in the country of the Moors?

What kind of voice addresses us here? What sort of intelligence lies behind it? To begin with, the narrative presence is demanding. The narrator simply assumes that we must already have considered the example of St. Theresa – and for that matter that we know who she was and what her significance was. (Do we really want to be classified as people who do *not* "care much" to understand the history and fate of human beings?) Yet how many of us actually have done so? The phrase "at least briefly" may seem to let us off the hook a bit; we are not, it seems, required to have spent hours on the subject. On another level, however, it only increases the rigor: the implicit demand is not simply that we have thought about St. Theresa, but that we have thought about her for exactly the right amount of time, which implies that we possess (or should possess) a comprehensive view of the general subject of human fate, one that tells us just how much time you need to spend on each example! All of this can feel a bit daunting. But one of the reasons we read Eliot is that we wish to be daunted. It is a privilege to be challenged in this way. We hope that the fine discernment we sense in the narrative voice is something we can come to share, just as we hope to learn from the specific examples of human strength and weakness that are presented with such depth and clarity.

The narrator's voice is demanding, but it is also inviting. The sentence we are considering is, after all, a question, and questions invite dialogue. And the voice, though it knows much, does not pretend to know everything. The "mysterious mixture" of humanity is mysterious even to it. There is something a bit extravagant (reflecting, perhaps, a quiet amusement or self-irony) in thinking of individual human destinies in history as the result of a series of "experiments" by the scientist Time. We may feel chastened that we have not sufficiently attended to St. Theresa, but we also feel reassured that such serious subjects need not be treated with utter solemnity, that there is room for wit and a play of mind.

But perhaps the chief reason why the voice seems inviting is that its intellectual rigor flows into feeling and emotion, as the sentence itself does, in its movement from the abstract personification of Time to the concrete picture of two toddlers. The narrator assumes (and demands) that we have thought for just the right amount of time about St. Theresa as a notable experiment in human destiny, but she also assumes that we will have smiled with some gentleness at this early chapter in her life. A truly adequate response to the fate of humanity will, it appears, include gentle emotion as well as rigorous intellectual analysis. We encounter here the same mind that tells us, in analyzing how his abstract ideology imprisons Bulstrode, that all doctrines must be checked "by the deep-seated habit of direct fellow-feeling with individual fellow-men," and demands that Dorothea learn to conceive of Casaubon's "centre of self" with "that distinctness which is no longer reflection but feeling – an idea wrought back to the directness of sense, like the solidity of objects."

The opening sentence of the novel moves from analysis to story. In doing so, it reminds us of why novels matter, and why the attempt to read them well matters. It makes sense that George Eliot, who began her career as a translator of philosophy and a commentator on the vigorous and varied intellectual life of her day, should have turned to the writing of novels. For it is only in the novel that the mysterious mixture of humanity as it travels through the experiments of time and history can be portrayed in its full intellectual and emotional richness.

Appendix: Free Indirect Discourse

Free indirect discourse is a mode of reporting thought and speech. It is an important technique for rendering the thoughts of characters in the novels treated in this book. It's worth pointing out, however, that the use of free indirect discourse (FID for short) extends beyond fiction – it was, for instance, once widely used in transcripts of Parliamentary debates. Since its critical discovery early in the twentieth century, it has gone by a variety of names in a variety of languages. For readers (and teachers) of the novel, there are few better ways to become sensitive to the presence and the significance of the voices in novels than to verse oneself in the workings of FID.

What is most interesting for our purposes about FID is that it is a mode in which the attitude of the depicted thinker seems blended with the attitude of the narrator, in varying proportions. The narrator seems to be trying to feel his or her way into the thoughts of a character and then to make those thoughts available to us as readers in the language of the character's inner, mental voice. In the process, narrators find themselves rendering a character's thoughts with a clarity and explicitness the character would be incapable of producing. This, in turn, often involves clarifying the larger implications of the character's thoughts. When that side of things develops, we begin to hear not only the voice of the character's thoughts, but the voice of the narrator thinking about those thoughts. We thus hear a blend of voices, which implies judgments about the thoughts of the character without directly stating them. If this aspect of FID sounds mysterious, think of the many social situations in which someone mimics aloud the voice of another person. If we laugh (or sneer), it's often because the values of the person mimicked have thereby been revealed. There is, to be sure, an important difference between such social mimicry and FID. Among them is that narrators do not indicate that they are moving into FID with the blatancy of mimics: it takes a bit of skill to recognize FID when it occurs. A negative view of the effect we are describing would be that narrators use FID in an attempt to sneak their judgments into the picture, while seeming simply to be presenting a character's thoughts without adding any judgment at all. This is doubtless one way in which FID might be used, but we do not consider it the normal use, because we tend to trust the intentions of authors and narrators, as well as the intelligence of novel-readers. In our view, FID normally suggests complex and subtle value judgments, allowing the reader to experience them and indeed to help produce them. Our talk of "blended" voices may remind our own readers, in this respect and others, of the Bakhtinian "dialogism" we discussed in our chapter on Thackeray, and in fact Bakhtin's collaborator Volosinov produced in the 1920s what remains one of the most valuable and stimulating discussions of FID.

Here is an example of FID. Toward the end of *Middlemarch*, the following passage appears, describing Tertius Lydgate as he comes to the conclusion that he must set aside his own intellectual ambitions and make a living instead, so that he can provide his wife with the support she needs (or thinks she needs):

> Poor Rosamond's vagrant fancy had come back terribly scourged – meek enough to nestle under the old despised shelter. And the shelter was still there: Lydgate had accepted his narrowed lot with sad resignation. He had chosen this fragile creature, and had taken the burthen of her life upon his arm. He must walk as he could, carrying that burthen pitifully. (800)

When the narrator tells us that "Lydgate had accepted his narrowed lot with sad resignation," we take this to be a simple report of a conclusion he has reached, not a report of his thoughts. We do not imagine that Lydgate says to himself something on the order of "I accept my narrowed lot with sad resignation." By contrast, the two sentences that follow do begin to sound like a rendering of his thoughts. We can imagine Lydgate saying to himself, "I chose her, and she is fragile. I must walk as best I can, carrying her pitifully." Yet the words on the page aren't quite the words we would imagine he thinks to himself. The reader will have noticed that our attempt to give a credible version of thoughts passing through his mind includes a number of alterations of Eliot's text. Would Lydgate really use the words "fragile *creature*" to think about his wife? Surely "creature" is the sort of word a narrator uses. For that matter, it seems likely that he would actually form in his mind an *image* of his wife's fragile beauty as he thought of her and his responsibilities toward her. In any case, it seems unlikely that he would have used the elevated diction of "burthen" in the verbal part of his thinking. "Burden" would be more like it. "Burthen" is, again, narrator language: it adds an element of dignity and pathos – in a word, it suggests judgments of *value*. What we hear in these sentences is partly Lydgate's mental voice and partly the narrator's voice.

This mixture of voices matters. If we read the final sentence with the feeling that we are hearing both Lydgate's voice and the narrator's voice beneath it, we may begin to ask ourselves just whose values it reflects. Who is saying that Lydgate "must" support his wife – Lydgate, or the narrator? In another context, the sentence might belong entirely to the narrator: "He must walk as he could, carrying that burthen pitifully" is, after all, something that the narrator might have said in a passage that had nothing to do with reporting Lydgate's thoughts. By the same token, in another context, the sentence might belong entirely to Lydgate. In the passage as Eliot wrote it, the question of whose voice we are hearing is less clear, but the issue of whose values the sentence expresses remains important. If the "must" simply reflects Lydgate's thinking, it could simply be yet another example of his delusions about women in general and his wife in particular, for his wife in fact is in many ways anything but "fragile." The notion that she is a "burthen" he must "carry" might then simply be one more example of his destructively conventional view of women. But if we are hearing the narrator's voice here, and that voice is *endorsing* this view of Lydgate's responsibility, then the situation becomes more complicated. Lydgate would then be right in thinking that he has a responsibility, even though he is wrong in some of the feelings that motivate that view – a situation that could lead to some quite intricate thought on our part about the sources of ethical conduct. How would we go about deciding whether the narrator is endorsing this view? By fitting this moment into the larger pattern of value judgments the novel as a whole has created by the time we reach this point. Of course, we run into interpretive problems like this all the time when we read fiction. We are (or should be) constantly asking ourselves whether a character's thoughts and actions fit in with the values structure of the novel as a whole. FID, however, not only makes a character's mental world seem vivid to us, its mixture of voices raises such interpretive issues in a particularly rich way.

Recognizing FID

There has been a good deal of controversy about the nature and significance of FID. (Some have even argued that narrative and character "voices" aren't involved in FID at all – a view we cannot accept.) Its centrally defining verbal characteristics, however, seem reasonably clear, though they require careful explanation.

Roy Pascal's description of FID provides a useful general summary of its major aspects:

> The simplest description . . . would be that the narrator, though preserving the authorial mode throughout and evading the "dramatic" form of speech or dialogue [i.e. "direct discourse"], yet places himself, when reporting the words or thoughts of a character, directly into the experiential field of the character, and adopts the latter's perspective in regard to both time and place. (9)

A standard way of providing a more specific characterization of FID is to contrast it with two other, more familiar ways of reporting thought and speech: *direct discourse* and *indirect discourse*. (This should not, however, be taken to imply that FID was derived from the other two or followed them historically.) Here are examples of all three of these modes, which we have created by taking two passages from *Middlemarch* that appear in the novel as FID and translating them into each of the other modes:

1 *Direct discourse*
   (a) Celia said to herself, "I always say just how things are and nothing else: I never do and never can put words together out of my own head. But the best of Dodo is, that she does not keep angry for long together."
   (b) Mr. Brooke said to himself, "Here is a fellow like Chettam with no chance at all."
2 *Indirect discourse*
   (a) Celia inwardly protested that she always said just how things were and nothing else; that she never did and never could put words together out of her own head. But she remembered that the best thing about Dorothea was that she did not keep angry for long together.
   (b) Mr. Brooke remarked to himself that it was amazing that a fellow like Chettam had no chance at all.
3 *Free indirect discourse*
   (a) [Celia inwardly protested that she always said just how things were and nothing else: she never did and never could put words together out of her own head.] But the best of Dodo was, that she did not keep angry for long together. (*Middlemarch*, 46)
   (b) Here was a fellow like Chettam with no chance at all. (*Middlemarch*, 40)

Here are two comments on the examples we have just provided. First, if you "translate" FID into indirect discourse, you are likely to find yourself needing to add words with direct evaluative force, because you will need to compensate for the meaning lost because indirect discourse (unlike FID) doesn't preserve the character's voice and idiom. (When we created example 2(b), we added the words "it was amazing" to register the surprise one hears in Mr. Brooke's voice in the FID version.) A character's "idiolect" (his or her characteristic mode of verbal expression), which can be preserved in FID, conveys a great deal of meaning. To give a simple example, the fact that the adult Celia still thinks of her sister as "Dodo" says something (in this case, a number of things) about her – as a first approximation, we could say that we learn that she's affectionate and a bit childish.

Second, a passage that seems to begin in indirect discourse can sometimes easily slide into free indirect discourse: the determining factor of when one begins and the other ends is how palpably we hear the individual character's voice in a passage. Thus the sentence we have placed in square brackets in 3(a) begins as indirect discourse, but after the colon it can be read as FID (it really does sound as if Celia is speaking it). By the time we reach the final sentence in 3(a), there is no doubt that we are reading FID.

It's worth adding that though the normal practice is not to put FID in quotation marks, some authors (particularly from the period before the middle of the nineteenth century) do use quotation marks for FID. Austen does this, though not often. So does Thackeray in recounting Bullock's panicked thoughts about where Old Osborne's money will go: "Bullock rushed from the city in a hurry. *'How much money had he left to that boy? – not half, surely? – Surely share and share alike between the three [of old Osborne's possible heirs, one of whom is married to Bullock]?'* It was an agitating moment." (For a full reading of the passage as a whole, see chapter 5.) The use of FID to render the thoughts we have put in italics (the quotation marks are Thackeray's) creates a place for the voice and judgment of the narrator and emphasizes his presence, laughing at and judging Bullock as the latter reveals his true nature out of his own mouth.

FID and Grammar

A careful look at the examples we have provided above will suggest some of the grammatical markers of FID. The most important ones involve verbs and pronouns. As compared to direct discourse (what the person would actually think to himself or herself) the tense of the verbs in a passage of FID undergoes what is called a "back-shift": present becomes past, past becomes past-perfect, past-perfect stays past-perfect because you can't shift back any further in English. In this respect, free indirect discourse is like indirect discourse but unlike direct discourse. Thus Celia would say to herself, "the best of Dodo *is*, that she *does* not keep angry for long together," but in FID, this becomes, "the best of Dodo *was*, that she *did* not keep angry for long together." The other main grammatical sign of FID involves changes in pronouns, in which first person pronouns ("I" and "we") become third person pronouns ("he/she" and "they"). In direct discourse, Lydgate would say to himself, "I must walk as I can." In FID, this becomes, "he must walk as he could." Or, to turn to *Persuasion*, what Wentworth actually said to himself when he thought angrily about Anne's refusal to marry him could be rendered, "She used me ill; deserted and disappointed me . . . she gave me up to oblige others. . . . Her power with me is gone forever." When the novel presents these thoughts in the mode of FID, they become, "She had used him ill; deserted and disappointed him . . . She had given him up to oblige others. . . . Her power with him was gone forever." Again, the reader will notice that "I" and "me" have become "he" and "him," and that the verbs have shifted back a tense (from, for example, "*is* gone" to "*was* gone").

Another sign of FID is that, even though it reports thoughts or speech, it does not preface that report by a verb of saying or thinking followed by the word "that." A report of Mr. Brooke's thoughts beginning "Mr. Brooke thought that . . ." could not be FID. But verbs of thought and speech can appear, without the "that," in FID in what are called "comment clauses" in the middle or end of a sentence. "Here was a fellow like Chettam with no chance at all, Mr. Brooke thought" could qualify as free indirect discourse, especially if it were imbedded in a longer stretch of free indirect discourse.

An alertness to grammatical markers can be helpful, but in the end, grammar will only take us so far in identifying FID, or for that matter in deciding what is and is not reported thought. On the latter score, consider the sentence, "Mr. Brooke was amazed that a fellow like Chettam had no chance at all." Is this simply narration that reports an event (the fact that Mr. Brooke was amazed), or is it an attempt to get us inside his head so that we can share his thought as he thinks it? It could be either, depending on the larger context in which it appeared. We'd need a fuller context to be sure. Identifying FID also depends on context, and particularly on how strongly the character's voice sounds in a given passage. In the sentence, "But the best of Dodo was, that she did not keep angry for long together," Celia's voice and idiolect are unmistakable. It is this, even more than the back-shift of the verb tense (direct discourse would give us "the best of Dodo *is*"), that tells us that we are reading FID.

Further Reading on FID

Fludernik, Monika (1993). *The Fictions of Language and the Languages of Fiction: The Linguistic Representation of Speech and Consciousness*. London: Routledge. (The best study to date; far-ranging and magisterial.)

McHale, Brian (1978). "Free Indirect Discourse: A Survey of Recent Accounts." *PTL* (3), 249–87. (Although this article is 40 years old, it remains the best place to start.)

Pascal, Roy (1977). *The Dual Voice.* Manchester: Manchester University Press.

Volosinov, V. N. (1986). *Marxism and the Philosophy of Language.* Translated by Ladislav Majejka and I. R. Trunik. Cambridge, MA: Harvard University Press.

Notes

Introduction

1 John Stuart Mill, *Newspaper Writings: December 22–July 31*, ed. Ann P. Robson and John M. Robson (Toronto: University of Toronto Press, 1986), 230.
2 Susan Lanser, *Fictions of Authority* (Ithaca: Cornell University Press, 1992), 15.
3 Gérard Genette, *Narrative Discourse: An Essay in Method*, translated by Jane E. Lewin (Ithaca: Cornell University Press, 1980), 185–211. Narrative focus is often referred to as "focalization." A "state of the art" guide to this and other terms used to describe narrative is the *Routledge Encyclopedia of Narrative Theory*, ed. David Herman, Manfred Jahn, and Marie-Laure Ryan (New York: Routledge, 2005).
4 Wayne C. Booth, *The Rhetoric of Fiction, Second Edition* (Chicago: University of Chicago Press, 1983).

Chapter 1 *Pride and Prejudice* and *Persuasion*

The quotations from Austen's novels in this chapter use the following texts: *Pride and Prejudice*, ed. Vivien Jones (London: Penguin, 1996), and *Persuasion*, ed. Gillian Beer (London: Penguin, 1998).

1 "Honoré de Balzac," in Henry James, *Literary Criticism: European Writers & the Prefaces* (New York: Library of America, 1984), 118.
2 William Nelles, "Omniscience for Atheists: Or, Jane Austen's Infallible Narrator," *Narrative*, 14 (2006), 118–31.
3 Raymond Williams, *The Country and the City* (London: Chatto and Windus, 1973), 116–17.
4 Lionel Trilling, in his Introduction to *Emma* (Cambridge: Riverside Press, 1957), suggests that in *Emma*, Highbury (presented in the pastoral mode of the literary idyll) serves the same kind of "ideal" function as the one I have argued Pemberley

serves in *Pride and Prejudice*. He connects the power of the "myth" of Jane Austen as person and author with the creation of this ideal response to crucial problems of modernity. This essay is reprinted as "Emma and the Legend of Jane Austen" in Lionel Trilling, *Beyond Culture* (New York: Harcourt Brace Jovanovich, 1965), 28–49.

5   Stanley Cavell, *Pursuits of Happiness: The Hollywood Comedy of Remarriage* (Cambridge, MA: Harvard University Press, 1981).

6   Adela Pinch, *Strange Fits of Passion: Epistemologies of Emotion, Hume to Austen* (Stanford: Stanford University Press, 1996), 160.

7   John Wiltshire, *Jane Austen and the Body* (Cambridge: Cambridge University Press, 1992), 157–9, presents an extreme version of this critique.

Chapter 2   *Waverley*

Quotations from *Waverley* in this chapter use the following text: *Waverley*, ed. Andrew Hook (London: Penguin, 1972).

1   James Boswell, *Life of Johnson*, ed. R. W. Chapman (Oxford: Oxford University Press, 1970), 389.

2   Henry James, Preface to the New York Edition of *The Princess Casamassima*, in *Literary Criticism: French Writers, Other European Writers, The Prefaces to the New York Edition*, ed. Leon Edel (New York: Library of America, 1984), 1094.

3   *Sir Walter Scott on Novelists and Fiction*, ed. Ioan Williams (New York: Barnes and Noble, 1968), 40–1. These comments appeared in the introduction Scott wrote for a reprint of Richardson's novels (1824).

4   Henry James, Preface to the New York Edition of *The Princess Casamassima*, 1094.

5   Georg Lukács, *The Historical Novel*, trans. Hannah and Stanley Mitchell (London: Merlin, 1962), 36–40.

6   Donald Davie, *The Heyday of Sir Walter Scott* (London: Routledge and Kegan Paul, 1961), 36–7.

7   For an extended attempt by one of the authors of this book to deal with such issues, particularly as they are raised by Said, see Harry E. Shaw, *Narrating Reality: Austen, Scott, Eliot* (Ithaca: Cornell University Press, 1999), 168–217.

8   Jonathan Rose, *The Intellectual Life of the British Working Classes* (New Haven: Yale University Press, 2001), 41–2. We are grateful to Christopher Shaw for this reference.

9   Hall's views on this and related subjects are conveniently collected and discussed in *Stuart Hall: Critical Dialogues in Cultural Studies*, ed. David Morley and Kuan-Hsing Chen (London: Routledge, 1996).

10   Robert C. Gordon, *Under Which King? A Study of the Scottish Waverley Novels* (Edinburgh: Oliver and Boyd, 1969), 109.

11   J. G. Lockhart, *The Life of Sir Walter Scott*, abridged edition (London: Dent, 1969), 156. This is Lockhart's own abridgement of the classic biography he wrote of Scott, who was his father-in-law, after Scott's death.

Chapter 3   *Wuthering Heights*

The quotations from *Wuthering Heights* in this chapter use the following text: Emily Brontë, *Wuthering Heights*, ed. Richard Dunn (New York: Norton, 2002).

1 The "cult of the Brontës," which has its shrine at Haworth Parsonage, owes its origins to Charlotte Brontë's far more popular novels, and most particularly to Elizabeth Gaskell's publication of the *Life of Charlotte Brontë* in 1857, but interestingly, tourist interest in the surrounding countryside was and remains tied almost exclusively to descriptions of natural settings in *Wuthering Heights*.

2 This last version owes a great deal to Charlotte Brontë, who in her preface to the 1850 edition portrayed Emily as an artist with little practical knowledge of human society but a deep and intimate connection with the natural world around her: "Wuthering Heights was hewn in a wild workshop, with simple tools, out of homely materials."

3 The reference is to Matthew 18.21–35, where Christ responds to Peter's query about how many times he must forgive his brother, that he must forgive him not seven times, but "seventy times seven" times. Brandersham takes this as a precise enumeration, making the 491st sin the first that need not be forgiven.

4 Though they routinely do so anyway, taking a single character (usually Cathy, Heathcliff, or Nelly) as the clear-cut center of value or of disapproval and organizing their reading accordingly. A surprising amount of even very sophisticated criticism of the novel can thus be sorted into the Blame Cathy school, the Vindicate Cathy school, the Blame Nelly school, the Vindicate Heathcliff school, and so forth. The temptation to stabilize the novel this way is difficult to resist (this chapter may well belong to the Vindicate Nelly school), but worth watching out for, as an unselfconscious indulgence in it will tend to flatten out the novel.

5 Though the novel is set in an earlier period, it was written during and just after the "Hungry Forties," when a prolonged depression in trade produced great suffering and political unrest among workers in the manufacturing areas around Yorkshire.

6 For a more detailed discussion of this subject, see Wendy S. Jones, *Consensual Fictions: Women, Liberalism, and the English Novel* (Toronto: University of Toronto Press, 2005).

7 Some psychoanalytic readings of the novel suggest that their "love" may actually reflect an infant's pre-Oedipal sense of undifferentiated union with the mother, both children having lost their real mothers.

Chapter 4   *Jane Eyre*

The quotations from *Jane Eyre* in this chapter use the following text: Charlotte Brontë, *Jane Eyre* (Oxford: Oxford University Press, 1975).

1 That it was also written by a woman was less evident to its initial audience, since it was published under the sex-obscuring pseudonym of Currer Bell, though, since this was soon known to be a pseudonym, speculation about the author's identity and sex was rampant.

2   See Elsie Michie, "From Simianized Irish to Oriental Despots: Heathcliff, Rochester and Racial Difference," *NOVEL: A Forum on Fiction*, 25 (1992), 125–40.

3   Brontë's ready linkage of moral and intellectual character to physical characteristics, racial or otherwise, is reflected also in her approving use of phrenology, a popular Victorian pseudoscience that linked individual character and talents to the shape of the head.

4   Carlyle, *Sartor Resartus*, 1831, ch. 9.

Chapter 5   *Vanity Fair*

Quotations from *Vanity Fair* in this chapter use the following text: *Vanity Fair*, ed. Peter L. Shillingsburg (New York: Norton, 1994). This text has the advantage of reproducing all of the drawings and initial capital letters Thackeray drew for the novel.

1   For a thorough and illuminating discussion of this, see Ralph W. Rader, "The Comparative Anatomy of Three Baggy Monsters: *Bleak House, Vanity Fair, Middlemarch*," *Journal of Narrative Technique*, 19 (1989), 49–69. We have also drawn on this brilliant article in our discussion of *Middlemarch*.

2   The classic exposition and critique of the injunction that authors "show" instead of "tell" is Wayne C. Booth, *The Rhetoric of Fiction*, 2nd edn. (Chicago: University of Chicago Press, 1983).

3   For an argument that George Eliot's narrator behaves in the same way, in response to Eliot's recognition that all of us are subject to the constraints of history, see Harry E. Shaw, *Narrating Reality: Austen, Scott, Eliot* (Ithaca: Cornell University Press, 1999), 236–52. Some eminent narratologists, including Gérard Genette, have objected strenuously to any such weakening of the line between heterodiegetic ("third person") narrators and novelistic characters.

4   Writings by and about Bakhtin are extensive. A good place to start would be Mikhail M. Bakhtin, *The Dialogic Imagination: Four Essays*, ed. Michael Holquist, trans. Caryl Emerson and Michael Holquist (Austin: University of Texas Press, 1981), especially the essay "Dialogue in the Novel." In our view, the best study of Bakhtin is Gary Saul Morson and Caryl Emerson, *Mikhail Bakhtin: Creation of a Prosaics* (Stanford: Stanford University Press, 1990).

5   For a more extended discussion of this passage, see Harry E. Shaw, "Why Won't Our Terms Stay Put? The Narrative Communications Diagram Scrutinized and Historicized," in *A Companion to Narrative Theory*, ed. James Phelan and Peter J. Rabinowitz (Oxford: Blackwell, 2005), 304–7.

Chapter 6   *Mary Barton*

The quotations from *Mary Barton* in this chapter use the following text: Elizabeth Gaskell, *Mary Barton*, ed. Shirley Foster (Oxford: Oxford World Classics, 2006).

1 Critics of the novel long presumed that direct address to readers by a narrator produced a distancing effect: by calling attention to the story's status as fiction. This is consonant with the modernist-inspired prejudice in favor of disappearing narrators. But Robyn Warhol was able to show that in nineteenth-century fiction direct address to the reader *can* have exactly the opposite effect, inviting the reader more directly to engage personally with the situations in the novel. "Engaging direct address," as she terms it, tends to be associated with female novelists (Gaskell is exemplary in this regard), although male novelists, most notably Dickens, also drew on it upon occasion. See Warhol, *Gendered Interventions: Narrative Discourse in the Victorian Novel* (New Brunswick: Rutgers University Press, 1989).

2 While lying mortally wounded and tormented by thirst, Sir Philip Sydney is said to have given to a wounded fellow-soldier a cup of water brought for him, saying "Thy need is greater than mine."

3 Shakespeare, *Henry IV, Part 1*, Act 4, Scene 2, ll. 34–9.

4 Angus Easson, ed., *Elizabeth Gaskell: The Critical Heritage* (New Brunswick: Rutgers University Press, 1991), 96.

Chapter 7   *Bleak House*

The quotations from *Bleak House* in this chapter use the following text: Charles Dickens, *Bleak House* (Oxford: Oxford University Press, 1987).

1 Compare this to *Middlemarch*, in which the units of publication, eight titled bimonthly "books," are also the main subdivisions of the finished novel.

2 *Westminster Review*, October 1853; reprinted in A. E. Dyson, *Dickens: Bleak House. A Casebook* (London: Methuen, 1985), 71.

3 *Blackwood's Edinburgh Magazine* 77, April 1855; reprinted in Dyson, *Dickens: Bleak House. A Casebook*, 87.

4 Though this last may be a matter more of expediency than of art on Dickens's part: unlike, say, the officials of the (invented) Circumlocution Office in *Little Dorrit*, the Lord Chancellor was a real, identifiable individual, who probably would not have taken kindly to being reduced to a villainous parody by the most popular novelist of the day.

5 Dickens, by forging an audience that stretched from the Dedlock class to, if not illiterate and destitute children like Jo, at least to the working poor, embodied another possible answer: "they are all reading Dickens."

Chapter 8   *The Warden* and *Barchester Towers*

The quotations from Trollope's novels in this chapter use the following texts: *The Warden*, ed. David Skilton (Oxford: Oxford University Press, 1980) and *Barchester Towers*, ed. Michael Sadleir, Frederick Page, and John Sutherland (Oxford: Oxford University Press, 1996).

1 Anthony Trollope, *An Autobiography*, ed. David Skilton (London: Penguin, 1996), 79–82; hereafter cited in the text.
2 *Anthony Trollope: The Critical Heritage*, ed. Donald Smalley (London: Routledge and Kegan Paul, 1969), 110.
3 D. A. Miller, *The Novel and the Police* (Berkeley: University of California Press, 1988), 107–45.
4 For "knowable communities," see Raymond Williams, *The Country and the City* (London: Chatto and Windus, 1973), 165–81.

Chapter 9   *Lady Audley's Secret*

The quotations from *Lady Audley's Secret* in this chapter use the following text: Mary Elizabeth Braddon, *Lady Audley's Secret*, ed. David Skilton (Oxford: Oxford World Classics, 1998).

Chapter 10   *Middlemarch*

The quotations from *Middlemarch* in this chapter use the following text: *Middlemarch*, ed. Rosemary Ashton (London: Penguin, 1994).

1 Scott was a favorite author of Eliot. She read him aloud to her father in the latter's final days, and George Henry Lewes, the man with whom she lived for a quarter of a century (they could not marry, because current laws prevented him from divorcing his wife, though they were completely estranged), gave her a set of the Waverley novels as a gift, and they read them together.
2 For "knowable communities," see Raymond Williams, *The Country and the City* (London: Chatto and Windus, 1973), 165–81.
3 When we discuss the "doctrines" underlying the novel, we tend, for the sake of simplicity of exposition, to attribute them directly to Eliot. It would be more precise to attribute them to the "implied author" (for this figure, see the Introduction).
4 Anthony Flew, *A Dictionary of Philosophy* (London: St. Martin's Press, 1984).
5 Peter K. Garrett, *The Victorian Multiplot Novel: Studies in Dialogical Form* (New Haven: Yale University Press, 1980). Henry James, Preface to the New York Edition of *The Tragic Muse*, in *Literary Criticism: French Writers, Other European Writers, The Prefaces to the New York Edition*, ed. Leon Edel (New York: Library of America, 1984), 1107.
6 Williams, *The Country and the City*, 173.
7 C. L. Barber, *Shakespeare's Festive Comedy* (Princeton: Princeton University Press, 1957), 15.

Further Reading

Our suggestions for further critical reading concentrate primarily on books and mention only a very small fraction of the available material. We begin with a list of studies of narrative technique in general, followed by works that cover more than one author. Then we move to works of particular interest for individual authors.

Works that comment substantially on the novels we have discussed in this book are followed by the initials of the title of the novel in question:

BH	*Bleak House*
BT	*Barchester Towers*
JE	*Jane Eyre*
LAS	*Lady Audley's Secret*
M	*Middlemarch*
MB	*Mary Barton*
P	*Persuasion*
VF	*Vanity Fair*
W	*Waverley*
WH	*Wuthering Heights*

Studies of Narrative, Narratology, and the Novel

An excellent tool for those who wish to delve further into issues of narrative theory is the *Routledge Encyclopedia of Narrative Theory*, ed. David Herman, Manfred Jahn, and Marie-Laure Ryan (New York: Routledge, 2005), which provides "state of the art" discussions of several hundred narratological terms and concepts and bibliographical references for further study. Another useful source is *A Companion to Narrative Theory*, ed. James Phelan and Peter J. Rabinowitz (Oxford: Blackwell, 2005), which contains essays on seminal issues in narrative theory by 35 current scholars in the field, including the authors of the present book. For a massively well-informed 50-page essay on developments during the past forty years, the reader may consult an essay by James Phelan which appears as a new, concluding chapter for the Fortieth Anniversary

Edition of a classic in the field, Scholes and Kellogg's *The Nature of Narrative* (Oxford: Oxford University Press, 2006). A useful anthology of selections by narrative theorists from Fielding to the present is David H. Richter, *Narrative/Theory* (White Plains, NY: Longman, 1996). Two recent critical anthologies focus specifically on the novel: Michael McKeon's *Theory of the Novel: A Historical Approach* (Baltimore: Johns Hopkins University Press, 2000) and Dorothy J. Hale's *The Novel: An Anthology of Criticism and Theory 1900–2000* (Oxford: Blackwell, 2006). What follows is a brief list of works on narratology and narrative theory that seem particularly relevant to the issues raised in this book:

Bal, Mieke. *Narratology: Introduction to the Theory of Narrative*. Second Edition. Toronto: University of Toronto Press, 1998.

Booth, Wayne C. *The Rhetoric of Fiction*. Second Edition. Chicago: University of Chicago Press, 1983.

Case, Alison. *Plotting Women*. Charlottesville: University Press of Virginia, 1999. BH, JE

Chatman, Seymour. *Story and Discourse: Narrative Structure in Fiction and Film*. Ithaca: Cornell University Press, 1978.

Chatman, Seymour. *Coming to Terms: The Rhetoric of Narrative in Fiction and Film*. Ithaca: Cornell University Press, 1990.

Culler, Jonathan. "Omniscience." In *The Literary in Theory*. Stanford: Stanford University Press, 2007, 183–201.

Lanser, Susan Sniader. *Fictions of Authority*. Ithaca: Cornell University Press, 1992. JE

Phelan, James. *Living to Tell About It: A Rhetoric and Ethics of Character Narration*. Ithaca: Cornell University Press, 2005.

Phelan, James. *Experiencing Fiction*. Columbus: Ohio University Press, 2007.

Rabinowitz, Peter J. *Before Reading: Narrative Conventions and the Politics of Interpretation*. Columbus: Ohio University Press, 1998.

Rimmon-Kenan, Shlomith. *Narrative Fiction: Contemporary Poetics*. Second Edition. London: Routledge, 2002.

Warhol, Robyn R. *Gendered Interventions: Narrative Discourse in the Victorian Novel*. New Brunswick: Rutgers University Press, 1986. BH, MB, VF

Studies of the Nineteenth-Century British Novel

Much of the most interesting writing on the nineteenth-century novel appears in books that cover more than one author. We list below a selection of significant works that contain analyses of one or more of the novels discussed in this book. For general background, see Daniel Pool, *What Jane Austen Ate and Charles Dickens Knew* (New York: Simon and Schuster, 1993) and *A Concise Companion to the Victorian Novel*, ed. Francis O'Gorman (Oxford: Blackwell, 2005).

Buzard, James. *Disorienting Fiction: The Autoethnographic Work of Nineteenth-Century British Novels*. Princeton: Princeton University Press, 2005. BH, JE, W

Garrett, Peter K. *The Victorian Multiplot Novel: Studies in Dialogical Form.* New Haven: Yale University Press, 1980. BH, M, VF

Gilbert, Sandra and Susan Gubar. *The Madwoman in the Attic.* Second Edition. New Haven: Yale University Press, 2000. JE, WH

Jones, Wendy S. *Consensual Fictions: Women, Liberalism, and the English Novel.* Toronto: University of Toronto Press, 2005. P

Kucich, John. *The Power of Lies: Transgression in Victorian Fiction.* Ithaca: Cornell University Press, 1994. BT

Langland, Elizabeth. *Nobody's Angels.* Ithaca: Cornell University Press, 1995. BH, M

Levine, Caroline. *The Serious Pleasures of Suspense: Victorian Realism and Narrative Doubt.* Charlottesville: University of Virginia Press, 2003. JE

Levine, George. *The Realistic Imagination: English Fiction from Frankenstein to Lady Chatterley.* Chicago: Chicago University Press, 1981. M, W

Lodge, David. *Language of Fiction: Essays in Criticism and Verbal Analysis of the English Novel.* New York: Columbia University Press, 1966. JE

Lodge, David. *After Bakhtin: Essays on Fiction and Criticism.* London: Routledge, 1990. M

Miller, Andrew H. *Novels Behind Glass: Commodity Culture and Victorian Narrative.* Cambridge: Cambridge University Press, 1995. M, VF

Miller, D. A. *The Novel and the Police.* Berkeley: University of California Press, 1988. BH, BT

Rader, Ralph W. "The Comparative Anatomy of Three Baggy Monsters: *Bleak House, Vanity Fair, Middlemarch.*" *Journal of Narrative Technique,* 19 (1989), 49–69.

Shaw, Harry E. *Narrating Reality: Austen, Scott, Eliot.* Ithaca: Cornell University Press, 1999. M, P, W

Showalter, Elaine. *A Literature of Their Own.* Expanded Edition. Princeton: Princeton University Press, 1999. JE, LAS

Tillotson, Kathleen. *Novels of the Eighteen-Forties.* Oxford: Clarendon Press, 1954. JE, MB, VF

Individual Authors

Austen

Butler, Marilyn. *Jane Austen and the War of Ideas.* Oxford: Clarendon Press, 1975. Reprinted in 1987 with an important new introduction.

Duckworth, Alistair. *The Improvement of the Estate: A Study of Jane Austen's Novels.* Baltimore: Johns Hopkins University Press, 1971.

Galperin, William H. *The Historical Austen.* Philadelphia: University of Pennsylvania Press, 2003.

Johnson, Claudia L. *Jane Austen: Women, Politics, and the Novel.* Chicago: University of Chicago Press, 1988.

Michaelson, Patricia Howell. *Speaking Volumes: Women, Reading, and Speech in the Age of Austen*. Stanford: Stanford University Press, 2002.

Poovey, Mary. *The Proper Lady and the Woman Writer: Ideology as Style in the Works of Mary Wollstonecraft, Mary Shelley, and Jane Austen*. Chicago: University of Chicago Press, 1984.

Southam, B. C., ed. *Jane Austen: The Critical Heritage*. London: Routledge and Kegan Paul, 1968. A collection of early critical writings on Austen.

Tave, Stuart. *Some Words of Jane Austen*. Chicago: University of Chicago Press, 1973.

White, Laura Mooneyham. "Jane Austen and the Marriage Plot: Questions of Persistence." In *Jane Austen and Discourses of Feminism*. New York: St. Martin's Press, 1995, 71–7.

We also recommend the essays Lionel Trilling wrote on Austen throughout his career, including, "*Mansfield Park*" (1954), in *The Opposing Self* (New York: Harcourt Brace Jovanovich, 1979), 181–202; "Emma and the Legend of Jane Austen" (1957), in *Beyond Culture* (New York: Harcourt Brace Jovanovich, 1965), 28–49; and "Why We Read Jane Austen" (1976; left incomplete at the time of Trilling's death), in *The Last Decade: Essays and Reviews, 1965–75* (New York: Harcourt Brace Jovanovich, 1979). In a different vein, Karen Joy Fowler, *The Jane Austen Book Club* (New York: Putnam, 2004) is an entertaining book that can illuminate one's reading of Austen.

Biography: Relatively little is known about Austen's life. The biographies prepared by her relatives are of more than period interest, though of course they can hardly be said to be objective. Her nephew, J. E. Austen-Leigh, wrote a "Memoir" that accompanies some editions of *Persuasion* (Penguin has however dropped it from its latest edition of that novel), and her brother, Henry Austen, wrote a brief "Biographical Notice of the Author," which prefaced the edition of *Northanger Abbey* and *Persuasion* that appeared in 1818. An interesting and reliable modern biography is Park Honan, *Jane Austen: Her Life* (New York: Fawcett Columbine, 1987).

Braddon

Brantlinger, Patrick. "What is 'Sensational' about the Sensation Novel?" *Nineteenth-Century Fiction*, 37 (1982), 1–28.

Cvetkovich, Ann. *Mixed Feelings: Feminism, Mass Culture, and Victorian Sensationalism*. New Brunswick: Rutgers University Press, 1992.

Matus, Jill. "Disclosure as Cover-up: The Discourse of Madness in *Lady Audley's Secret*." *University of Toronto Quarterly*, 62 (1993), 334–55.

Tromp, Marlene, Pamela K. Gilbert, and Aeron Haynie, eds. *Beyond Sensation: Mary Elizabeth Braddon in Context*. Albany: State University of New York Press, 2000.

Biography: For a study of Braddon by a celebrated book collector with an encyclopedic knowledge of nineteenth-century fiction, major and minor, see Robert Lee Wolff, *The Life and Fiction of Mary Elizabeth Braddon* (New York: Garland, 1979).

Brontë (Charlotte and Emily)

Allott, Miriam, ed. *The Brontës: The Critical Heritage*. London: Routledge and Kegan Paul, 1996. A collection of early critical writings on the Brontës.

Eagleton, Terry. *Myths of Power: A Marxist Study of the Brontës*. London: Macmillan, 1975, 97–121.

Glen, Heather, ed. *The Cambridge Companion to the Brontës*. Cambridge: Cambridge University Press, 2002.

Homans, Margaret. "The Name of the Mother in *Wuthering Heights*." In *Bearing the Word: Language and Female Experience in Nineteenth-Century Women's Writing*. Chicago: University of Chicago Press, 1989, 68–99.

Michie, Elsie. "From Simianized Irish to Oriental Despots: Heathcliff, Rochester and Racial Difference." *Novel*, 25 (1992), 125–40.

Miller, J. Hillis. "Emily Brontë." In *The Disappearance of God: Five Nineteenth-Century Writers*. Cambridge, MA: Harvard University Press, 1963, 157–211.

Miller, J. Hillis. "*Wuthering Heights*: Repetition and the 'Uncanny'." In *Fiction and Repetition: Seven English Novels*. Cambridge, MA: Harvard University Press, 1982, 42–72.

Moglen, Helene. *Charlotte Bronte: The Self Conceived*. New York: Norton, 1976.

Newman, Beth. "'The Situation of the Looker-On': Gender, Narration and Gaze in *Wuthering Heights*." *PMLA*, 105 (1990), 1029–41.

Spivak, Gayatri. "Three Women's Texts and a Critique of Imperialism." *Critical Inquiry*, 12 (1985), 243–61. JE

Yeager, Patricia. "Violence in the Sitting Room: *Wuthering Heights* and the Woman's Novel." *Genre*, 21 (1988), 203–29.

Biography: Elizabeth Gaskell's *Life of Charlotte Bronte* (1857) is still an engaging introduction to Charlotte and her sisters, though certainly one shaped to meet the perceived requirements of Victorian propriety. Of modern biographies, Winifred Gerin's extensively researched and sensitive biographies of each significant member of the Brontë family are a vital resource. For a modern rewriting of *Jane Eyre* with a difference, see Jean Rhys, *The Wide Sargasso Sea*.

Dickens

Collins, Philip, ed. *Charles Dickens: The Critical Heritage*. London: Routledge and Kegan Paul, 1971. A collection of early critical writings on Dickens.

Dyson, A. E., ed. *Dickens's Bleak House: A Casebook*. London: Macmillan, 1969.

Jaffe, Audrey. *Vanishing Points: Dickens, Narrative, and the Subject of Omniscience*. Berkeley: University of California Press, 1991.

Miller, J. Hillis. *Charles Dickens: The World of His Novels*. Cambridge, MA: Harvard University Press, 1958.

Newsome, Robert. *Dickens on the Romantic Side of Familiar Things: Bleak House and the Novel Tradition*. New York: Columbia University Press, 1977.

Page, Norman. *Bleak House: A Novel of Connections*. Boston: Twayne, 1990.

Shatto, Susan, ed. *The Companion to Bleak House*. London: Unwin Hyman, 1988.

Welsh, Alexander. *Dickens Redressed: The Art of Bleak House and Hard Times*. New Haven: Yale University Press, 2000.

Biography: A Victorian biography of great value is John Forster, *Life of Charles Dickens* (many editions), written by one of Dickens's close friends. Fred Kaplan, *Dickens: A Biography* (New York: Morrow, 1988) is also recommended.

Eliot

Bodenheimer, Rosemarie. *The Real Life of Mary Ann Evans: George Eliot, Her Letters and Fiction*. Ithaca: Cornell University Press, 1994.

Carroll, David. *George Eliot and the Conflict of Interpretations*. Cambridge: Cambridge University Press, 1992.

Carroll, David, ed. *George Eliot: The Critical Heritage*. London: Routledge and Kegan Paul, 1971. A collection of early critical writings on Eliot.

Chase, Cynthia. "The Decomposition of the Elephants: Double-Reading *Daniel Deronda*." PMLA, 93 (1978), 215–27.

Graver, Suzanne. *George Eliot and Community*. Berkeley: University of California Press, 1984.

Hardy, Barbara. *The Novels of George Eliot: A Study in Form*. London: Athlone Press, 1959.

Hertz, Neil. *George Eliot's Pulse*. Stanford: Stanford University Press, 2003.

Levine, George. "George Eliot's Hypothesis of Reality." *Nineteenth-Century Fiction*, 35 (1980), 1–28.

Welsh, Alexander. *George Eliot and Blackmail*. Cambridge, MA: Harvard University Press, 1985.

Biography: The standard biography remains Gordon Haight, *George Eliot: A Biography* (Oxford: Oxford University Press, 1968).

Gaskell

Anderson, Amanda. *Tainted Souls and Painted Faces: The Rhetoric of Fallenness in Victorian Culture*. Ithaca: Cornell University Press, 1993.

Easson, Angus, ed. *Elizabeth Gaskell: The Critical Heritage*. New York: Routledge, 1991. A collection of early critical writings on Gaskell.

Flint, Kate. *Elizabeth Gaskell*. Plymouth: Northcote House, 1995.

Gallagher, Catherine. *The Industrial Reformation of English Fiction, 1832–1867*. Chicago: University of Chicago Press, 1985.

Schor, Hilary. *Scheherazade in the Marketplace: Elizabeth Gaskell and the Victorian Novel*. New York: Oxford University Press, 1992.

Spencer, Jane. *Elizabeth Gaskell*. New York: St. Martin's Press, 1993.

Williams, Raymond. "The Industrial Novels: *Mary Barton*." In *Culture and Society*. London: Chatto and Windus, 1958, 87–91.

Biography: The best modern biography is Jennifer S. Uglow, *Elizabeth Gaskell: A Habit of Stories* (New York: Farrar Straus Giroux, 1993).

Scott

Cockshut, A. O. J. *The Achievement of Sir Walter Scott.* London: Collins, 1969.

Ferris, Ina. *The Achievement of Literary Authority: Gender, History, and the Waverley Novels.* Ithaca: Cornell University Press, 1991.

Hayden, John O., ed. *Scott: The Critical Heritage.* London: Routledge and Kegan Paul, 1970. A collection of early critical writings on Scott.

Lukács, Georg. *The Historical Novel.* Translated by Hannah and Stanley Mitchell. London: Merlin, 1962.

Millgate, Jane. *Walter Scott: The Making of the Novelist.* Toronto: University of Toronto Press, 1984.

Shaw, Harry E. *The Forms of Historical Fiction: Sir Walter Scott and His Successors.* Ithaca: Cornell University Press, 1983.

Trumpener, Katie. *Bardic Nationalism: The Romantic Novel and the British Empire.* Princeton: Princeton University Press, 1997.

Welsh, Alexander. *The Hero of the Waverley Novels.* Princeton: Princeton University Press, 1992.

Wilt, Judith. *Secret Leaves: The Novels of Sir Walter Scott.* Chicago: University of Chicago Press, 1985.

Shaw, Harry E., ed. *Critical Essays on Sir Walter Scott: The Waverley Novels.* New York: G. K. Hall, 1996. Contains a selection of essays on Scott, and its introduction provides a review of major books on Scott.

Biography: Scott's son-in-law J. G. Lockhart produced a multi-volume biography of Scott, complete with a large selection of his letters; he subsequently edited this down to a one-volume edition, reprinted in Everyman's Library as J. G. Lockhart, *The Life of Sir Walter Scott* (London: Dent, 1969). Though it is subject to the problems of any "in-house" biography, it has a grand narrative sweep and is full of insight into the man and his times. The standard modern biography is Edgar Johnson, *Sir Walter Scott: The Great Unknown* (New York: Macmillan, 1970); this corrects many factual errors in Lockhart.

Thackeray

Ferris, Ina. *William Makepeace Thackeray.* Boston: Twayne, 1983.

Fisher, Judith L. *Thackeray's Skeptical Narrative and the 'Perilous Trade' of Authorship.* Aldershot: Ashgate, 2002.

Harden, Edgar F. *The Emergence of Thackeray's Serial Fiction.* Athens: University of Georgia Press, 1979.

McMaster, Juliet. *Thackeray: The Major Novels.* Toronto: University of Toronto Press, 1971.

Rawlins, Jack P. *Thackeray's Novels: A Fiction that is True*. Berkeley: University of California Press, 1974.

Tillotson, Geoffrey and Donald Hawes, eds. *Thackeray: The Critical Heritage*. London: Routledge and Kegan Paul, 1968. A collection of early critical writings on Thackeray.

Trollope, Anthony. *Thackeray*. London: Macmillan, 1879 (and reprints). This brief study is interesting for what it reveals about both novelists.

Biography: The standard biography of Thackeray remains Gordon Ray's two-volume work, *Thackeray: The Uses of Adversity, 1811–1846* (New York: McGraw-Hill, 1955) and *Thackeray: The Age of Wisdom, 1847–1863* (New York: McGraw-Hill, 1958). A more recent biographical study is Peter Shillingsburg, *William Makepeace Thackeray: A Literary Life* (Houndsmills: Palgrave, 2001).

Trollope

Herbert, Christopher. *Trollope and Comic Pleasure*. Chicago: University of Chicago Press, 1987.

Kincaid, James. *The Novels of Anthony Trollope*. Oxford: Clarendon Press, 1977.

Lansbury, Coral. *The Reasonable Man: Trollope's Legal Fiction*. Princeton: Princeton University Press, 1981.

Peters, Catherine. *Trollope's Universe: Shifting Worlds of Imagination and Reality*. New York: Oxford, 1987.

Polhemus, Robert M. *The Changing World of Anthony Trollope*. Berkeley: University of California Press, 1968.

Smalley, Donald, ed. *Anthony Trollope: The Critical Heritage*. London: Routledge and Kegan Paul, 1969. A collection of early critical writings on Trollope.

Biography: For Trollope's life, see his own *Autobiography* and also N. John Hall, *Trollope: A Biography* (Oxford: Clarendon Press, 1991).

Index